English people

English people

The experience of teaching
and learning English
in British universities

COLIN EVANS

Open University Press
Buckingham · Philadelphia

Open University Press
Celtic Court
22 Ballmoor
Buckingham
MK18 1XW

and
1900 Frost Road, Suite 101
Bristol, PA 19007, USA

First Published 1993

A catalogue record of this book is available from the British Library

0 335 09359 0 (Paperback)   0 335 09361 2 (Hardback)

Library of Congress Cataloging-in-Publication Data
Evans, Colin (Colin H.)
    English people: the experience of teaching and learning English
in British universities / Colin Evans.
        p. cm.
    Includes bibliographical references and index.
    ISBN 0-335-09361-2. — ISBN 0-335-09359-0 (pbk.)
    1. English philology — Study and teaching (Higher) — Great Britain.
2. English teachers — Great Britain — Attitudes. I. Title.
PE68.G5E82   1993
420'.71'141—dc20   92-36207
                                                            CIP

Typeset by Graphicraft Typesetters Ltd, Hong Kong
Printed in Great Britain by Biddles Ltd, Guildford and King's Lynn

English people is dedicated to
Elias Ellis Evans of Llanllyfni and Abertridwr.

It's a nice way to spend your life, but it's an odd experience to try to communicate to anybody. (20)

Contents

Preface

> How intermittent is our good Jocelin; marking down, without eye to
> *us*, what *he* finds interesting! How much in Jocelin, as in all History,
> and indeed in all Nature, is at once inscrutable and certain; so dim,
> yet so indubitable; exciting us to endless considerations. For King
> Lackland *was* there, verily he; and did leave these *tredecim sterlingii*, if
> nothing more and did live and look in one way or the other, and a
> whole world was living and looking along with him. There, we say, is
> the grand peculiarity; the immeasurable one; distinguishing, to a really
> infinite degree, the poorest historical Fact from all Fiction whatsoever.
> Fiction, 'Imagination', 'Imaginative poetry' &c. &c., except as the vehicle
> for truth, or *fact* of some sort, – which surely a man should first try
> various other ways of vehiculating, and conveying safe, – what is it?
> (Thomas Carlyle, 1843, *Past and Present*)

This book, like its predecessor *Language People*, is a contribution to what
the anthropologist Geertz calls 'an ethnography of the disciplines'. It is one
of those 'full-length canvases of notable subjects', the exhibiting of which
Becher (1989: 28) sees as one way of furthering our understanding of
disciplinary cultures and thereby of higher education in general. As he
says, such 'concrete exemplifications' are still very rare. And yet, behind
(buried underneath?) the abstract titles of the higher education literature,
Research and Higher Education, *Restructuring Higher Education*, *Access
and Institutional Change*, *Academic Freedom*, behind the statistics and the
accounts of governance are individual men and women, staff and students,
living their lives within academic communities which are largely unstudied
qua communities and sites of experience. The 'absence of documentary
and ethnographic information about the routines of Literature teaching in
Higher Education', which Tony Davies referred to in 1982 (in Widdowson
1982: 35), has not, to my knowledge, been remedied in the meantime.

My project is to redress the balance somewhat, in favour of the concrete
– individual students and teachers, unique experiences and unique voices,
what Carlyle calls 'the grand peculiarity'. The reader will find in this book

a great deal of direct quotation. I make no apology for this. I am concerned to offer an alternative to that form of knowledge production which entails reducing multiple voices to manipulable statistics. Save in the unlikely event of this becoming *A Book at Bedtime*, the reader will not hear, as I did, the accents, the hesitations, the silences, the sudden fluency as something became real, nor (save in the even less likely event of my selling the film rights) see the people and the rooms where I spoke with them.

I do not disguise the fact that this book is my cake. I baked it to my recipe. But there are in it generous quantities of fruit and nuts which I neither created nor modified in the oven. This means that the reader can engage with the material and respond to it in ways that may be tangential to my own.

I am all too aware of the epistemological problems (including the fact that there is a sense in which I did, by being who I am, 'create' the responses). What is the truth-status of one extract from one interview given by one English person to one interviewer (white, male, fifties, linguist, Welsh) on one particular day? The answer to this question deserves a book to itself. All I can say here (with acknowledgement to David Armstrong, who offered me this formulation) is that my concern is less with the question 'How representative is this?' than with the question 'What does this represent?' In this perspective, a statistically minority view may be highly significant. I am also conscious that there is a homology between this position and that of the producers of the material with which English People largely work (writers of fictions who also describe things that are by no means 'representative' or 'typical' in a statistical sense). This book, in a way, is a 'metalogue'.[1] It mirrors and enacts its own subject matter – which is fundamentally concerned with questions of representation and with the appropriate way to communicate experience or to discuss reports of experience. I will add that practitioners of the alternative approach – statements of the type '73.6 per cent of those who filled in the questionnaire agreed that English was a "soft option" compared to 26.4 per cent who thought it was "an intellectual challenge" ($N = 104$)' – have, as they will agree, their own epistemological and presentational problems.

I offer here an arboretum and, as in *Language People*, I have numbered (and sometimes named) the trees.[2] However, to pursue the metaphor, my interest is in the wood. I am under no illusion that by the end of this book I will be able to give a succinct statement of what the experience of English People essentially is, or what the discipline essentially means. But I hope to have explored some general tensions which go beyond the experience of any individual, which are relevant for all English People and for all people concerned with higher education and the humanities.

There is also the international wood. This book is the first step of another project which overlaps the disciplinary one. It is a case study in the ways in which nations seek, more or less successfully, to transmit a national language and culture, and thus a national identity, through an educational system. France is the obvious point of comparison but there are very interesting issues raised by all the European countries. 'English' as a discipline is unique because of the profound homologies between it and the life of the nation. As we shall see in Chapters 8 and 9, the problematic of disciplines is the same as the problematic of nations: the concepts of boundary and category, and of group and sub-group are common to both. English is the scene of a basic tension between on the one hand the individual and the private (symbolized by the act of silent reading) and, on the other, the public (represented by the institution). The drama of the humanities and of their flagship, English, is to do with taking that private experience across a boundary into a public institution, as the drama of citizenship is to do with accepting restraint on individual freedom.

All of this is not totally unconnected with the themes of *Language People* but there is a difference of scale. Some statistics may demonstrate the sheer size of the phenomenon of higher education English. There were, in 1991, 16,468 students of English in British universities. Of these 1,334 were post-graduates.[3] There were also 9,890 students of English at polytechnics and colleges in England (of whom only ten were post-graduates).[4] This makes a total of well[5] over 26,000 students who at this moment see themselves and are officially categorized as English People. This is roughly double the number of Language People and it represents a huge resource and a huge investment. The experience of these highly selected young people (and they are predominantly young) is of crucial importance for the future.

The whole group of English People comprises all those living who have ever been students of English. But a sub-group of these is particularly significant. They are the English People who stayed on in higher education and became lecturers and professors, examiners, writers of books, teachers of English teachers. There are 916[6] of these in universities in the United Kingdom and about 500[7] in polytechnics and colleges.

My hope for this book is that it will be of value to all these people as a portrait of their discipline against which they can set their own experience. I would particularly hope that the proportion of the 50,000 or more[8] boys and girls who, having passed English A or AS level, go on every year to higher education, will be able to use this book as a means of enhancing their learning about the world they are entering. I see the ability to engage in this kind of meta-reflection about the subject as an essential feature of the experience of higher education.

A female student in Newcastle told me, 'When I chose to do English, I had no idea it would be 80 per cent female.' (105) Had she read this book she would have at least known that. Another respondent, a final-year student, said that she regretted 'not knowing what sort of a set-up this place is before I came, not being told what goes on. You just study without thinking about it for two years. It's just now I'm beginning to appreciate what I'm doing.' (64) I would like to speed up that process of self-awareness.

The position of staff is different. But there is little mobility in the system,[9] and a civic university lecturer may well not have much idea of what life is like in a polytechnic or in Oxford. Indeed, even within a department, people do not share their experience very extensively or intensively. As one respondent said of a colleague with a different view of the subject: 'He and I hardly ever talk and certainly never talk like we have talked separately to you.' (7) Staff may also have only a partial awareness of students' experience – and vice versa.

This book is like a big seminar where a hundred participants can speak and be heard – by themselves and by anyone else who cares to eavesdrop.

My method is the one I developed in *Language People* except that, for resource reasons, I was not able to use the inter-group activity. Because the phenomenon was larger than modern languages I increased the number of institutions I visited and the range. In all, I interviewed 50 staff and 53 students. The interviews were semi-structured and lasted between one and two hours. They were all recorded. I visited the Universities of Cardiff in Wales, Oxford and Newcastle in England, Stirling in Scotland and the Polytechnic of North London. One of the weaknesses of this study is that I was not able to include colleges of higher education, although I am aware from various contacts that institutions like Crewe and Alsager and Bradford and Ilkley Community College represent very significant aspects of the subject. One of the rare published accounts of innovation in teaching and learning in English comes from the College of St Paul and St Mary, Cheltenham (Miall 1989). My research is skewed then in the direction of the universities (in the pre- and post-binary sense).

My only excuse is the need in an exploration like this to collect and analyse the data over a very short period of time. What my respondents say may cover a long period (my oldest respondent was in his eighties) but they all said what they said during the period April 1991 to January 1992. Even so, some parts of the photograph are blurred because the subject moved. In particular, the binary line went out of shot. I have not modified the references to 'polytechnics' or 'public sector' in the text; I conducted my interviews in the 'Polytechnic of North London', not in the 'University of North London' and I therefore refer to 'PNL' in the text, though the reader should understand this as shorthand for 'the former PNL, now the University of North London'.

I was able to carry out the research in this necessarily short time thanks to a sabbatical from the University of Cardiff for which I am grateful. My colleagues in the School of European Studies at Cardiff accepted willingly the extra commitments that my absence entailed. I received a grant of £2950 from the Nuffield Foundation, which covered all the expenses of the field-work and the preparation of the database and the book. Cynthia Holmes of the Universities Statistical Record was extremely helpful, as were Trevor Knight and Tricia Hammond of the Department for Education Analytical Services Branch. Carol Bretman gave unstinting support with the word-processing in the midst of her own difficulties as an English Person and a mature, single-parent student. The Muir family also gave secretarial help. In Oxford I received help and hospitality from Ann

Jefferson, Peter Agulnik and Maggie Campbell; in Stirling from David and Caroline Punter and Neil and Jenny Keeble; in PNL from Pat Jackson and Trevor Jocelyn; in Newcastle from Ken and Katy Robinson. The DUET project group and the CESC 13 team at the Grubb Institute offered me opportunities for thinking collaboratively and in public. Jean Verrier and his students and colleagues at the University of Paris 8 helped me see English People more clearly by getting me to look at French People. Barry Palmer read the whole manuscript with his legendary scrupulousness and empathy, and various chapters were read in draft by John Bazalgette, Tony Becher, Roger Ellis, Carol Evans, Valmai Evans, Robert French, Peter Hawkins, Roy Jones, Anthony Packer and Norman Schwenk. I am sincerely grateful for their honest feedback.

Ray Cunningham commissioned the book although it was hopelessly hybrid and the title was ambiguous. The Open University Press staff were, at all stages, good practice personified.

My wife, Carol, provided insights from a tribe I have yet to study and whom I call 'Psycho-People'. My friends put up with me during a period when, although I had not entirely ceased to be a member of the human race and continued paying my subscriptions, I did not actually attend the meetings. My gratitude is heartfelt.

My greatest debt, however, is to the staff and students who made time to speak to me and who trusted me to represent them. My hope is that I have been able to justify that trust.

part one

Joining

one_____

Origins

> In history, as in Nature, birth and death are equally balanced.
> (Huizinga, 1924, *The Waning of the Middle Ages*)

Historians

Like the Druids and the Christmas tree the subject 'English' has always seemed more ancient than it is. Baldick (1983: 3) records the astonishment of English undergraduates on learning 'the comparative novelty of their chosen subject within the history of higher education', and comments: 'It would seem that the study of English Literature is accepted by most of its practitioners as a "natural" activity without an identifiable historical genesis.' It is, he says, 'a discipline unconcerned to examine its own history', and Graff and Warner (1989: 3), writing of English in the United States, maintain that 'The history of its own development as an institution has up to now had no serious status as a field within literary studies.'

My sense is that this is not a chance oversight, a regrettable hiccup in the process of scholarly digestion, but an essential part of the activity of legitimation and establishment. People's experience of any entity or situation is associated with the state of their knowledge of how that entity came into existence or how they came to find themselves in that situation. It may well be in some cases that their experience is in fact largely determined by their lack of knowledge, or by their firm belief that they do not need such knowledge of origins: things always were (and therefore always will be) thus. More frequently, they have ready to hand a particular narrative which they share with other individuals and which they use to make sense of the entity and to give meaning to their present experience.

The search for origins is ambiguous. On the one hand, if it can be demonstrated that the origins of X go back very far indeed, this gives X power compared to more recent confections – so it is in X's interest to assert the origins and make them ancient (conversely, revolutionaries need to seek and destroy them, as the French revolutionaries dug up the bodies of the ancient Kings of France, buried in the tombs of the Basilique Saint Denis). On the other hand, to admit to having origins at all is to admit to being in history, and therefore contingent; it is to weaken the claim to be timeless, natural and thus immune from change. Establishments have usually tried to claim distant origins followed instantly by eternal timelessness. Right-wing history has usually been written *in extremis*.

Exactly the same phenomenon can be observed with respect to the university as a whole. A historical awareness is only one form of general self-awareness. There has been resistance to self-study in higher education: while maintaining a quasi-monopoly on this kind of research, the academy on the whole has chosen not to pursue it. Historical reflexivity is inimical to profession-building since this depends, to a large degree, on occulting real origins (how many dentists' surgeries display pictures of fairground extractions?) and on leaving institutional or pedagogical processes unexamined. The aim is, after all, to construct a body of 'scientific', 'detached' knowledge, knowledge which will be true at all times and in all places. To suggest, say, that the French predilection for rectal temperature-taking is cultural rather than scientific is to weaken the medical profession. There is also a need to play down conflicts between sub-groups – which is nevertheless a large part of the reality of the profession.

It is in fact unlikely that the experience of any 'English People' in the past two centuries was ever one of complete consensus. As Graff and Warner (1989: 2) say, there may have been more consensus in the past in higher education, since most of the consensus challengers were excluded from the institution, but their collection of accounts written by the early practitioners and professionals shows indeed 'a welter of conflicts, debates, and contradictions'.

Baldick (1983) and Graff (1987) are themselves two of the authors who have recently challenged this claim to timelessness. There were earlier accounts of the rise of English at Cambridge (Potter 1937; Tillyard 1958) and also at Oxford (Firth 1929; Palmer 1965). But it is in the past decade only that histories like those of Baldick and Graff have become more frequent (though it is still hardly a 'field' within literary studies). Mulhern's study of *Scrutiny* (1979) takes up historically exactly where Palmer left off, but geographically describes a different universe – Cambridge. He addresses basic issues about the past and future of the subject from a particular (Marxist) narrative position, but avoids the left's subsequent anti-Leavis excesses.

Mathieson (1975) also focuses very much on 'Cambridge English' and the Arnoldian tradition, but is particularly concerned with the impact of this idealistic tradition on secondary schools and the fallible human beings who teach in them. Baldick is also concerned with this particular 'missionary' tradition, but his emphasis is on the work of the founders, Arnold, Newbolt, T. S. Eliot, I. A. Richards and the Leavises. Doyle's thesis, finally published in the New Accents series in 1989 under the title *English and Englishness* covers the whole ground, from Arnold to McCabe, with an emphasis on the issues of Englishness and nation-building. Bergonzi in *Exploding English* (1990) gives a personal account, based on his own wide institutional experience since 1955 when he became a mature student at Oxford. His is similar to the accounts my respondents gave me in our interviews. His emphasis is on the impact of structuralism in the 1970s and, more generally, on theory. As we shall see, this is a part of the subject's history which has had considerable significance for my respondents. Easthope's books, *British Post-structuralism since 1968* (1988) and *Literary into Cultural Studies* (1991), describe the impact of theory and, as the title of the more recent book indicates, extend a particular narrative into the future.

Some of my respondents have been significant actors in this story; others are actually engaged in writing histories of the subject – some have published work in the field. All, like Bergonzi, have their own personal histories that are in relation to (and are indeed ultimately constitutive of) the larger history with which they are, to a greater or lesser extent, familiar.

Most of the accounts, both written and oral, are from the left because, as I suggested earlier, the establishment's interests are best served by disguising process and origins.[1] There is, however, an interesting exception: George Watson in *The Discipline of English* (1978: 10) agrees that 'no one can know a subject if he knows nothing of its history, or misunderstands that history'. He goes on to produce a narrative which has the period 1945–59 as a high point of prestige for the subject in the form of New Criticism. The story since 1960 he sees as a decline, although the decline is, he says, partly or wholly to be welcomed, because modishness is not a good thing for a subject which is essentially elitist, and the subject's claims were in any case during this period overweening. The 1960s, he says, were a 'period of lies'. The *nouvelle critique* was vitiated by subjectivism. The future lies in scholarship; the real mission of English is historical research and the search for objective truth. Watson's book is clearly an example of the *in extremis* right-wing history I referred to above.

Writing at this time, I am fortunate to have been able to draw on all this work and all this reflection. My aim is to understand the experience of students and teachers of the subject today: I start from their experience and their accounts. But my intention, as I have said, is to see both the individual trees and the wood. And the pathbreaking historical work of the past few years is of great value for this.

I am aware that in mentioning these recent book-length histories I have sequenced them: Firth and Palmer up to 1894; Baldick up to 1932; Bergonzi and Watson for the structuralist period of the 1970s; Easthope for post-structuralism. This mirrors another sequencing, which goes: classics, philology, Cambridge English, New Criticism, structuralism, post-structuralism, cultural studies. Yet another could be Oxford, Cambridge, polytechnics. I have done this almost unconsciously, although I was convinced many years ago (by Huizinga in *The Waning of the Middle Ages*) that history is not in fact like this; sequencing is just the line of least resistance when attempting to write it. My particular method does alert me to this chronological reification, as the following exchange with a respondent demonstrates:

- When I was doing English in America in the sixties there was a knock-down fight in the department between the young lecturers and the people concerned with the aesthetics of English in a pure form. That was the battle that was going on, it was all very open and savage.
- Who won?
- Nobody won. It's still going on. (13)

Tensions

It seems to me that the history of the subject is best seen as a field of opposing forces or tensions. These are lived dynamically by individuals and these individuals are, consciously or unconsciously, members of particular groups which represent one aspect of a tension at one time. The group conflicts are rarely resolved; they are rarely even articulated. Aspects are not eliminated but go underground or become avatars.

This is true, I believe, of any discipline. But 'English' is not a subject like the others. 'Physics' can never have the same relation to 'English society' as 'English' does, since English refers both to the language of English society and to its cultural and social reality.

I shall now attempt a preliminary overview of these forces, which I see as having determined the experience of English people and which will underlie the subsequent chapters.

United Kingdom

The most extensive, historically, is the opposition between England and the rest – the slow thousand-year process by which Picts, Frisians, Angles, Saxons, Danes, Normans, all the original inhabitants save the Celts – lost their separate tribal identities, and became amalgamated and absorbed, as the Kings of Wessex extended their domain towards the fringes. It is this process of 'internal colonialism' which produced the British state – by incorporation (Wales in 1536) or by merger (Scotland in 1707, Ireland in 1801). That this is indeed a question of forces in tension and not some inexorable flow is borne out by the fact that Scotland is now seriously considering leaving the Union, that Northern Ireland's status is, to say the least, in question, and that the Welsh language and identity are powerfully alive.

This tension is connected with the subject English in two ways. First, as one of my respondents – an eminent literary historian – pointed out, a major part of the very material of the subject was produced by 'marginals', in order to investigate the question of their national identity and their relation with metropolitan identity (Walter Scott is an example). Second, the question of which English language texts to study is one that foregrounds the issue of metropolis and periphery: the question 'Which texts?' becomes 'Whose texts?' The subject itself is radically different according to whether the answer is 'the whole community's texts' or 'the dominant group's texts' or 'subversives' texts' (see an early article by Graff 1980: 345).

Empire

'English' is inseparable from Empire, and the great process of imperial withdrawal is a crucial aspect of the discipline. In 1855 'English' became one of the subjects in which candidates for the Civil Service of the East India Company were examined (and the most important in terms of marks allotted: Palmer 1965: 46). One of my respondents gave what I came to see as a commonly held view of the 'invention' of the subject:

> It was a means of introducing people without a public school classics background to university and it was established for them. It was also about the civilizing of the Indian population. Since missionaries were not allowed to enter India (they caused more unrest) Imperial Britain wanted a secular educational structure which could provide Western moral values: so Milton and Donne were exported to India to serve that project. This was why English literature was first invented. (7)

> If you've got Shakespeare you don't need to use force. Shakespeare is worth a couple of regiments of infantry. (15)

So English was the language of the Empire and English literature was its Bible. But today the Empire writes back. English has become plural – 'Englishes'. An Irish respondent said: 'These other societies are doing their own thing in English, magic realism or whatever. It's not something you can easily handle from your own culture, even though it's in English.' (23) So the end of Empire may mean the end of 'English': 'What you are asking me to talk about is starting not to exist. Its boundaries have been changed. "English people"? That phrase has started to move.' (20)

Classics

The reason why English was even considered as a selection procedure for the Indian Civil Service was to do with another vast theme – the break-up of the pedagogical empire of the classics. It is difficult today to grasp the sheer massiveness of the Latin/Greek disciplinary hegemony.[2] It is a perfect example of the phenomenon of an establishment with a venerable origin and no history, which I referred to earlier.

The history of the rise of modern languages in its broad (American) sense of foreign and native language in Europe and America is quite simply the history of the defeat of Latin and Greek, their dethronement as mandarin subjects. It would be possible to list all the episodes of the long and bitter retreat as Latin and/or Greek ceased to be a requirement for matriculation or for entry to this or that institution or profession. There was the Civil Service entrance examination already mentioned (and the public examination concept has been a powerful weapon used against classics[3]); then the founding of the English Honours School at Oxford in 1893, which is the best documented of the battles (Firth 1929; Potter 1937; Palmer 1965) and perhaps the most crucial, because of Oxford's status as the very citadel of Classics and Greats. Defeats in Cambridge, culminating with the Tripos of 1926, came later and more gradually.

The whole story epitomizes the way the most deeply entrenched and apparently eternal empires will eventually collapse when they cease to be functional and adaptive, when whatever original sense of ultimate purpose they had has vanished, leaving empty rituals. But it is also symbolic of the sheer stubborn endurance of empty rituals in the world of education. There was certainly a time, as Raymond Williams (1961: 161) says, when Latin was vocational. But that is not the same as being functional. The educational objectives of effective speaking and writing, the national purposes of pride and unity and the commercial purposes of trade could all have been better attained from the beginning of the sixteenth century through the vernacular, and few indeed were those subsequently whose reading ability in Latin or Greek became such as to give them what we would call a literary or a humane education. On the contrary, the classics, in their university and public school fortresses, blocked the road of all educational reform which aimed at an adaptive relation with the real world and with real knowledge. For centuries classics served no purpose whatsoever other than that of social and educational filtering.

At this stage the reader should perhaps pause and devote a minute's silence to the memory of all those school-children who suffered from the obduracy and self-serving of the classicists. It is worth noting, at this early stage of this study, that English was a major participant in a long war of pedagogical liberation. 'There is a real case for it having been an oppositional subject.' (26)

After centuries in which the self-evident necessity of the classics went unchallenged, the early nineteenth century saw a sustained and bitter attack. There were two arguments: (a) the familiar one made by the Mechanics' Institutes that it excluded the study of science and technology and left Britain inferior to Germany (Mathieson 1975: 21); and (b) (shared entirely by the proponents of the technological argument) that classics also failed to provide the liberal and humanizing education which was by now its sole justification and which all agreed was necessary in a technological and mercantile age (Dixon 1991: Part 1).

The attack was upon the upper class alliance of public schools, Oxbridge and the Church, and was conducted by middle-class propagandists (particularly in the *Edinburgh Review*). This group was motivated, as always, not only by intellectual or patriotic feelings, but by a political awareness on the part of one group that they were being excluded by another established group. Classics was the means by which one group sought to hold on to power and privilege, and English was the means by which other social groups attempted to wrest that power from them. The strength of the entrenched position can be gauged, however, from the fact that the war lasted for most of the century; from the Edgeworths' articles in the *Edinburgh Review* in 1808–11 to Farrar's remarkable collection of essays in 1868, or T. Huxley's *Science and Culture* in 1887, the arguments continued to be made powerfully (Farrar's own attack on Greek and Latin verse composition is a splendid polemic) and the public schools and old universities continued successfully to ignore them. Mathieson sums up (1975: 24):

> For a century and a half then . . . critics attacked a curriculum limited to the study of classical texts. The universities and public schools, however, stubbornly resisted successive series of critical articles and the recommendations of commissions and scientists. They maintained their unshaken confidence in what they believed to be the superior humanism of the classics and the truth of the faculty theory. Public school headmasters, distrusting the notion of progress through scientific discovery and application, were unimpressed by references to foreign competition, suspicious of the anti-religious associations with the scientific cause, and untroubled by any need to provide their pupils with the means of earning their living. They continued therefore in those ways by which they had succeeded in the past in producing Christian Gentlemen.

One can see in this debate generations of schoolteachers gritting their teeth and hoping the classics will 'see them out'. Cogent argument in British education has always been the David to the Goliath of vested interests.

I have presented this opposition of English and classics as a war between two sides – as it was. But this is a simplification: inevitably many of the 'English' camp were classicists: progressives in any debate are likely to be disaffected products of the established regime and therefore formed and imbued by it. In the actual process of debate, compromises will be reached, deals will be struck. When it comes, not to argument and debate, but to actual practice – syllabuses, curricula, examinations, pedagogy – the victors will dispose only of the weapons abandoned by the vanquished. The automobile convincingly defeated the carriage but started out looking suspiciously like a cart without a horse.

So English is in many ways an avatar of classics. This phenomenon is, as I have said in *Language People*, most evident in modern languages where the standard university exercises, particularly 'prose composition' and 'unseen translation', were taken over direct from the dead languages and have survived as ritual, intact and virtually unchallenged, until this day, in spite of their almost total irrelevance to the practicalities of advanced language acquisition. But it is also apparent in the way that texts are approached: 'close reading', 'practical criticism', *'explication de texte'* are the avatars of classical teaching methods. In short, it seems that educational contents may be changed – albeit with difficulty – but educational forms are much more resistant. So Milton became the object of study, replacing Homer, but in the classroom the time was spent in the same way. Marsh wrote in 1893:

> In 1845 . . . I made my experiment of teaching English like Latin or Greek – hearing a short Grammar lesson, the rest of the hour reading Milton as if it were Homer, calling for the meaning of words, their etymology when interesting, the relation of words, parsing when it would help, the connection of clauses, the mythology, the biography and other illustrative matter.
>
> (In Graff and Warner 1989: 25)

The central problem for English was that, compared with the classics, it was not punishing.[4] It was 'roses without thorns' (Rollin 1934, in Palmer 1965: 12) and children might actually derive enjoyment from it. This says a great deal about the fundamentals of the educational system. There must, by definition, be a gap between what the teacher knows and can do and what the student knows and can do – how else to justify the salary of the teacher? The gap between someone who knows a foreign or ancient language and one who does not is self-evident and can always be adjusted: if the students can translate Agatha Christie, give them James Joyce. But vernacular literature poses a problem. Palmer shows how the main objection to English at Oxford, Cambridge and in the public schools was that English was, in modern parlance, a soft option. This is why, even when it had found some legitimacy, it was despised – known as the 'courier Tripos' in Cambridge, and relegated to an inferior place in public schools.

Philology

Thorns were at hand, however, at least for the universities. As Eagleton (1983: 29) puts it, 'making English unpleasant enough to qualify as a proper academic pursuit' is 'one of the few problems associated with the study of English which have since been effectively resolved'. Anglo-Saxon was invented in 1876 with Sweet's reader.[5] As Marsh said, 'The early professors had no recondite learning applicable to English, and did not know what to do with classes in it. They can now make English as hard as Greek.' With Anglo-Saxon and with a suitable textbook, English really could become 'the poor man's classics' (and the poor woman's) (Graff and Warner 1989: 27).

To succeed, a discipline has to meet both internal and external demands. Anglo-Saxon was the means of pursuing internal, professional, scientific research while still teaching 'literature' to students. Graff and Warner (1989: 5) put it excellently:

> It was the scientific model of research that justified philological studies of literature to other professionals inside the university, it was the

civic and humanistic claims of literature that justified those studies to outsiders.

In order to gain acceptance a subject has to be shown to be 'hard' and this means not only hard for students (examinable, usable as a means of exclusion and inclusion, passing and failing) but also hard for researchers, hard in our modern sense – part of the 'hard' sciences. A bizarre consequence of this was that, for a period, the centre of 'English' was Germany since it was the philologists (the ancient tribes I call the 'Philogs' in *Language People*) who were laying claim to controlling the discipline of English, and the capital of Philog country was Berlin. Germany, said Perry in 1935, possessed (in the 1880s) 'the sole secret of scholarship' (Graff and Warner 1989: 139). The conflict here was between the philologists who had received a training as comparative linguists in graduate school and in Germany, and the classics professors who were gentlemen amateurs. Philology was the downfall of the classics because it took classics' own claims (to be 'hard') and professionalized them.[6]

Professionalization: 'A career for clever men'

Professional versus amateur is another powerful tension and the history of disciplines is in large part the history of professionalization. It is salutary to remember that lofty discussion about what to teach, how to teach, what to research and how to organize disciplines, is founded on the needs of individuals to survive and prosper financially and psychologically. The struggle between classicists and would-be English teachers was a struggle about jobs: the Professor of Latin at Oxford, Thomas Case, saw this clearly in 1887. Students, he said,

> will be withdrawn from the Final Classical examination by the ease of an examination in one Modern Language with the result that all classical studies, philological, philosophical and historical, will suffer a common martyrdom because there will be a constant pressure to appoint teachers of modern languages in the colleges instead of classical teachers. The consequent outcry for modern teachers in the colleges will partly diminish the classical staff and partly their stipends, and that too in the face of declining revenues and the difficulty of offering clever men a career.
>
> (In Firth 1929: 71)

There is a certain amount of satisfying, remunerated professional work to be done, and there is competition for it. But the essence of professionalization is that things that were previously unpaid become paid: a good contemporary example might be psychotherapy. If writing and talking about vernacular contemporary literature (or the cinema), which people had always done, can be professionalized, the amount of paid work will increase (though there is still competition). This aspect of the discipline is frequently understated; English is a good example of an amateur area that has become professional. All the respondents in this book, students and staff, as well as the author and a large proportion, I suspect, of the readers and reviewers, are beneficiaries of that process; but they also share to different degrees what might be called professional guilt – the feeling attached to getting money for something you would be doing anyway and which other non-professionals (in some cases volunteers) are doing free out of the goodness of their hearts or from pure love of the subject.

So the rise of English is part of a modern phenomenon of professionalization and institutionalization. The subject gains respect from other members of the institution. This is why certain events have disproportionate significance: the founding of Chairs, first in London, 1828, 1835;[7] then in Scotland, 1862, 1865, 1893; then, more symbolically, in Oxford, home of Greats, and in Cambridge; then in provincial universities. A Chair is the symbol of a legitimated discipline. The role of the university is to legitimize. As Tapper and Salter (1992: 4) write, universities are 'the keystone of the whole educational edifice'. They 'have always been the institutions at the top of the educational hierarchy', so 'they make the ultimate decision on how knowledge should be organized and what status should be attached to different knowledge areas. . . . Once sanctioned . . . changes are passed down the educational pyramid.' The means used is the establishment of Chairs. The more the university uses its legitimating power, the more powerful it becomes. The rise of the university feeds on and is fed by the rise of professionalization, in a long symbiotic process. This is one of the special features of the profession of university teaching: it *is* a profession, but one whose function is to a large extent to legitimize other professions and disciplines. This is the reason for focusing on English in higher education. It is not that there is no contest between the university's power to define and the power of other groups – notably the government but also secondary education. Nevertheless, the university's power is the more ancient and defines the nature of the contest. It is the university's power which, at one remove, is exercised through the other essential stages in the process of profession building: the foundation of the English Association in 1906 and the establishment of professional journals, such as the *Review of English Studies* or *Scrutiny*.

Democratization

The Education Acts of 1870 and 1944 are peaks in a whole mountain range of legislative Acts which progressively established the notion that education was both a right and an obligation, while weakening the idea of segregated national schooling for discrete social classes. The 11-plus selection examination, which separated the grammar school cheese from the secondary modern chalk, was abolished in the early 1960s and comprehensive schools were created. In 1991 the division between polytechnics and universities was eliminated as part of the same trend. Here, as elsewhere, it is not a question of some inexorable movement but of a tension and a conflict. The public schools continue to exist, Oxbridge still has prestige and there are powerful forces, overt and covert, demanding a return to selection and resisting democratization – that is, the incursion of certain social classes into privileged territory reserved for other social classes. This development of state education had as its driving force English. In a phrase which has become famous, Low in 1867 made the link: 'I believe it will be absolutely necessary that you [the House of Commons] should prevail upon our future Masters to learn their letters' (in Mathieson 1975: 30).

In 1921 the Newbolt Report (paragraph 9) made the move from functional literacy to literature:

> For English children no form of knowledge can take precedence of a knowledge of English, no form of literature can take precedence over English literature: and . . . the two are so inextricably connected as to form the only possible base for a national education.

The result is, as Doyle (1989: 2) says, that it is now 'difficult to imagine a system of education in . . . any English-speaking country which is not founded on the teaching of English'. Whatever the qualifications, whatever the rearguard actions designed to preserve certain territory for certain privileged groups, or to designate certain forms of English as unmarked and others as marked, the rise of English as a subject is inextricably connected with this process of emancipation.

Yet here again we are dealing with a tension, not an inexorable movement. English is used inclusively but also exclusively. One of my working-class respondents had recently done a degree in English literature at Ruskin College. There he found his fellow students frequently hostile to the subject for reasons he describes:

> Literature is used to stratify and divide. It marginalizes and excludes working people. It can alienate them whether they know it or not. Usually it taught them to exclude their own backgrounds and to extol all the virtues of the middle-class thing. (63)

This is a fundamental tension. For George Watson to say that the historical, objective study of formal aspects of great works is the core of the subject is perfectly reasonable given a prior consensus about which works are great. Once the question 'Who decided that this particular text should be studied in this way?' is raised, then Watson's case is open to all the elements.

Emancipation of women

If English was generally emancipatory, it was particularly so for women. Women were excluded from the professions partly by the device of being excluded from Latin and Greek (and mathematics). They seized on English (and modern languages) as substitute qualifications. At Oxford in the early years there were almost four women students in English for every man: at Cambridge the proportions were even higher. From its very inception English was a feminine subject. So another tension of the subject is between notions of masculine and feminine. In America, said Babbitt in 1908, literary courses are known as 'sissy' courses.

> The man who took literature too seriously would be suspected of effeminacy. The really virile thing is to be an electrical engineer. One already sees the time when a typical teacher of literature will be some young dilettante who will interpret Keats and Shelley for a class of girls. As it is, the more vigorous and pushing teachers of language feel they must assert their manhood by philological research.
>
> (In Graff and Warner 1989: 112)

Theory

The final tension that is significant in understanding this subject in its historical context is one originally described by Terry Anderson (1968). It is the absence in British intellectual life of what he calls the category of the totality. Classical sociology and Marxism on the Continent were 'global theories of society articulated in a totalising conceptual system'. This is what is missing, says Anderson, in British sociology, philosophy, history, political theory, economics, psychology, aesthetics, psychoanalysis and anthropology. In other words there is a hostility to systemic thinking. (Anderson defines totality as 'an entity whose diverse structures are bound together in such a way that any one of them considered separately is an abstraction. It is not an aggregate sum of parts.' This is what I call 'system'.) Anderson attributes this to the fundamental fact that Britain has for centuries had freedom from revolution, invasion, occupation, civil war: 'This history is so natural to most Englishmen that they have never registered how supernatural it has seemed abroad' (Anderson 1968: 16).

Indeed. I am writing this chapter in Paris. A house nearby has on it a plaque indicating that it was used to produce false documents for the Resistance, and that on a certain date the inhabitants were arrested by the Gestapo. The cinemas are showing *La guerre sans nom*, in which Tavernier allows the young conscripts of the Algerian war, now men in their fifties, to tell their stories for the first time. In the absence of debacle and crisis, the solidity of the overall structure could be taken for granted, and British intellectuals have been able to enjoy the luxury of discrete empirical investigations. (It could be, however, that Anderson fails to acknowledge the extent to which this history is also in part the *result* of a refusal to think in a 'totalizing' way.)

The one disciplinary exception to this rule, claims Anderson, is literary criticism: literary criticism became the 'displaced home of the totality . . .

driven out of any obvious habitats, the notion of the totality found refuge in the least expected of studies' (p. 56).

He is referring to 'Cambridge English'. Much of the historical work on English which I cited earlier is in fact devoted to this aspect of English – particularly that of Mulhern, Mathieson and Baldick. 'Cambridge English' defeated philology at Cambridge in 1918 thanks to a timely *non sequitur*, the discrediting of things German after the war. It represented a complex, but powerfully coherent, response to social trends. Its very coherence, as Anderson says, makes it remarkable in British intellectual life. 'English' was consciously designed and propagated as a response to social conflicts described above and as such shared the kind of totalizing impulse Anderson refers to (though the motive is to avoid the debacle rather than understand it after it has happened). English would be a centripetal force binding together the various parts of the kingdom and, more urgently, the different social classes, thereby preventing upheaval and revolt. It would, by replacing classics, both respond to and take further the process of democratization. It would fulfil the transcendental functions which religion was increasingly unable to fulfil in a secularized society. English teachers would be missionaries or preachers or priests in the savage industrial outback, explicating the word, providing a redemptive moral sense, softening the rigours of the mercantile state. It would compensate for the loss sustained by ordinary people as a result of the industrial revolution – a loss of spiritual value, creative freedom in work, community. It would provide, as classics never could, a common culture.

This discourse was, from the beginning, part not so much of a philosophical debate as of a socio-political activity. Arnold was Inspector of Schools; the most powerful text of the movement was a government report, the Newbolt Report. As Anderson says of these aspirations and of Leavis, who seemed to him to be their spokesman:

> With him English Literary Criticism conceived the ambition to become the vaulting centre of humane study and of the University. English was the 'chief of the Humanities'. This claim was unique to England; no other country has ever produced a critical discipline with these pretensions.

'Cambridge English' is indeed in one sense 'theoretical'. Richards in particular was no narrow empiricist. He wrote that 'good theories will protect us from worse' and that 'we shall in any case use theories' (quoted in Russo 1989: 311). In a note to *Practical Criticism* (Richards 1929: 347) he talks of a 'General Theory of Critical Relativity'; the book is 'field-work in comparative ideology' (p. 6). His enterprise, which Graff (1987: 133) calls 'therapy for ideologically based miscommunication', is clearly aware of the ideological basis of criticism. But Eagleton (1983: 46) is surely right to refer to his basic positivism and to compare his scientific leanings with Leavis's almost religious intensity. Leavis was famously reluctant to theorize his practice and Richards himself emigrated, leaving behind him not a theory but a practice – 'practical criticism'. In retrospect, Anderson's idea of Cambridge English as a totalizing project seems premature. Ideological yes, theoretical no, practical certainly.

Before 1929 Cambridge English did not provide any answers to the question of what an English teacher was actually to do in a classroom or, more fundamentally, what could be *said* about texts that was not philological or historical. Richards's lectures provided an answer to the latter question which could be applied to the former. He gave students copies of unattributed texts and asked them to 'comment freely in writing upon them' (1929: 3). His brief does not seem to have been any more precise than that, though his lectures must have had an effect on later 'protocols', as students realized what he was concerned with and what the difficulties of criticism were. His work consisted of reading what the students said and lecturing on the poems and the protocols. His immediate aim was to describe the difficulties inherent in reading complex, ambiguous texts and expressing one's responses to them. His ultimate aim was to train people to do these things better. He was not, it seems to me, primarily concerned to teach students to distinguish good from bad, Donne from Woodbine Willie (although his occasionally ironical comments on the protocols might indicate the contrary). 'Poems . . . after all, are only sets of words . . . It is the quality of the reading we give them that matters, not the correctness with which we classify them' (Richards 1929: 348–9).[8]

It is clear that this is a very powerful teaching prospectus. Richards alludes in conclusion to the social need for this kind of ability, the need to 'resist' as Leavis would put it, but he avoids catastrophe-mongering. The project, as he presents it, needs none. He has demonstrated a need and a way of meeting it.

This particular set of beliefs, allied to this particular pedagogy and practice, has dominated English for decades both at university and at school level. As Eagleton (1983: 31) says, 'There's no more need to be a card-carrying Leavisite today than to be a card-carrying Copernican.' To what extent it still dominates will be one of the themes of this book.

As for Oxford, there is not even a hint of theory, and empiricism rules. Cambridge is in fact seen by Oxford as dangerously tendentious. Professor Thomas moved from Cambridge to Oxford: 'When I moved here I thought that the very negative vibes I received from my colleagues were because I was a Marxist. I gradually realized it was because I was from Cambridge.' (23)

Anglo-Saxon is still a compulsory undergraduate subject at the university of Oxford, part of 'Oxford English': 'from Beowulf to Virginia Woolf', a concept of the subject which owes a great deal to the essentially historical values of the philologists – scholarship rather than criticism. However, as we shall see, Oxford is also the last refuge of the amateur, the gentleman, the unprofessionalized (though fee-earning) man of letters.

While the genus Oxford English can best be studied in Oxford, it is by no means confined to that university. The early Chairs in provincial universities like Newcastle or Durham were filled by Oxford men; the copy of *Past and Present* from which I took my epigraph for the Preface was 'purchased from the library of Cyril Brett M.A., Professor of English at the University of South Wales and Monmouthshire 1921–1936' and is signed 'C. Brett, Wadh. Coll. Ox 15/10/07'. It is a tradition which lives on. A respondent who did English in Edinburgh in the 1960s recalled: 'We had to date a Scottish text within fifty years and fifty miles.' (4) And in University College London, at the same period a respondent was studying Anglo-Saxon up to 800 and old Norse. (41)

The real alternative to the empirical tradition did not exist when Anderson published his article. This alternative is opposed to Oxford English and Cambridge English and is known as 'theory'. This conception – anti-empirical, totalizing, predominantly Marxist – goes against the whole grain of British intellectual life in the way and for the reasons described by Anderson. Professor Dover narrates it like this:

> It once seemed possible, when Leavis was a noise in the land, to think that there was an autonomous discipline which was about maturity and judgement and all these things. But when that broke down and people got sceptical about those values, there was a vacuum at the heart of English studies and all sorts of other disciplines rushed in, linguistics, stylistics, and after that an influx of continental theory, a great range of things which were nominally English studies but which less and less looked like literary study. (15)

And an Oxford don sees the institutional reasons:

> In the polytechnics, the humanities could re-invent themselves from scratch because they didn't have the dead weight of a tradition, and they were locked into an institution which didn't really care that much what they were doing, so they could exploit their marginality. (23)

Chapter 7 will be devoted to this issue of theory.

The world of English

'English People' have a history, as we have seen. The large group of those who, throughout the centuries, have thought of themselves or been thought of by others as 'English'; the smaller group of those who, throughout the centuries, have thought of themselves as teachers or students of a discipline called 'English'; all have histories in the sense that they are aware of themselves as individuals and groups who have lived certain tensions and had certain experiences.

They live in a world in which the territorial integrity which was achieved in the nineteenth century is now threatened, constitutionally (Scotland) or unconstitutionally (Northern Ireland); a world in which the Empire writes back and also comes to stay, so that native-speaker students and teachers of English, even in England, even in London, especially in London, have black skins, brown skins, yellow skins, and the whole history of English colonialism can be present in an 'English' lecture room; a world in which the very question of Englishness is problematized, since English, the language, is spoken throughout the world and can in no way be seen as the mother tongue of English people alone, while the subject English is studied in Scotland, Wales and Ireland but also in America, Australia and Africa (to mention only the A's); a world in which classics has been eliminated as a force, the war is over (English won) and the nineteenth-century propagandists of the *Edinburgh Review*, Rev. Farrar and the proponents of the Oxford English school would be well pleased (scientists like T. Huxley might be less sanguine); a world in which Anglo-Saxon is still compulsory at Oxford, in which democratization continues, in which polytechnics become universities, in which Oxford and Cambridge and the public schools continue to thrive while 11-plus selection stirs in its grave, in which literature teaching is a profession, while there is universal concern about the future of the practice of reading books, in which master narratives in search of totality seem discredited worldwide, vindicating, it seems, British empiricism, while critical theory remains the dominant force in the discipline of English.

This world is in permanent movement but at a given moment an individual can produce an account from his or her own perspective, and another individual can attempt to account for the accounts. This book looks at this world at one particular moment in time. It is in no way a summation; at no time did I have the omnipotent fantasy that I might master all the discourses, take up a position on all the debates. The 'metalogue' aspect of this project, which I referred to in the preface, is relevant here: my own position within all these discourses is no different from that of the people whose experience I attempt to relate. The truth status of my text is epistemologically similar to the truth status of the literary texts which constitute their materials. There is no fixed, external point, no fulcrum from which to move or understand the world, only positions in time and space which one occupies and to which one gives a title – on this occasion *English People*.

two

Choice

Risk, Ignorance and Imagination.

(Heap *et al.*, 1992, *The Theory of Choice*)

Creative choice

While I was, with some trepidation, contemplating this chapter, reviewing the life choices of over a hundred idiosyncratic English people, I came upon a book which promised succour – *The Theory of Choice* (Heap *et al.* 1992): 'Where consequences are certain and costs are equal, a rational agent chooses by the measure of what outcome he or she most prefers' (p. 311). The authors state that on the assumption of such *instrumental rationality* we can describe human choice mathematically. But they recognize that in real life, alas, the consequences are not certain and costs not equal. They also see that human beings are usually engaged in existentially inventing the ends:

> People are less certain about their objectives and the environment in which they operate . . . than the people who are fully described by a set of well defined objectives. This more elusive idea of the individual has, unsurprisingly, proved to be much less mathematically tractable than the instrumental ('rational choice') version. Consequently there are fewer theorems and elegant proofs.
>
> (Heap *et al.* 1992: 3)

In other words, a decision is not usually a calculation at all but a judgement, 'a stab at representing what we regard as worthy . . . and this somewhat heroic quest is often reduced into a messy and arbitrary kind of "muddling through" ' (p. 23). The context of this *expressive rationality* is well summed up by a chapter heading which I have taken as my epigraph.

This notion of expressive rationality corresponds fairly closely to my sense of the way in which my respondents chose to be English People. It required me to abandon any hope of theorizing their process of choice.

The reader will indeed find here no 'theorems and elegant proofs', rather glimpses of the way in which, out of the muddle, some kind of order emerges.

There is certainly a sustained attempt at rational calculation on the basis of objectives, consequences and costs. We know from the limited amount of quantitative research carried out mainly in the 1970s that schoolchildren can, when faced by a questionnaire or a grid, make distinctions. We also know that when these ratings are compared English emerges as unique since it is the only subject which is ranked first in terms of *both* 'social benefit' *and* 'freedom' (Duckworth and Entwhistle 1974). It is also perceived as 'easy' compared to other subjects like French, physics and chemistry, and it appears that girls in particular choose according to perceived easiness (Keys and Ormerod 1976). Yet individuals, even those who have completed questionnaires, still find that the actual choosing is calculation, supplemented or undermined by creativity, by trial and error and by chance, what E. Ginzberg calls 'an unplanned exposure to a powerful stimulus' (Williams 1974: 74).[1] Having made their choice, the students themselves are often still trying to understand it (and using the interview with me to this end): 'I wanted to talk to you because I wanted to find out about it. I've never really thought why I did English, or why I came to Newcastle. I wanted to find out for myself what I was going to say.' (102) A staff respondent, towards the end of his career, can conclude: 'It's all a process of drift, you know.' (14)

The road not taken

My respondents are now or have been students in higher education. Their choice of English was rarely forced: with the important exception of the group of access students, they were high achievers, successful all-rounders at school. They could have chosen most other subjects. A comparison with those subjects throws light on English as a choice.

Science and mathematics

Some could have chosen science and mathematics. Professor Wagstaff did physics, chemistry and history at A level, and began a Cambridge degree in mathematics, before realizing that although he was very good he would not be the best. Dr Lake, an American, did a first degree in chemistry and English; she chose chemistry because she 'wanted to do something tough, not the squashy subjects women do'. But she took a seminar in the theory of comedy and found it 'much more interesting than memorizing the periodic table'. Dr Daniels, at 16, was prevented from becoming a scientist by a combination of events: a swimming accident before a science exam and falling in love (there does seem to be a positive correlation between falling in love and choosing English). In a literal sense, English is more laid-back than science: 'You could not relax because you were on these high stools all the time. In English you could lean back.' (100) The basic distinction between science and English, though, is for them that in English 'there are no right answers' and this allows creativity: 'In physics the questions are right or wrong, there's nothing creative about it.' (93) This is the essential 'freedom' element. In Liam Hudson's terms, English people are 'divergers' rather than 'convergers'. One would expect them, faced with his tests, to be able to find any number of uses for a brick (Hudson 1966; see also *Language People*: 66, Table 3.2 for portraits of the converger – the modern linguist – and the diverger).

Modern languages

The choice between modern languages and English interests me particularly. My initial hypothesis (prejudice) that English People were not good at languages was disproved. Many have the inquisitiveness, the delight in eavesdropping, the love of the exotic which characterize Language People. Only one respondent (interestingly a linguistician) said he was 'poor at languages', though several said they were specifically poor at 'pronouncing French'. 'I could have done languages if it had been German.'

Modern languages figures in the short-lists of many of my respondents. Here is the story of a woman Fellow at Oxford. It will also serve as an illustration of the uncertainties from which the decision emerges:

> I was going to be a modern linguist. It was a flip of the coin in my case. Then I applied to Cambridge to do French and German but my French wasn't terribly good. When they turned me down, I thought I'd change university and subject. I also applied for German and management studies and also Chinese, but coming here I thought I'd stick to what I'm quite good at, which is English. (31)

The choice of English over modern languages can be based, as here, on caution. But the more positive side is an overriding interest in literature (which, as I showed in *Language People* (p. 33), linguists tend not to have). Many respondents said that their early serious reading was in fact foreign literature in translation. High achievers, as we saw with regard to mathematics, want to be the best, and one problem with modern languages is that there is a clear criterion of best: native-speaker fluency. Dr Mason actually had a degree in French and English and she had offers to do research in each. 'My French, though reasonable and fluent, was never going to be top class. People would always have seen the odd awkwardness so I thought no, I'd better do English.' (53) She also had an eye on the future job: 'I couldn't face the thought of teaching French language day in day out, marking all those proses' (this shows, incidentally, how the practice of a discipline can determine recruitment into it). English offers more freedom but also more challenge: 'The reason I'm not a language person is that English was a more challenging discipline. I always enjoyed translation but it was a relief from the much greater effort involved in analysing literature.' (53) This mixture of caution and readiness to accept challenge seems typical of English People. For example, many of my Language People respondents had bilingual backgrounds which they used to give them an advantage; but Martina, who has some of her Czech father's language ability, like him, sees language simply as a means of studying other things, such as literature. (101)

History

The choice between English and modern languages is an either/or one. But English is also a means whereby other subjects can be pursued in more personal, immediate ways. This is the transgressive aspect of the subject:

> What got me into English was love of the past. We were on holiday once near Tintagel. My father said we were going to see an Arthurian battlefield. I thought when we got there I would be able to pick up bits of armour and arrowheads. When we got to this field it was completely bare. My initial reaction was a great disappointment. Where are the shields? Then I remember registering 'If there aren't any shields lying around, this battle must have taken place a long time ago.' (29)

The obvious question is, why did he not do history? The answer gives an insight into the nature of English:

> The problem with history at school and undergraduate level is that you are dealing an awful lot with secondary sources. With English all of your contact is with primary texts. So if you are really interested in the past there can be no better way of going into it than via these primary documents. (29)

The characteristic of English as a subject is that students deal with the original materials and are able to respond in personal and original ways. The subject is more democratic, in the sense that the student's relation to a literary text is much freer than a student's relation to most other school materials, where the teacher's mediation is all-powerful. English People have the idea that their materials are actually more significant even than the historians' primary documents. English is 'history plus the unconscious': 'With the creative text, driven by the unconscious, you end up with a richer record of someone's experience – beyond the conscious experience – than you get in an historical text.' (11)

In general English represents an escape route from learning impersonal *facts* which most school subjects – science, history, economics, modern languages – typically require:

> There was a lot of emphasis on rote-learning in our school, and testing. You had to know the details of the Treaty of Utrecht, and I didn't want another three years of that. (43)

I've always been more interested in ideas than brute facts. I was always interested in personalities and the clashes of ideology, big ideas, colonialism, nazism, whatever, never been one for the small detail. (76)

Philosophy and psychology

English enables the combination of big ideas and personal experience:

English is a much better subject than philosophy because the issues you deal with are more general, and relate to your own experience. English makes you more perceptive. It makes quirky bits of the day more interesting. It's trying to ground your experience in something that is relatable. (83)

English can be construed positively as being capacious:

It's not just studying literature, it's studying psychology, philosophy, history, economics, politics. You are studying your perception of culture and your perception of forces on your life. It's more of a practical subject than, say, psychology. Studying literature you can come up with psychology you can apply to yourself. I think what swayed me about English was it did allow you to bring in a lot of other interests. As a discipline it was less fenced-off. (61)

English is actually closer to people's lived experience, their personal lives, but also closer to their imaginative lives. It seems too that the subject English is used by high achievers as a means of resisting the fundamental aspects of the school system: strong framing and classification in the Bernstein (1972) sense; premature choice and labelling; fact-based learning. So there is a sense in which to choose English is, for better or worse, to avoid choice, to avoid crossing the threshold into the world of categories. As Rosen says, it is 'the least subject-like of subjects' (in Protherough, 1989: 8).

This makes its status highly ambiguous and it is possible to construe it negatively. Professor Dover, for example, sees it as a non-subject. Like classics, he says, it indicates general, not specific, aptitude. Not everyone would agree with his conclusion, which is that 'if you're good at English it probably means you ought to be diverted to another subject. Being good at English is a cry for help.' (15)

Influence

Teachers

A great deal of 'help' *is* offered to pupils. These choices are not made in solitude. They are made in contexts where powerful others are intervening. Garratt's (1985) conclusion that school and family have little influence is not confirmed by my evidence:

It's extraordinary, the power that is benignly wielded at that age. I wanted to be an actor, and at the age of 13, the teacher said, 'Oh you can't be an actor, actors are not very clever,' and I thought, 'Well I'd never thought of that before,' and I never considered being an actor again. (45)

Teachers have great and lasting influence. One of the best parts of the interviewing was to hear vivid descriptions of teachers, some now in their twenties, others long dead:

Excitement and love for something, that sort of thing is catching. (87)

Witty, dashing. He was terribly interested in our own writing. We worshipped him. (3)

An absolutely brilliant teacher who wasn't interested in syllabuses . . . I remember furious debates about *Paradise Lost*. Sometimes she would lose her temper and leave. It was terrific because we talked about it as though it mattered. (5)

Schools, it seems, often have two contrasted teachers: one had a 'Laura Ashley-style teacher – long skirts and quiet with a passion for Gerard Manley Hopkins' together with a 'flamboyant medievalist' in 'beaten-up desert boots and a scruffy suit'. (3) There was a junior school teacher who had the whole class writing serious poetry (25); an access teacher who encouraged a man with no academic qualifications to get A level and then do a degree – 'The first week I wrote half a page of A4 and I was stuck. She said, "What you've written is really good"'; a Leavisite teacher in Manchester who 'worshipped Leavis, a terrific teacher' (24); a Marxist in Leicester who discussed Derrida and Barthes and race and power relations in the classroom – 'I was taught about power and struggles, we didn't deal with anything as bizarre as character.' (107)

Family

Another force is the family, which means class, race and religion. One respondent was born in England of professional-class Bengali parents who were anxious that she should master the English language but were against her doing English at university: 'They said, "Imagine. You are going to walk in and say I'm your English literature teacher. Get real. What sort of job do you think you're going to get?"' (71) This brings us to an issue which will be important in this book: the question of who English People are. The Bengali family do not see English literature as helping their daughter's career. For them (and also for her, even after her degree in English at Oxford) there are problems about a person of Indian origin teaching English literature. They are aware that the link between effort and results is much less predictable and much more culturally determined than it would be in a subject like physics or economics. Their concern is more with integration than aspiration. In an analogous way, working-class parents can be opposed to aspiration: 'Everything I aspired to was beyond their dreams.' (48)

There are complex relationships here between class, nationality and religion, but on the whole, for whites, the subject was seen as a vehicle for upward social mobility, perhaps a more effective means of acquiring middle-class status than others. Whereas for middle-class children English might be transgressive in the sense that parents would be expecting their children to become professional or business people, for working-class or lower middle-class parents the fact of post-16 education is enough in itself, without distinction of subject, and the 'cachet' is a bonus:

> There was respect for the idea of culture in the traditional sense: 'this is a cultured person because they know about art and literature or music', so there was a certain cachet in the sense of someone who read Shakespeare. (43)

For Dr O'Hare, a Protestant from Dublin, English represented the sense of tradition: 'It was perceived socially as a prestige thing. It was snobby, antiquey. It gave a superiority: "Gosh, I'm studying English".' (1)

School system

Individuals' choices are individually influenced: by this teacher, this parent. But pupils, teachers and parents operate within systems and, however rebellious or transgressive the individual or the subject, some aspects of the system are almost impossible to resist: for example, the type of school–secondary modern, comprehensive, public school, grammar school.

My staff respondents are predominantly lower middle-class grammar school products. They contrast themselves with previous generations and with upper-class people whom they see as having a different relation to culture. Dr Wilton admits: 'I have never been at home in the subject. I come at it from the outside,' and he compares himself with a different class of English Person: 'She was the high Tory daughter of a diplomat, a home which has Johnson's dictionary in its original edition. She was ill at the age of 12 and read the whole of *The Faerie Queene*.' (2) The contrast is between home and school, insiders and outsiders; the suggestion is that in this subject the institution cannot compete with the advantages of birth. But it can try. The grammar school's emphasis on upward mobility through competition (examinations) and hard work has marked them:

> I was enormously hardworking, ridiculously so. So I didn't make many friends, except the few who would put up with me the way I was. (57)

> I was very much a high achiever in school, I was driven, too much so I think. I would, in the sixth form, spend three or four hours an

evening doing homework. All I wanted to do was to go to university, I thought: 'It's the only way out of this council estate'. (25)

Pleasure was not precluded but it had to be upwardly aspiring pleasure – literature itself, of course, but also classical music, the Hallé in Manchester, for example: 'It was a great pleasure, but it was a matter of seeking social definition too.' Popular culture did not count: 'I was in Manchester in the year of the Beatles. I feel a complete idiot in retrospect because I missed all that. It wasn't serious stuff.' (24)

Another powerful aspect of the system is imposed subject-choice or options. Some of the examples I have given above are of people who effected their choices outside the British system. The life histories of these non-British respondents are significantly different, because the system in which they worked never demanded the stark choices that the British one does. As Dr Lake said: 'Chemistry and English, that could only happen in America.' One effect may be to make the British feel superior: 'When I went to teach in the States I felt so superior, so scholarly, because I had been trained in such a narrow range at such an early age.' (45)

The price paid for this superiority is the premature closing down of avenues and the result is splitting. In order to choose between mathematics and English the young person has to be defined as not good at either one or the other:

> I have never been happy about having to choose English or maths. If I had stayed in Ireland I would probably be an engineer now, because the leaving certificate is like the international baccalaureate. English was my favourite, but other subjects too. (24)

Choice between subjects, in other words, is free and, for above-average pupils, unforced. But the choice itself is compulsory and the freedom is exercised within a very constraining and splitting system which excludes creativity and imagination from the sciences and locates them exclusively in the arts. Protherough's survey (1989: 34) shows that little has changed in this respect since the 1973 NFER study: 'The majority of those [from his sample] who . . . were selected for university had followed a more conventional arts grouping at school. Half had done History with English, and 40% with French.' So the British combination of A level and university entrance forces young people to make quite dramatic choices early on. They may spend part of their careers seeking to integrate parts which the system has forced them to separate and split. Dr Kelly worked for a year for IBM because he felt he had 'unused numeracy'. (24)

> It's like what happens to children. You have two daughters. One's pretty, one's clever, and the clever one can't be pretty and the pretty one can't be clever, and you ruin their lives like that; it's the same with the arts/science divide. By not doing well in maths I was fulfilling someone's expectations, including my own. (45)

Choice of university

First there is the subject choice made within the constraints of the educational system and under the influence of teachers and family. Then there is the choice of a place where this choice will be furthered and made virtually unalterable, where it becomes character.

To do English, rather than a vocational career subject like law or accountancy, is already a risk (though, as we have seen, more for middle-class pupils). One way of reducing the risk is to do it in the most prestigious institution possible – Oxbridge not civic, civic not polytechnic. When it comes to university choice we are still very much in the area of expressive rationality: calculation mixed with fantasy.

Oxbridge

Which is the most prestigious place to do English? Most people think it is Oxford. Some think it is Cambridge. Everyone thinks it is Oxbridge. Why is this so? The days are over when Jocelyn Stephens, a pupil at Eton, could be seen rowing at Henley by a Cambridge don and offered a place to read English at that don's college with no qualifications or interest in the subject.[2] There is a bar which everyone must jump, and it could well be set at its maximum height (three A's at A level). But those who have jumped it or will jump it are still rigorously selected. So it is very difficult to get into Oxbridge. So it is very desirable to get into Oxbridge. So Oxbridge is perceived as the best – which means that if you see yourself as the best or others see you as the best you want to get into Oxbridge. And if you do get into Oxbridge you are the best:

> I wanted to go to Oxford, because I had this mental image of it as the best place to go to. I've always had this drive to excel. It was the idea that it was the best that was important, which is a sad admission to make really. I wanted people to admire me for going to Oxford. (76)

Here is a revealing example of how torn Oxford students can be about the situation (my emphases):

> Gowns I don't really mind, it gives me a certain sense, *I'm almost loath to admit*, of achievement. *I'm sure it's not a good thing, but it is.* I think there are a lot of people here who would lie and say gowns are not on, and the rest of it, but at heart they like the fact that they are at Oxford as opposed to anywhere else. It gives you the sense, *it's a horrible phrase*, of being at the top of your generation. *I'm aware of the fact that it's fallacious*, but at the same time it doesn't make me feel bad. *Whether it's true or not*, employers seem to think that. There are still so many companies that still take a set quota from Oxford and Cambridge. *I am sure that's wrong*, but I'm quite prepared to take advantage of it. (76)

The important point is that the reality – good, bad or indifferent – of what actually goes on in Oxbridge is largely irrelevant. It operates in fantasy as a self-fulfilling prophecy. The system will ensure that people who are highly motivated and see themselves confidently as the best will form the student body (and staff body, since the same process operates). I am not suggesting that there is no reference at all to reality – the quality of teaching, the library and so on – I am saying that the reality aspect is subordinate. A professor who did not go to Oxbridge but whose children did said:

> With the present set-up, if you're offered a choice of a place in Cardiff or a choice of a place in Oxford, you'd be well advised to take Oxford, not because you'll get a better education but because it'll carry more weight. (15)

So school-children and their families and teachers make guesses about whether they are Oxbridge material; they make decisions about who they are. Here is a student who underestimated herself in A-level terms but still assessed herself as not Oxbridge:

> I didn't apply to Oxford and Cambridge before my grades because I didn't think I was good enough, but then when I got three A's, my mother was livid. She said, before you do anything else, sit down to make sure you don't want to go to Cambridge or Oxford. And I said no, I'm not one of those types. They're very intellectual and I didn't class myself as that at all. (94)

It does happen that, like Robyn Penrose in David Lodge's *Nice Work*, a pupil will decide against Oxbridge on instrumental grounds, excluding fantasy:

> I didn't want to go to Oxford or Cambridge, I wanted to go to the most modern or progressive courses in the country, incorporating a lot of new ideas about language, sociology of language and things like that. I wanted to be in a more real place. (101)

Some students feel that even if Oxbridge's intellectual demands can be met, there are social demands which cannot. This is often the conclusion of a working-class or of a Northern pupil:

> There were 30 at the interview and they chose four. A lot of the others were from private schools. They turned up in their nice little tailored suits. I had a long green skirt that I bought from a chain store, with a nice blouse and a knitted jumper that I'd had made for my birthday. And yet I got an A in English literature at A level. I could do the work, there was no question about that. I wasn't posh enough. (91)

There is a striking contrast in this family:

My brother did voice lessons and he doesn't speak with a northern accent any more. He doesn't say he's from Manchester but from Cheshire. He did all this to get into Oxford, and I thought 'No way, if they want me they want me for who I am, and the way I talk.' (91)

Oxford is the south, another world:

I don't think I would have fitted in at Oxford. I preferred to stay up north. I've got a friend in London and I visited him last weekend, and the train stops at Banbury and then a certain type of person gets on. I've nothing against them, it's just they seem to rub me up the wrong way. (95)

There is some awareness that this rejection may not be wholly rational: 'I turned down their offer in the end. I regret that to a certain extent. It may have been inverted snobbery. It would have been a good career move.' (43)

It can also happen that a pupil from a famous public school will resist school and family pressures:

I went to the interview and told them there that given the choice I would rather go to Newcastle. They wrote to the school and said that they weren't accepting me because I'd expressed a wish to go else-where, which the school didn't like at all. It's the type of school where the headmaster has to stand up in front of the parents and say we got so many people into Oxford this year, so he was rather disappointed. He did say he admired me for my honesty, which is a polite way of saying 'I wish you hadn't said anything'. (95)

The position of the colleges is that everyone gets in who is bright enough. This means that the colleges make genuine efforts to attract pupils from comprehensive schools. But somehow these efforts founder on the twin rocks of the colleges' own problems – the tutorial system restricts dramati-cally the kinds of students you can take, since the last person you want in a tête-à-tête for an hour is the deep silent thinker – and the comprehen-sives' own assumptions.

You are constantly finding this frustrating experience with the Oxford interview. You think you are dealing with very clever people from comprehensive schools, and it's not showing. You do everything you can, but if they are reading less sophisticated stuff, and if they are tongue-tied at interview as they would be, because they are terribly in awe of the whole thing...In competition with the Winchester sixth who come in with lots of interview practice, especially in subjects like English where articulacy is everything, there isn't a lot you can do about it. (24)

They do not get the students they are looking for in Oxford because there is so much snobbery about Oxford. It's the schools' block, not the colleges'. (44)

So we come up against another related issue – that of the public schools and their link with Oxbridge. Pupils from public schools and from a particular background are more likely to feel that Oxbridge is their place. Professor Thomas recalls his time in Cambridge:

> Everyone in Cambridge seemed to be over six foot and brayed rather than talked, and elbowed the locals off the pavement. It's changed – Oxbridge students would now have at least a wash of democracy. In those days they didn't. They were very visibly the ruling class, the arrogance was very upfront. I detested the place. For a long time after, I got a sinking feeling in the stomach going there. It indelibly marked me as the scene of a certain trauma. Here, in Oxford, I've taken people and wondered if I'd done them a favour. (23)

And Professor Leigh recalls Oxford:

> Oxford was frightening. I didn't retreat into reading, I retreated into being in love, another form of copping out. There were all these bright, wonderful, glittering people. They might have been upper middle class, I don't know, but they had confidence and you had the feeling that they were doing bright, glittering things, and you could never do them, you didn't know quite what they were. And so you sat around a lot drinking Nescafé with the other no-hopers. (17)

However, it was pointed out to me that, while to go to Oxford may be conformist for someone with a certain public school background, to do English is not:

> The teaching body of my generation, drawn from the grammar schools, are teaching a significant number of stylish public school people. It's tripartite – grammar school, comprehensive school, public school. The public school boys are terribly nice people. They wouldn't be doing English if they didn't have some kind of idealism. They are not just money-makers. They are often in opposition to becoming accountants. They are often the most politically alert. (24)

Civic

Selection for civic universities is also rigorous. The bar is set higher for English than for any other subject.[3] I was told that almost all of Newcastle's first year had three A's: 'They are very sharp; they are an elite bunch.' (53) Here too there is a high proportion of public school pupils:

> Here I'm considered as one of the lowest of the low because I didn't go to a public school. I'm among the minority here having been to a comprehensive. (92)

> I went to Henderson, which is the hall of residence which has a Sloaney reputation, and there were a large number of people there

who did nothing to hide the fact that they came from public school.
I don't make any attempt to move out of that section of society. Last
year I lived with three boys. One went to Uppingham, one went to
Harrow, one went to Eton. They're all lovely people. (102)

There are still requirements over and above A level, though the balance
between candidate and institution is more equal than at Oxford. Civic
university entrance resembles a marriage market where potential partners
size up each other's charms, real and imagined, before making or accepting
a proposal. It is all a very private, unpredictable business. An article by Ian
Robinson (1983) gave a rare indication of how a selection procedure was
operated in Swansea at that time. There was the factual test (Who wrote
the following? Give approximate dates for the composition of . . .) and a
piece of practical criticism (Which of these is the better poem?), and then
a search for sensitivity, via the interview. But, as he says, 'I am only
speaking for myself. In our department we all do what we think best.' So
there is in fact no way for us (or the teachers and students) to extrapolate
even from this rare account.

In any case, students are making their initial selection according to
various criteria: their own hypothesized ability (in terms of A level) is only
one; the actual course is another ('I would have done this course anywhere' (95)); there are non-academic considerations, especially the geo-
graphical situation of the institution and the type of institution it is.

Polytechnic

Here is a middle-class student from a public school, currently at PNL:

My history teacher in school told me not to go to PNL because it was
a bit political. She said they all live in communes. (82)

A university student:

It's people's perceptions. You don't tend to link something like English literature with polytechnics. I always viewed them as being more
technical. (95)

The abolition of the binary line may mean that in the future (but when?)
these images will alter. But at the moment there is no doubt that most
sixth-formers see polytechnics as less prestigious, a safety-net if their self-
perception happens to be over-optimistic.

Only exceptionally independent-minded pupils will choose civic over
Oxbridge on course grounds. In the same way, only the exceptional will
choose polytechnic over civic:

I wouldn't have gone to a poly. I wasn't independent enough in the
kind of values that were around, to have been able to have made a
choice to go to a poly, even if I'd known about them. (75)

So far we have considered high-achieving pupils who followed the conventional route from their school to university or polytechnic, via interviews and A levels. But what of the children who left school at 16 or younger? Self-belief has negative as well as positive aspects. In the same way that a prerequisite for becoming an Oxbridge student is a belief, in yourself and others, that you have it in you to be one, so the belief that you are incapable of certain kinds of study precludes you automatically from that world. Here are some very different English People from those we have met so far.

Paula is a working-class single parent who went to a secondary modern school in the north of England:

> We weren't even given the option of doing O levels. In the end I decided to train as a hairdresser. That lasted three months. After that I did over 60 jobs. (81)

Richard left his secondary modern school at 16:

> It never entered my head not to. I had friends in the grammar school, it never entered their heads not to go to university, or not to become a doctor or whatever. That's the set-up. When you go at 11 you know what's in front of you. (81)

David was in a further education college and saw the class contrast very clearly:

> I had real problems. I had working-class parents who said, 'Reading's all very well. What are you going to do with an English degree? It's a waste of time, get married, get a job.' But I was meeting people who had been told by their parents that university was the obvious thing to do. I'd go to their houses and they would say, 'Help yourself to the food, Mummy won't mind. If you want to borrow any of Dad's books, help yourself,' and there would be all these books on the shelf and my parents had five between them. (90)

All these students are currently doing degrees in English at the PNL. They got there by access courses or threshold courses at places like Paddington College. They did an A level in English. And when they were convinced that they could do the unthinkable, a degree in English, they applied to polytechnics. And they applied to do English because English was the only choice, the only thing they were 'qualified' to do. It was the life-line. This is also a form of transgression: 'You work with 20 Irishmen on a jack-hammer and you don't see yourself studying the subject English at all.' (83) Throughout the years of unsuccessful schooling and the years of brief, dead-end jobs, the fact of being a reader and a writer persisted:

> I loved English literature, I loved reading books, even in the primary school. The teacher used to read a story. I could hardly wait to the

end of the day, and I could have stayed there all night. The spark was there, but it wouldn't light. With sparks like that you need someone near you to be wafting. (81)

They got accepted into the polytechnic, not because of their A-level scores but because of their persistent enthusiasm for 'natural' reading.

It is worth signalling here the fact that the polytechnics deal centrally with two aspects which are very marginal in universities. One is race. The ethos of equal opportunities has permeated PNL:

It's an inner-city institution, local students. We don't encourage people to come from far away. The staff and students are very mixed, because the population of London is very mixed, but there is a shared view and a great deal of tolerance. (40)

It's just accepted that it's a multi-cultural college. You almost forget that there are places where there are no black faces. If I went to Oxford that would strike me as very strange. We've probably got a good representation of different races and cultures within the polytechnic. (89)

But PNL does not work miracles:

If I get this degree it will make me more confident, but it will never make me middle class. I could never be accepted as middle class, could I, because of the colour of my skin. (80)

The other aspect is age. The most striking thing about PNL compared to any of the institutions I visited is the number of mature students (the policy is 50/50) and the satisfaction this gives the staff: 'The students are brilliant. We have a cross-section. Instead of going for A Levels, the institution has gone for returning students, and it has produced this exciting, wonderful group of students.' (47)

Some, as we have seen, are treating this opportunity as a life-line. But there is another group and it seems appropriate to end this chapter on choice with them. Florence is in her late fifties. She took early retirement after a successful nursing career which had culminated in her running a large hospital. But now she is doing what she had been dissuaded from doing over 30 years ago, a degree in English. For some students the choice of English is a compromise between the need to earn a living and the need to satisfy personal aspirations; for a number of fortunate mature students there is no need to compromise. English is indeed a preparation for life, but for life after work. Another student, in the same age-group, puts it like this:

My mother is working class. She is 83 now and through lack of education she has had no inner resources on which to draw. I realize more and more how important our inner lives are. And I love literature. (70)

'Loving literature', reading, perhaps writing: the choice of English as a subject, at whatever age, is based on these specific personal interests. But how do personal aspirations interact with institutional demands? This is the core question we will examine in the next chapter.

*three*_____

Reading and writing

English children

> I, as a child, it is not too much to say, was in some way kept alive by
> fictions. I was asthmatic and spent much time in bed. I read Scott,
> Dickens, Jane Austen, I lived in those worlds. I told myself long tales
> of other lives. I also retold my own life to myself to make sense of it.
> (Antonia Byatt, 1991, *Passions of the Mind*: 21)

Reading

One of the easier parts of writing this book was coming up with the
hypothesis about what kind of children English People were and then
confirming it. English People were: only children ('It made for a lot of
reading. I lived in imagination mostly, and I had all sorts of imaginary
companions' (5)); or late-born ('My parents were relatively old by the time
they had me. None of my family were readers, but I was. I think it was
because my sisters were so much older than me' (89)). They lived in
remote places ('a farm in the middle of nowhere' (77)); or they were
cloistered in some way ('My mother was a very hysterical, paranoid person. We weren't allowed out, my brother and I. We didn't have a television until the age of eight and I was never allowed to see anything that
kids want to watch' (90)). Others were ill and convalescent ('Years spent
as a TB patient' (6); 'sickly, heavily mothered, missed a lot of school' (13)).
They were romantic and solitary ('Generally solitary and shy, dreamy, a
lot of time on my own in sensuous melancholy' (22); 'lonely, full of fan-
tasies and imagination, quite shy' (5)).

There are examples that modify this expected picture. There were
working-class children for whom reading was a beacon on a bleak land-
scape: 'Reading spread my world . . . pure escape.' (89) There were: a front-
row forward from a South Wales grammar school – 'It was not done to
be sensitive' (2); children of large, intrusive families who would read, not

to escape from solitude but to retreat into it (11); children at pre-TV boarding schools. (21) There were tomboys: 'I used to go out and beat up all the boys in the neighbourhood and then go back in and read some *Black Beauty* and *Heidi*.' (6) And there are happy childhoods: 'amazingly happy. I grew up in the countryside, I didn't have much of a social life. It was a fairly thoughtful childhood.' (65) This last example shows how the key may be not so much loneliness as the capacity for being alone.

Another hypothesis easily confirmed concerns precocious reading: 'Phenomenal. At the age of seven I had a reading age of 14 plus. It was off the scale. I sat in, reading constantly, I had read *Treasure Island* before I started school.' 'All the time, from a very early age, walking to the bus, on the bus, at the bus stops, at every meal' (9); 'in the bath' (82); 'under the bedclothes with a torch'. (60) 'I've always been a reader. I would read sauce bottles'. (6) 'The first thing I ever learned to do was to read. They used to sit me on my potty with books.' (106) There are family stories: 'We went on holiday in a motorbike and side-car. My father drove into a ditch and I didn't move my head from the book.' (56) There is the absence of an ending: 'One of the traumas of my third grade, at about eight, was having a murder thriller taken away from me. It was called *The Back Bay Murders* and they took it away because they thought it was too grown-up. I have never found out who did it.' (13)

It is not just the precocity but the intensity. Here is an account of reading *King Lear* at age 15: 'The amazing passion, amazing feeling, it was the ultimate – death, people falling around going mad. Everything you'd ever wanted.' (65) A striking fact is that siblings (in this case a twin (98)) are often not like this at all: 'She hardly ever picked up a book. She was interested in science.' (98)

There are rare exceptions to precocious reading: 'I didn't read until I was nine. I taught myself. I was getting desperate.' (86) But this exception reveals something which may be prior to reading – a relation to language in its spoken form, to the human voice:

> It came from my Dad listening to Edith Piaf, and Richard Tauber and Al Jolson. 'Listen to this,' he'd say. He was shining, and I thought Wow! and I paid attention. (86)

Initially, the voices are family voices: 'A lot of my younger books have got voices to them. Winnie the Pooh is my grandfather, my mum is Bambi.' (88)

The family attitude to language and books is fundamental and it varies greatly:

> The whole family has been interested in language games. My brother and I used to find sentences we liked. One I remember particularly, 'Great newts and salamanders wallowed in the mud amidst the eternal gloom cast by mammoth ferns.' I got this into an essay when I was about eleven. (56)

The house was full of books. There was a calf-bound edition of the *Waverley* novels and my father used to read them. He used to read me the *Lays of Ancient Rome*, and I can remember parts of them. (55)

This respondent finds a striking image for the process of taking in and giving out: 'Once you're steeped in it, you're like peat full of rain. Someone steps on it and it squeezes right out.' (55) By contrast, there was a more arid world: 'There were no books in the house apart from Jane's Book of Planes and an incomplete Shakespeare. My mother didn't like going to the library because she might incur debts.' (51)[1]

Writing

I cannot remember writing with the same intensity as reading. Reading then, it seemed, didn't require any effort. (89)

For a small child, the physical demands of writing are greater. Dr Paisley's mother taught her to read and write but the child was left-handed, badly coordinated. She 'wrote' stories, but in her head, or she told them to her brothers and sisters at night. (53) She nevertheless had written a novel by the age of nine. Professor Patterson (55) had written a story by the age of five and got his mother to type it out, whereupon, thus encouraged, he began an epic. One respondent actually had in his office and proudly showed me the (unpublished) novel he had written aged ten. Recent technology has made things easier: 'My father's office is strewn with the poems that I used to type on his computer when I was little.' (94) In some rare cases writing took precedence over reading:

There were not many books in the house. Writing was a surrogate for reading. I was always interested in writing. The act of writing and the practice of writing was more important than the content. (23)

Adolescence is an important stage for writing: 'Around 13 I wrote short stories, confessions. I remember a line: *When I write I am mad.*' (22) I had vivid glimpses of how adolescents used writing not for vicarious escape but as an active way of dealing with distress:

[As a child, pre-14] I was very upset about the things I found myself writing. I did a lot of tearing up. It was too painful. I wasn't happy with myself and all that came out in the writing. It was too personal, I couldn't really bear it, I didn't quite know how to handle what I was putting into words. (3)

This adolescent writer was making sense of his feelings through writing – a painful activity. The experience of reading did not require the reader to be articulate about the nature of the experience, or to specify what the identification was, or what it was that was being evaded. But the writing experience could confront the reality.

The core may be not so much writing as inventing, relating (in both senses of the word): a student, now in a creative writing group, remembers telling and hearing stories in secondary school. But this activity still did not cross the boundary into the English class. It took place in needlework:

> I remember being in a group of about four, and we used to make up stories. Stories broaden your experience without your actually having to live things like abuse and rape. Fairy stories are concerned with dealing with these subjects, but in a fantastical world. I have vivid memories of a couple of my friends who had abortions while we were at school, and it was only in that environment that they came out. (105)

Transgression

Reading and writing start in the family and meet various needs. But they are also pre-eminently school activities and, even at an early age, the school/home, public/private boundary is problematic. Transgression consists of crossing the boundary but refusing the institution's definitions:

> I went into the school, and they tried to give me the Ladybird reading books, and I had to bring in a signed letter from my parents saying that I'd read them all. They said it has to be on your report that you've read a particular series of books and got through those. (106)

In some cases the only reading experience was the school. A working-class student:

> I remember *The Old Man and the Sea*. It's still with me, that book, but the reading was just in the school. I don't remember taking books home. It didn't occur to me to buy one, or take one off the shelf. Outside school was football and pop music, and then drinking and girls. (81)

For most English People, the characteristic of reading and writing as activities and of English as a subject is that, in Bernstein's (1972) terms, the framing is particularly weak. Whereas Ohm's Law is a school notion, rarely evoked domestically, even over a blown fuse, reading as an activity crosses the boundary very easily: a child sees adults engaging in it all the time, if not at home then in trains and buses or on the beach. With writing too the framing is relatively weak although the instrumentality is greater because writing is the way a child's reading ability gets converted into school capital.

The child who has derived private satisfaction from reading and writing crosses the boundary of an institution. English as a subject is characterized by an extreme duality. On the one hand is core instrumentality in the sense of basic literacy and decoding. This is the aspect of English which gets it high ratings on the 'social benefit' scale, since English represents two of the three Rs; this is the aspect which the state is legitimately exercised about and which it will wish to standardize. On the other hand is the non-utilitarian, potentially subversive fantasy, represented by reading and writing imaginative literature.

English People, after acquiring the core, are concerned with this latter aspect. English is one of the arts, like music, drama and art, subjects which live marginal, transgressive lives in the largely utilitarian institutions that are schools, subjects which are allowed by the institution to put into question the instrumental values of the institution and, by extension, other values as well. Students who eventually go on to study English are transgressing by resisting a particular, dominant notion about the role of work and money in a person's life. Mark illustrates well a certain deferential contempt for material success:

> I've got a sort of resentment of people in accountancy, finance or economics, people who go into that kind of profession. I'd like to have some kind of comfort but I don't think that earning money comes into it at all. If there's ever a school reunion in a number of years there'll be people turn up with a BMW and I'll be there with a battered old bike. But that wouldn't worry me at all. I'll turn up with some pride with my bike and park it, trying not to scratch the cars. (95)

Some may have a goal, but it has to be distant, such as becoming a writer or opera singer. Some simply have no vocational goal and are postponing crossing the boundary of the serious world of employment (or unemployment):

> I'm quite happy to sit back and say for three years I don't have to decide what I'm going to do. I'm quite into going off travelling. I'll go abroad for a few years. I'm all about broadening my experience. If you are going to write you need to know a lot. (97)

> If you want to do something vocational you have to know what you want to do, and I didn't have any idea. (105)

They are also saying something oppositional about school and university, that these places are not solely about vocationality or meeting the state's need for specialized manpower, that the self is not to be defined solely in terms of social insertion:

> I don't think it's a preparation for work at all, I think it's a preparation for the rest of your life. It's of far more value to me than any job I would ever do. Any job I get is not going to have anything to do with English, because English is to do with me, and not my work. (107)

Some see a revolutionary aspect to this:

> It's a Bahktinian notion, literature as a carnivalesque experience against those forces, which are positioning you as a productive unit,

as someone whose *raison d'être* is to produce cars and go home and sleep until it's time to get up and produce and consume again. (43)

The student or teacher of English is siding with the creative writer. And, as Sartre says, in *Qu'est-ce que la littérature*, the relation between literature and money is arbitrary:

> The writer's activity is not *useful*, it is even *dangerous* for society to become aware of itself, since what is useful is defined precisely within the parameters of society as it is, its institutions, values, aims. If society sees itself and especially if society sees itself *being seen*, that means a challenge for established values and authority.
>
> (Sartre 1947: 128; my translation)

Literature itself is transgressive and students of literature are accessories after the fact.

English is also (the two things are connected) seen as the flagship of spiritual values:

> Literature is another world. I'm not very comfortably at home in the world of getting on. Art represents an alternative realm. Schiller has a poem about God giving out gifts; he gives the poet no gifts but says he can go to heaven whenever he wants. This perpetuates one's out-of-key relation with the world, but it does mean there is an alternative, another perspective beyond worldliness, at least as important. (22)

For some, religion can be this other world, but for the majority art and literature are the opposition to materialism, the market and *Homo oeconomicus*. 'In a rampantly instrumental society you will turn to something else for solace or ultimate value, and literature is that.' (23) English is both transcendent and transgressive. To do English is to affirm things beyond worldliness and also to deny seriousness, to be self-indulgent, pleasure-seeking. One respondent, now a professor, recalls that her father, a scientist, wanted her to be a scientist like him. She started to do science and then reverted to English without informing her parents:

> Doing English was transgressive. It was also something I was ashamed of, because it was so pleasurable, an escape. When I was applying to university I thought 'English is too much of an indulgence, I can't go on with this. I'll do history. History is hard.' I did two terms of history and couldn't stand it and went on to do English. (17)

Sometimes the institution encouraged the transgression:

> The headmistress saw me after my A levels and said I should go to university. 'I'll have to do Latin and French,' I said, 'won't I?' She said, 'But you'd rather do English wouldn't you?' I said 'Yes, but I didn't think I could because I liked it so much.' She said, 'That's all right.' It seemed self-indulgent. (5)

Accommodation

How do English People manage this tension, between personal and public, self-indulgence and work, transgression and establishment? Since staff are actually, for better or for worse, in the world of work, their position is significantly different from that of students, and in this section I shall consider the two groups separately.

Students reading

At the heart of the decision to 'read' English is a relation to books:

> I always open a book with great excitement. I walk around Dillons in a state of ecstasy. It's someone's soul between the two covers. It is something very, very exciting. (88)

Books are the precious, scarce resource:

> Cost is a big factor in what you can read and what you can't read. One of the books we had to buy for one story in it was £8.99, and I have £24.00 a week. The library had three books and there were 60 of us. (91)

But reading does not always mean ecstasy. There is a great sense of guilt:

> I know that I should be reading and I feel bad that I'm not reading all the time. But even so I haven't come to university just to read books, there are other things that I want to do. (102)

They have the sense of a task which is completely unbounded, which is out of proportion to a human life: 'I'm only a little person. There's only so much I can cope with.' (105) 'I feel at times as if I can keep swimming and swimming and swimming and I'll never get to the horizon.' (102) 'If you pick up one book, someone will say to you: Have you read a big clump of books clustered around this one that you're focusing on. It's just forever.' (60)

It is the switch from school reading to university reading that produces this shock: 'I had no preparation for the brief intensity with which you do things here [in Newcastle]. You get over a book in a week whereas at A level we spent three months on each text and wrote ten essays on it.' (94)

There is a clear mismatch between their notion of what is reasonable and that of their teachers. A lecturer in Stirling:

> I wish more of them enjoyed reading. Generally they regard the reading imposed on them as excessive but it isn't. It seems to be very light. Hardly more than one book a week. (7)

Another teacher says they are becoming like students of French, reading only what they study: 'Students should read a lot more than they study. In one's own language one should have read very large amounts.' (18)

So students are faced with the dizzying notion that you can never read enough to satisfy the institution:

> In the vacation before I came up I had a letter from the senior tutor at college, telling us to change our way of reading. You couldn't labour over it, you couldn't afford to waste time on the actual reading. (48)

English is extreme in this respect:

> I read *Little Dorrit* in four days in two-hour stints, that was hard graft, and it's back to back Dickens. You finish with *Little Dorrit* at nine in the evening and then you start another one, getting at least the first chapter done, that's psychological. The English Faculty library allows books out for one week, whereas German allows them out for four weeks, that's indicative of the demand. (78)

And Oxford represents the extreme of the extreme. Here is a particularly scathing critique of the concept of unbounded reading and writing:

> What was supposed to happen was that you had a concept of literary history which had key figures in it, but it has so many key figures so what you have to do is to pick key key figures. If you are diligent you say 'I'm supposed to cover this person's life-work in seven days, and that's just not feasible.' (71)

One Oxford don sympathizes: 'There's too much to read in the three years and that generates a lot of puzzlement and despair among the young people because it's undo-able, therefore they find some way of pretending to do it.' (29)

The solution seems to be 'speed-reading'. Students are certainly capable of feats of reading: 'I read *Bleak House* in the library in two days, 900 pages. I was slightly tired after that.' (64) This is clearly a professional skill which may be problematic for the kind of student who says 'I'm a sporadic reader not a prolific reader.' (68) And a surprisingly large number claim to be slow readers:

> Slowly, that's how I read. I'm so slow it's terrible. An average chunk is ten minutes, and the most I've ever read for in a chunk is about an hour and a half. The middle third is the most difficult third and of course for the bigger novels the middle third is going to last far longer. (61)

This slowness is not always merely a technical weakness. There is a sense in which it is from choice. The reader wants to savour the experience, to control it:

> I don't ever skip bits. I can't really skim-read like a lot of people do, I tend to read it word for word, and if there's a dramatic pause in the actual scene that I'm reading about, I tend to pause as well before

going on to read the next sentence. I suppose I really try to get into it, that's why I enjoy it so much, I soak up every word, and sometimes I re-read a page just to go through that, to enjoy that sense of being there. (65)

Students continue to make a distinction between reading for work and for pleasure. But in practice they become professional in spite of themselves:

Whenever I picked up even a crummy book for enjoyment or to vegetate with, I found myself analysing it. I'd like to just read it and leave it alone, and not have it worry my brain. But you'll just nonchalantly be going through it and something will go 'Beep!' and you'll think 'Oh, no', and then you'll start thinking about it. (60)

The ideal is that this reading should be pleasure: 'If you are not reading the things you read for work for pleasure you are on the wrong course.' (88) 'Like most people, I did my reading for a good read and I still do, of course, for escape, enjoyment, but academic study's a different ball game. It didn't make it any less enjoyable, in fact it made it more so.' (63)

Work enhances pleasure. The distinction goes. But this ideal is difficult to achieve. On the one hand, there is the demand for integrity, an authentic reading experience, which implies free choice, immersion, consent, identification: 'I have to be able to submerge myself into a text. I've got to enjoy the text to be able to read it.' (106) On the other hand is the notion of what is 'imposed', of 'force'. 'Sometimes now I have to sit and force myself to read a book. That was something I hadn't done before.' (106) Some students accept the constraint: 'You should force yourself to read things you don't enjoy.' (102) Others are doubtful:

This book by Rebecca West, because I had to force myself to sit down and read it I didn't enjoy it so much. I had not chosen this book off the shelf, it was on the list. (91)

The distinction is between a non-purposive activity and a purposive one. The purposive one alone seems self-defeating. Rather like riding a bicycle, you have to get up speed to have the experience:

Every time I read a text now I've got a pad and I make notes, that slows it down. I also think it deadens it, because you have to stop reading it. I was reading *Farewell, My Lovely*, I was really into it, but I was stopping myself reading so I could make notes so I could say something in the tutorial. (100)

But to be totally non-purposive is not to join the institution. One solution seems to be multiple readings: 'The second time, the third time, the fourth time you read a book if it's a good book you'll carry on noticing things that you didn't notice before.' (66) But this can add to the pressure and to the guilt if you think you have not only to read all the books in the world but to read them at least twice.

In most cases the circle is squared: students accommodate to the requirements of the institution and they remain readers. One student horrified his
business-studies flatmates by handing in the dissertation which signalled
the end of his degree requirements and going immediately to the library to
start reading *Middlemarch*. (65) This example seems to encapsulate neatly
the way in which students play with the boundaries: he has finished his
degree, so the novel is not *work* but he reads it in the library, the workplace.

Students writing

Creative writing
The sense of loss is more apparent in the writing than in the reading.
Students manage on the whole successfully to transfer their early reading
pleasures to the classic set texts of the institution. They experience guilt,
they feel pressured, they have to make compromises, split things off, but,
as we have seen, they also see positive gain. It is harder to hang on to non-
academic writing than to non-academic reading. Another way of putting
this is to say that writing is where the boundary between the personal and
the institutional is strongest. In all the institutions I visited (except Oxford)
there are options in creative writing. In Stirling it is the most popular one,
heavily over-subscribed. But, in the absence of this institutional frame, few
manage to hang on to their creative activity.

A student used the activity of writing poetry to prepare her for the move
from a remote farm to Oxford University. By writing about her experiences of lambing, for example, she was able to make those experiences
valuable and transportable across the boundary. She literally brought them
with her. Once at Oxford, however, she gave up writing: 'My own writing
has fizzled out. I don't have the angst any more.' (77) Another Oxford
student: 'I used to write books. It was knocked out of me well before
university. I feel sad about that. I write occasionally now, but I'm very
reluctant to share it with anybody.' (75a) So the writing is abandoned or
becomes purely private, shown to no one.

Academic writing
The primary boundary is that between silence and speech. Students start
from their own strong feelings about life or literature and these are inarticulate. Even a straightforward experience of fiction can end in inarticulacy:
'*Sons and Lovers* was the first book I read. I thought it was amazing but
I found it difficult to speak about.' (80) There was a great deal of evidence
of people being very powerfully affected by reading works – Sartre, Eliot,
Rilke, Auden – that they could not 'understand'; that is, they could not put
into words what they felt:

> The first poet I read was Auden and I couldn't understand the things
> he was saying and yet the way he wrote was so cohesive as opposed
> to actually having a meaning. It was like 'Wow what's going on?'

Every time I want a touchstone for why I do English it's W. H. Auden. (83)

This phenomenon is particularly connected with poetry – with voice and rhythm. It is possible in this way to cross the boundary into speech mimetically, without producing another discourse: 'I could actually recite poetry. I didn't have a clue what it was about.' (2) 'I loved reading aloud, intoning it. The first book I bought for myself was Eliot's poetry. I didn't understand much of it, it's wonderful music.' (51) 'One day when I was quite small I went to a cupboard and found a book. Inside was something I'd not seen before, a slanty script written in lines, and I started to read it and it jingled and I read it and read it.' (41) To poetry should be added the experience of drama – 14-stone rugby forwards combining enthusiastic assassination of Caesar with speaking Shakespeare's lines, lines which they might not have been able to paraphrase or analyse.

To enter the institution it is not enough to have had a powerful experience: the experience has to become commentary. But how? The gap between private reading and public utterance is mysterious:

There was a sense in school and all through university when I didn't know what I was supposed to be doing with these texts. People that I got a lot of pleasure out of reading. I knew that I was interacting with them in some way but hadn't the language to describe that process. It did feel like it was some kind of magical thing, that you somehow had to know how to talk about these texts. No one was going to tell you what you were meant to be doing, what you were meant to be saying, and for a long time I felt quite lost. (58)

The feelings about writing are very strong: 'The initial act of putting pen to paper, it's the opposite of opening the covers of a book.' (88) This fear can be disguised as something else: 'I have to admit that I'm lazy . . . well not so much lazy as afraid.' (66) What is this fear? Basically it is the fear of exposure, of exposing personal feelings and of being judged. This feeling is strongest with regard to creative writing, but expressing one's feelings about a reading experience provokes similar anxiety.

That's my truest response to literature, it's to say 'Yes, that's what it feels like'. But it means laying yourself open. How can you do that? How can I? I know there is a part of me that says 'That's not appropriate', or 'It's pearls before swine'. I'm embarrassed to have strong responses. (111)

A particular characteristic of English is that students are beginners in a difficult trade, 'raiding the inarticulate': 'Learning to write what you mean is really very tough, I'm nowhere there yet.' (79) And they are in daily contact with the achievements of the greatest practitioners of that trade. This produces a sense of inadequacy. 'You become so overawed that you are inhibited, so don't do it yourself.' (43)

Far from helping students overcome these legitimate fears by acknowledging them and developing, for example, techniques for 'raiding the inarticulate' and for controlling and limiting self-exposure (which is what
all writers do), the institution tends to solve the problem by banishing
the personal altogether and dismissing students' attempts to overcome it
themselves.

I asked Diana, an Oxford student, if she would write in an essay 'This
text is important because of this aspect of my life.' She replied: 'I'd be shot
on the spot if I did that. You are such a small fish that anything you
particularly think must be couched in: "one", "the reader", "it is thought
that". If you write "in my opinion", that usually gets a line through it.'
The result is the abandonment of the notion that the course could produce
integration or that serious matters could be dealt with in the institution:

> I've taken a degree like a job. I have my own personal life. It's
> teaching me to deal with things that are outside myself. Seeing things
> in an objective way is what is required of you. I tend to keep things
> at arm's length and not get too involved. I remember doing Sylvia
> Plath and getting too involved in it, and I did awfully badly, whereas
> the things that didn't interest me so much I can dissect, my writing
> is clearer. If you do feel deeply about Wordsworth, I say go and do
> a maths degree. (77)

Students' attempts to be personal within the institution are not well
received:

> The first essay I did, I didn't get any mark, not even an F. The guy
> who marked it said, 'I can't give you a mark for this, it's . . . creative.'
> Not an E, not an F – nothing. (87)

They often feel that, far from learning to articulate more clearly the personal,
they are losing touch with it:

> When I started writing here, I just wrote essays off the top of my
> head, and the tutor kept saying, 'Give a bibliography,' and I would
> say I hadn't consulted any. But I'm now writing using critics. I'm
> really worried because I feel I'm losing that ability to write what I
> feel. I feel better about writing my own views than these high-falutin
> ideas that someone else is coming up with. At times when I was
> writing my own ideas they didn't sound as good as what the critics
> had said, but I thought these are my ideas and I'm going to put them
> down. (102)

What emerges from this is that the institution has a particular and
exclusive view of knowledge and that this tends to exclude the process of
learning to make the inarticulate articulate because it does not recognize
any value in the inarticulate. The only experience which can count is that
which can be articulated according to the institution's rules, and they are
analytical. A lecturer puts it like this:

You can be a fully paid up member of an English department and not be concerned with fiction but with ideas. English does that to you; you're forced to be analytical, you're not allowed to be creative in your appreciation of literature, they're forcing you into the analytical camp but insisting that you have your first allegiance to creative texts. It's a duping; it's a frequent experience of people coming as undergraduates. They love reading and they really get culture shock because they do their essay and almost break down into tears at the beauty of the passage they're reading and they get a low mark. (1)

The problem starts before university:

I have been Chief Examiner at A level for a long time, so I know it from the inside. A-level reading is fundamentally very simple decoding of content. I think that's a sad loss, that they can't enjoy this in a precognitive way. (51)

All this is part of the wider issue of the arts in general within the education system. In school, potential university students are channelled into the most cognitive subjects. English People were in fact often very good at art or music or drama. But 'people who wanted to go to university didn't do art. Art was sneered at.' (64)

Here is another tutor's view of the process:

They disappear into the tunnel of exams, and at 12 they've stopped drawing, they've stopped writing stories. Post A-level students are like old rubber bands that have been stretched and stretched and they don't snap any more. (13)

The university merely continues the process:

They come with a hunger to read and it gets knocked out of them in our course because we put them through a period of sensory deprivation and they come out of it changed, cannier, more sophisticated, but they've lost a lovely light in the eye and in the heart. (22)

The loss of innocence may be the entrance price. English is offering an accommodation between the risks of the (precognitive) arts and the security of the (analytical) institution, between, one might say, the uncanny and the canny.

Here too there are accommodations, and squarings of circles, losses and gains. Patrick, after getting a first, is going to be a dancer: he produces a very thoughtful balance-sheet of the whole process, from the point of view of someone who has just completed it:

I've done well within the system, but it always felt like a struggle. It often felt insincere. Dance is different. Like in English I work hard, I train hard, but it isn't intellectual. It seems more personal, more happy. Dance means I don't have time to think about it, I just do it. (72)

It is as if he has paid for his academic identity and now can be free. But this solution involves oscillation. The ideal would be that students, in their written academic response to their own lived experience and to their reading, might be enabled to 'dance' more, to find disciplined spontaneity and integration.

Staff reading

The staff position is more clear-cut. Their career choice has been made and it is possible to see how the tension between the cognitive and the pre-cognitive, between personal (which does not pay the rent) and institutional (which does), is actually lived.

The question of the private nature of reading and of the text becomes more urgent when they realize that they may actually be responsible for bringing it over the threshold and breaking the spell. The fears are very strong:

> I was afraid the academic study of English might interfere with my very intense relation with it. I was afraid of violation. There were books which I resisted teaching in case it took away the magic. You need to keep your own personal space inviolate. (22)

One solution is to keep literature private, to preserve the right not to speak about it. These are the English teachers who in fact become 'language people'.

> I was emoting. I was passionately in love with Hamlet and still am, but as far as my approach to writing about it was concerned it was very analytical, very much a linguist's approach. My essays were methodical, it was something I had control over, in all the emotional turmoil when you are 17. (56)

Others have the same conflict as the students between institutional reading and what they usually call 'natural reading', 'reading in an undesigning way as a human being'. (22) 'I read Dickens in my teens, it was my most natural reading experience, I loved it. I'm not as natural a reader as some. My wife retreats into a book and gets lost in it completely, I don't do that.' (24) It is interesting that this respondent seems to have transferred the 'natural' aspects to music. As his reading became institutional, 'music took over'. 'Now I'm a professional reader, I just read for work. I can't read things that are not improving me. I can't read detective novels. Every page I read I've got a sense of "What can I use this for? How can I show off with it?"' (24)

As with the students, the work–pleasure opposition can be resolved: 'It's rare I pick up a book that isn't connected with a course. But that's not to say I'm not getting pleasure. I'm not reading for pleasure, but I do enjoy reading. It's one of the nicer aspects of the job.' (43)

We should remember that for staff it is not only the profession that threatens 'reading for pleasure':

> The important thing in my thirties and early forties was raising kids. In the job I just marked time. I was lucky to get through a book. I'd see these books that I couldn't finish piling up round the house. (13)

The student panic at the vastness of what must be read does not seem to surface among the staff, though there are slow readers among them as well. The highest praise is still 'He's read everything', 'He's read every scrap of published poetry in the eighteenth century.' (27) The game played in Lodge's *Changing Places*, where academics earn points by owning up to major works they have not read, still strikes a fearful chord. But what has happened, I think, is that staff have read enough to make it seem for practical purposes as if they have read everything. Students do not have this luxury.

Staff writing

Many lecturers see their position as being humbly in the service of creative writers: 'I'm not creative. I study literature because I admire it. So I want to be as close to it as I can.' (5) 'I think of myself as a non-creative person, an enjoyer of things. I don't think I could write a poem to save my life.' (6) This respondent sees that being non-creative 'might be a reason for not being in this job in the eyes of some people', but for people like him the institution offers a relatively conflict-free, traditional role as mediator, explicator.

Many others saw themselves not essentially as servants of writers (teachers or critics) but as writers themselves. And they saw the institution as a place where this ambition could be realized.

> My priority was to write poetry. I came here to be a writer. I refused to write criticism. I gave a lecture entitled 'Should literature be studied at the university?' They thought I meant: was literature good enough to be studied in the university? I meant: did the university deserve to have literature? (13)

> I came here to be a writer. I got this postgraduate award and I thought I'm going to get there and bunk off. I had this quiet submerged desire to be a writer. (48)

But writing is risky in all sorts of ways and there is an inherited streak of caution in these institutional would-be writers:

> At the age of 11 I had to put down what my career would be. I put: author, playwright, poet. My mother made me strike that out. I put: lawyer, teacher. (19)

> I was more on the imaginative side, but I went for the scholarly side, which I now regret. I was anxious to please. I'm a writer who hasn't

had the guts to do without a monthly guaranteed pay cheque. Too much the dutiful little Scottish boy. (55)

The range of possibilities for living this opposition is considerable and there is a great deal of ambiguity. Indeed, the recent research selectivity exercise has forced departments into taking uncomfortable decisions as to whether poems, novels and reviews in *Penthouse* are or are not 'research output'.

Professor Duke earned money from writing while he was still an under-graduate and earned his living from writing after that (including reviews for *Penthouse*). He converted a book into a PhD in six weeks when the need for a salary became urgent: 'You live hand to mouth as a writer but sooner or later your family says: everyone else has got a house.' He had some difficulty getting the job – 'They were afraid I'd write a funny novel about them' – but eventually succeeded. He produces books – fiction and non-fiction – but never writes for academics: 'I write for general readers.' And he doesn't feel part of the department: 'I'm down this end of the corridor, with the fire-extinguisher and the oxygen resuscitator.' He feels that creative writing is something which is seen as all right for students 'but if you are a member of staff, you mustn't get caught at it'. And yet 'someone who's a whizz at writing critical works but can't write a line of poetry or fiction is like someone teaching surgery who says "My God, I wouldn't operate on a patient, he'd die." Someone who doesn't write novels can tell you about the novel but some things you only know if you've written one.' For him the teaching is very much ancillary: 'I am a writer who does some teaching. If I suddenly made a lot of money out of a book I'd stop.' He sees what he does in the university as 'work'; his writing is 'an alternative to working for a living'. He will retire soon from 'work' but not from writing:

> Retiring from writing is like retiring from life. You can retire from teaching but not from writing. I've got so many things I want to write about. It's the most important thing in my life. I work a 16-hour day quite often, the one thing that seems to get easier as you get older is writing. The last novel I did I wrote in four weeks. I had to stop myself at the end of a day. At three in the morning I'm bashing away. Its like being a junky. (21)

Writing for Professor Duke is clearly a way of staying outside the institution while having most of the advantages of being inside. Such accommodations may become harder to achieve in the future.

He also represents the outside reality of literature (readers and writers) to the institution in a way which may be necessary but which is resisted. Another respondent points to the same tension with respect to drama: 'It is a weakness that our treatment of the drama is overwhelmingly literary. There should be someone who knows how to put on a play.' (52)

Others have positions which are more ambiguous. Some continue to write non-academically for therapeutic purposes, throwing it away when the need is past. Some write knowing the institution disapproves: 'Poetry is not part of your production as far as the university is concerned. It's an indulgence. You're not getting on with the job.' (24) Some have simply given up, but have twinges of nostalgia about what might have been:

> I did a lot of writing around the age 24–25, and I was filled with nostalgia the other day because a story that I wrote was referred to as being 'quite extraordinary'. It filled one with thoughts about directions not taken . . . It's not part of my life any more. Some small element, one hopes, filters into the criticism and makes it more than just arid. (52)

Some police the boundaries:

> There was always a sense that if I studied English I would learn how to write creatively. I learned that that was an inaccurate assessment of what I would get out of studying English. It might have in fact been better if I'd done philosophy or history and kept that separate. I've thought a lot about how to bring together critical and creative writing. I've reached a point now when I do them separately. I don't try to muddle up the genres. (58)

What is being dealt with in this conflict between academic writing or criticism and creative writing is the problem of the unconscious or, less controversially, of the imagination – that which is not under rational control, that which is not under any control, in fact, since it represents a primary freedom. So the materials themselves are clearly the product of something which is not cognitive, which is powerful but inarticulate, and yet they are being approached solely through the cognitive and the analytical. Professor Pool puts it like this:

> I think that denial is quite crucial, envy too. There is an extremely difficult and touchy relationship between my self as a critic and my self as a potential writer. I don't think we go round slagging off writers, but it's quite a massive act of control, and I think that if one was to look harder at the notion of the unconscious, and at the notion of what is repressed, then it might well be that the writers remind us of the freedom of the imagination. We police it in a sense. Looking at the pedagogy, we actually control the boundaries of what people are allowed to do, to speak. (9)

Integration

Students

The complementary notions of *boundary* and *identity* are at the heart of the discipline. Individuals, disciplines and institutions derive their identities from firm, clear boundaries which separate self and other. And within each identity are further boundaries which constitute roles associated with various activities: work, leisure, etc. This is the necessary social process of differentiation. English offers an escape from this process. The activities of reading and of writing involve a kind of merging, a dissolving of the constructed self, a loss of identity which is not experienced as loss or as threat but rather as consolation and reintegration. This is what is meant by the references to the magical.

This dissolving of boundaries, typical of the act of reading, can be part of life. Life can be seamless and integrity is possible: 'I put T. S. Eliot on when I'm doing the dishes, "Let us go then you and I". The trick is not to exclude things from your life and bracket them off.' (87) In Britain at least, remarkably, and for the moment, this seems a possible strategy:

> I could get a job in journalism, teaching, personnel, or even accountancy. They want you with English or history degrees, it gives you a wider scope. (91)

> It's demonstrable that English students go out and do all sorts of things rather well. Being articulate is important, not just being articulate in the sense of finishing your sentences, but in the sense of having thought things out very clearly before they start the sentences. Very crudely, it gives power. (45)

> I think English is still widely perceived as a subject in which you can neatly combine a fair bit of enjoyment, a fair bit of ability to move around, not be too confined in a straitjacket, and pretty good employment prospects at the far end. (9)

Staff

Staff grapple with the problem of the boundary between the academy and the world, between professional reading and the 'natural' reading which must underlie it, between themselves as teachers and critics and the authors they study or the writers they attempt to be. They share with the students and with the writers the sense of a never-ending battle against the inarticulate:

> Anybody who works with language knows how frustrating, how agonizingly inadequate, it is. You are trying to reach for things that you know are there and you just can't get them, you can't grasp them. (13)

And, like the students, they see the possibility of integration. Here is an account of how the 'magical', dissolved aspects of reading can be reconciled with the analytical needs of the institution and society:

> Aristotle in his *Poetics* talks about the ability of the text to take the mind captive. These phrases, 'I couldn't put it down', 'You get lost

in it'. You watch someone reading a book on a bus. They're smiling. If you lose touch with that as literary critics in academe you might as well give up. The two things are not incompatible. You internalize the critical capacity to such an extent that you can do the two things simultaneously. That's a very difficult skill indeed. (51)

The same is true in writing (though there is a hint here of the denial and the rivalry with creative writers that Professor Pool referred to):

Writing English prose is very difficult anyway. If you can produce decent prose, that's a creative achievement. (12)

I don't feel as I did when I was young that there is a great gulf between creative writing and other kinds. I don't feel that what I am doing is as secondary as I would then have felt. Whether I feel that because it's a way of bolstering me up in what I do, I don't know. (7)

There's the struggle to get it right, the pleasure of the struggle, the absorption – whether you are writing poems or an academic book. (17)

We will be looking further at these questions in Chapter 7, when we consider the question of theory, and in Chapters 8 and 9, when we look at the concepts of boundary and identity with regard to discipline and nation. But our immediate step is to consider the way that for staff and students the activities of reading and writing are translated into the institutional experience of teaching and learning.

four

Teaching and learning

In the big stockyards, where pigs, cows, and sheep
Stumble towards the steady punch that beats
All sense out of a body with one blow,
Certain old beasts are trained to lead the rest
And where they go the young ones meekly go.

Week after week these veterans show the way,
Then, turn back just in time, are led themselves
Back to the pens where their initiates wait.
The young must cram all knowledge in one day,
But the old who lead live on and educate.
(Anthony Thwaite, 'Lesson', in *The Stones of Emptiness*:
Poems 1963–66)

Forms

The institutional forms in which teaching and learning occur are surprisingly few in number and highly traditional: there is the *lecture*, where the individual speaks to a silent audience; the *tutorial*, where a teacher and a student meet in dialogue; the *seminar*, where the tutor meets with a group (though, confusingly – and revealingly – the seminar is often referred to by the Oxford term: tutorial). As for written work, here too the range is no wider: the students write critical *essays* and very little else. The essay may be read out in a tutorial or seminar by the student but usually it is read, assessed and returned with comments by the teacher. Assessment is based largely on these literary essays, written in students' own time or in an examination room. We will examine these forms one by one, considering the experience of both the student and the teacher.

Lectures

I have used the word 'teacher' in this chapter so far, and this is how the role is named by the unions (Association of University *Teachers*, National Association of *Teachers* in Further and Higher Education), but the term actually most in use is 'lecturer'. This is not merely semantic. Lecturing is to teaching what the missionary position is to sexual intercourse. For some academics, lecturing is specifically defined as *not* teaching: a lecturer from Newcastle (subject unknown) wrote to the *Education Guardian* (29 October 1991):

> I am not a teacher. I am not employed as a teacher, and I do not wish to be a teacher. I am employed as a lecturer, and in my naivety I thought that my job was to 'know' my field, contribute to it by research, and to lecture on my specialism. Students attend my lectures but the onus to learn is on them. It is not my job to teach them.

Oxbridge dons (who may or may not be 'university lecturers') would agree. Indeed, an aspect that distinguishes medieval Oxford from modern civic universities is the peripheral role of lectures. It may well be in a teacher's career interest at Oxford to give a lecture series but students are not encouraged to attend, still less to see this as their main resource.

In Oxbridge or in Newcastle (in Australia or in Zimbabwe), however, a lecture is a lecture. An individual stands before a silent crowd and speaks. Some are good, some are bad; some do not like doing it, some like doing it it very much:

> The lecturers [at Cambridge] were amazingly variable. There were people there who should never have been lecturing at all and clearly not only couldn't but who visibly shook with fear at doing it. (9)

The fear comes from the public performance element, which can be extraordinarily stressful. The comedienne Marti Caine would be physically sick before each show and once said she was thinking of finding an easier way of earning a living – 'like being a mercenary or something' – and many lecturers would sympathize. Dr Linsey may be understating her initial difficulties and current doubts: 'I found standing up in front of a big group of people extremely difficult to begin with. I prepared very carefully but I felt a sense of strain. Now sometimes I feel I don't have enough to say to justify all these people's attention for this period of time.' (58)

This same assertion of self and theatrical display is what can give the most intense satisfaction:

> It's an ego trip for me. I love giving lectures to huge audiences. I don't like one-to-one teaching very much, I suppose that's because there isn't an audience. I'm best at standing up without any notes and lecturing for 50 minutes to very young and highly uncritical people who don't realize what a fast one I'm pulling on them. I was taught by people who could do that, wonderful mountebanks. It's show-business, it's Frank Sinatra. I don't particularly like sitting in a room by myself writing, you force yourself. It's the price you pay for being able to stand up and display yourself. I'm nearly 60 and I still like it. (15)

Not everyone is so unabashed: 'I don't like lecturing as much as I used to. I got a sense of power by doing it. It's a very false situation.' (16) '[It's] a strange ritual, no real feedback, no quality control.' (20) '[It's] the most boring medium ever devised. The lecture's been pointless since the invention of printing.' (21)

Comments like these come from civic universities and I detected, particularly in Newcastle, a general lack of enthusiasm and conviction for this form in the places where it has been most dominant – which is unfortunate in present circumstances. A former head of department told me he thought the department had lost faith in lecturing 'and yet we are going to do more and more of it because we won't be able to cope with the numbers except by lecturing'. (53)

Students share the view that the good lecture is theatrical. Here is a student account of a lecture given by the 'show-business' respondent quoted above:

> We would have liked to stand up and give an ovation. The air was electric, everyone was riveted, it was fantastic. He appeared and he talked about the poem. He read it. He's an actor and he spoke the words so beautifully and then he said, 'What if I don't read it like this, what if I read it like this? This word changes its meaning. And this one.' It made me want to look at more. (70)

But such experiences seem rare: the same student is scathing about other lecturers: 'I would like to know how university lecturers are selected. Communication must be an important part of their job, and if you can't communicate what's the point? They could be given the benefit of a course on how to put yourself across.' (70) 'The lectures [at Oxford] are awful. Some are well attended because they're such a relief in relation to the rest of them.' (74)

There is a great deal of criticism about technique:

> He was reading out the foreword of the Penguin Classic. I find that insulting. (90)

> Dull basically, dull. People fall asleep in lectures. Obviously they're not trained, they just can't hold your interest, that's the major criticism. I think if I was going to give a lecture, the first thing I would do would be to put up the structure of it, and you would have that on one side. That would help the people taking notes. (97)

When the performance is disappointing the audience asks: 'Why do it at all?'

> We go to the lectures and then it's just regurgitation of the lecture. You don't learn to think that way. (83)

> Why aren't we just going to the library and reading books if there's no communication? (70)

Students are also shocked at some of the prejudices displayed: 'He denigrates homosexuals, train-spotters, and people who wear white shoes.' (70) For others it is the monologic aspect that is frustrating.

> If you hear a lecturer mention one of your favourite writers you want to say 'Hey, have you read this?' but you can't. If you say something they say, 'That can wait for the seminar.' You say 'No, No, I feel it now.' (83)

> The majority seem to have so much material to get across in the 50 minutes, that there isn't space. Professor X allows time for someone to interrupt, but so far no one has. (70)

Students are ambivalent: one teacher in the PNL, acting on her scruples about lecturing, tried to reduce the number of lectures and met resistance: 'They want the lectures. It's the format they've been used to.' (48) Some very independent students are critical of other students' dependency and passivity: 'I want to get this subject out of my system, to talk about it. There aren't all that many students who are into this kind of thing. They would prefer to sit and be lectured to.' (83)

This ancient phenomenon of the lecture is in fact quite mysterious. It has indeed survived the invention of printing (and television and tape-recording). It is ubiquitous, and books demonstrating its ineffectiveness (Bligh 1971; Gibbs 1982) have not changed much (except perhaps to contribute to the loss of conviction described above). The extreme resistance among lecturers to the use of visual aids, even in the form of a simple outline as suggested by the student quoted above, cannot be explained simply by lack of training or of awareness of how the human brain most efficiently takes in information. There must be a deeper reason for the fact that in the average lecture room, ostensibly dedicated to the furtherance of the text, the only written word publicly on display is the word 'EXIT'. It seems to me that the lecture, as practised in universities throughout the world, is actually *in competition with the written word*, and is dedicated symbolically to the defence of pre-Gutenberg orality. It is in this sense a profoundly reactionary form, both ante- and anti-book (although *manuscripts*, in the form of lecture-notes and essays, being pre-Gutenberg, are compatible). Linked to this is the unconscious rivalry between writers and lecturers alluded to in Chapter 3: far from being at the service of the writer in their lecture-rooms, lecturers are competing in their own (ancient, oral) way. I believe these are the forces at work and they work in conjunction with the more conscious desire for self-display which we have already noted. Small wonder that the form survives but small wonder too that there is this sense of malaise about the whole activity.

David Punter, in a rare discussion of these issues as they affect English, calls lecturing a 'passive–aggressive mode of relating'. The lecturer, he says, is invested with fantasy power and the student is allowed child-like irresponsibility while being habituated to powerlessness (Punter 1986: 218).

This analysis applies whatever the quality of the lecture; it applies particularly perhaps when the performance is successful. It confirms my view that the lecture is an assertion of power – over writers, over students.

The tutorial

Punter (1986: 217) affirms that the 'one-to-one encounter is now very rare'. This may be true in civic universities but, to my surprise, I found it still flourishing at Oxford (sherry withal). My assumption was that, in the current climate, a teaching staff–student ratio of 1:1 was not likely. And one Oxford fellow did indeed offer the opinion that it was 'an outrageous luxury'. (27) In fact, I sat in on several such tutorials: they are the basic teaching mode. There has, it seems, been a move to tutorial pairs, and it would seem that one to two is now as frequent. The 'class' – a tutor with seven or eight students – is 'a progressive idea in Oxford', (23) but it usually only happens when the tutor (not necessarily for progressive reasons) wants to reduce the number of contracted contact hours and is able to square this with his/her college. It would be wrong to see the one to two tutorial as a different form, a small seminar:

> The pairings are never teams. They are put together because they will compete. One of the private pleasures of dons is working out who they are going to pair up and inflict on each other. (74)

In the same way, even where, exceptionally, there are six or seven students, the underlying tutorial model interferes:

> What's missing is collective responsibility for discussion. They expect to be able to hold forth for ten minutes because they think that you want to hear that. (34)

The pattern of the tutorial is also, it seems, unchanged. I sat in on what I believe was a typical event: one student (white, male, 20) in the tutor's book-strewn room, overlooking the quad. The student read an essay on a rather obscure aspect of Tennyson; the tutor took notes during the reading and then used them to comment on the essay, getting up from his armchair every now and again to take down a book, making suggestions for further reading and for the examination. The student during this time did not say a great deal. When he left, Dr James commented: 'It's a lot of effort doing that for me, as you can see. Twenty of those a week is quite wearing. It's a job for young people, not people like me.' (29)

Other respondents were negative about the essay-reading aspect but confirmed its ubiquity:

> I very rarely have students read essays, it seems to be an old Oxford trick, to use up the time without having to do anything. They often feel cheated if they don't get to read essays because everyone else does it. (27)

Some undergraduates I spoke to were mildly positive. They appreciated the contact with an expert:

> You're sitting there with someone who knows a huge amount about the subject and who, if you are lucky, is concerned to let you learn about it in your own way. (75)

And they see the tutorial as potentially useful for the examination:

> I enjoy it. I don't think it's particularly effective, but I like yacking on about things. I don't think it particularly teaches me very much. Sometimes you can get invaluable stuff when a tutor moves in on a particular part of your essay and opens it up for you. They can give you that edge when you come to write the essay for the exam. (76)

But there was also a great deal of criticism of the system, particularly the *ad hoc* nature of the arrangements:

> Dr X, the don who was the reason for my choosing that college, left when I arrived. They had a replacement who was only here for a year. The person who interviewed me for Anglo-Saxon had retired by the time I arrived. The person who took me for the first term then got a sabbatical . . . (75a)

Even where the tutorial arrangements are stable, luck still plays a big role, because the number of tutors a student meets in the course of a career is limited (five or six at the most) compared with the other institutions. A student may find a tutor difficult: 'For the first few tutorials she didn't look at me, she sat staring out of the window smoking all the time. There are some strange characters at Oxford.' (72) And even having a star as your tutor is not without its problems, because so much is invested in the one brief weekly encounter:

> In my first year I had Eagleton as my tutor. He's very very famous, there were five or six people in a group vying for a famous person's attention. I felt irrationally antagonistic to the other people in my English set. It was just madness on my part. I'd see him for one hour a week and I would be trying to plan how you could say all the right things in that time. (71)

The language that students use about the tutorial experience is quite strong: 'There is no escape. There's only you in the room. You become quite paranoid.' (77) 'The whole first year was an experience in inadequacy.' (72) There is a lot of suppressed anger: 'The tutor has been overbearing and not really let me speak. He always had a theory and you spent the whole of the tutorial trying to find out what it was. That made me cross.' (77)

There is a range of personal ability and style among tutors. I certainly observed tutorials where there was openness, attentiveness, awareness on the part of the tutor and enthusiastic readiness to contribute on the part of the students. What is more relevant is the system within which whatever personal skills and qualities a tutor has are exercised. If you are famous and if students have come specifically to study with you there is no way of avoiding those projections and no obvious way of dealing with them within the tutorial, even assuming that you are aware of the phenomenon (and you do not have to be famous to receive projections). The power relations in a tutorial are different from those of a seminar because there is no student group. A postgraduate tutor:

> You have such authority as a teacher in your office, you can get out of any challenge. Your authority gives you 101 ways of evading any remark. In a classroom they have solidarity. (74)

A former don, now in a civic university:

> I don't miss that [the tutorial]. I always thought that was a mistake. The students are not ready for it, they can't take it, they are not equipped for this one-to-one thing, they haven't done the reading, they're frightened, it's much better for students to be in groups where they talk to each other, where they develop a common expertise, and where they learn from each other. The undergraduates aren't brilliant, most of them. Most of them are frightened. It's an absurd system. (50)

The tutorial can produce intimacy: 'the tutorial situation is notoriously intense, and leads to all kinds of abuse. The slightest twitch, you know it. If they have stayed in bed for three days you know it.' (27) Or it can produce a purely social urbanity, 'chatting in cultural ways as the English gentleman is supposed to do'. (74) In either case, things can work well or badly. There can be successful intimacy and unsuccessful; there can be skilful or unskilful social occasions. The point is that both intimacy and social exchange are extraneous to the concept of a teaching or academic role: 'It's a social situation, and, as in any social situation, you have to keep the conversation going, but that's completely false because it's an academic occasion.' (25) What counts is the interpersonal, not the professional, and one can see how this can be a preparation for a life where personal connectedness (even in clearly dominant/submissive ways) is more important than bureaucratic fitness.

This absence of a teaching role may suit some students very well since it enables them virtually never to join the institution and facilitates a mutually satisfying collaboration between those who do not want to teach and those who do not want to be taught:

> I saw my tutor about four times a term, and that was the lot. I never did want to be taught. I was never bored, lots of friends. I never went to lectures. He was an idle tutor, often away. Smashing. He didn't bother me and I didn't bother him. (21)

Oxford didn't make a great deal of difference. I got taught hardly anything, I got an education but it was very unstructured. That suited me tremendously well. (45)

So the tutorial system enacts dramatically the paradox at the heart of English: the subject should not need teaching. The sort of person who should be doing it should not need much more than a library and (optionally) the company of like-minded people. To need more than that casts doubt both on that person's fitness and on that person's conception of the subject. Dr Ford was at Oxford around 1970: 'There were good scholars, but it was intellectually moribund; you could come out of Oxford untouched.' (52)

I would suggest that to 'come out untouched', or at least to think that you did, is not a sign of the system not having worked, but a sign that it did work. There is a paradoxical similarity with the pedagogy of Freire and Illich, who feel they have succeeded when the peasants say: 'We did it ourselves.'

This minimalist notion is rare, in its extreme form, but it is not so long ago that students dropped in for their weekly tutorial without making appointments, and the link between work done for a tutor and the actual examination is very flimsy. The whole concept of a structured course, course materials, syllabus, objectives, criteria and so on, is basically foreign to an ethos devoted to blurring the boundary between the world and the subject, that is, to denying professionalization. Task and role are made invisible. So are power relations:

> That's why Oxford isn't very keen on the lecture, because the power relations are out in the open. The ideological point of the tutorial is in its concealments of those power relations. So for someone formed in a liberal sixties pedagogy it fits, because it doesn't obviously involve putting you in a dominant role. It's more like a conversation etc. But then you can be blind, and many tutors are blind, to the concealed power dynamics of that. (23)

The lecture outside Oxford and the one-to-one tutorial in Oxford are examples of ancient pedagogic forms surviving largely because they are ancient, and because they meet institutional needs over and above the requirements of a process of knowledge acquisition and professionalization; indeed, in the case of the tutorial, one of the prime needs is to protect against professionalization. The most regrettable thing is that Oxford, unlike many other institutions today, actually could still resource seminars of six or seven students, has the kinds of students who would thrive in such a format, and does not have the distraction of a massive lecture-based transmission model. The tutorial system leaves students without experience of peer-group challenge and support, and has tutors pointlessly overworking, devoting six hours to what could actually be done more effectively in one, and reducing needlessly the opportunities offered: 'If you went over to seminar methods you could have 50 per cent more people studying' (31) (though you might also have to abandon the college-residence system – which is another issue).

Oxford denies the professionalization which comes from effective economic teaching and clings to an ancient aristocratic (private tutor) mode. A Canadian who studied in the USA said: 'Oxford squanders its resources hugely, both financial and human. That's what I admire about the American system. The university as a whole uses its intellectual resources better.'(74)

Both traditionalists and radicals deplore the tutorial but despair of ever changing it:

> It's not very productive, this university. It's locked into the sacred cow of the tutorial. I've been campaigning for 15 years for it to be diminished. You must go into seminars. Faculty won't listen, they just thought I was a cranky maverick. We must rationalize the job, but it's not going to happen in my lifetime. That causes me to feel that really I would like to leave. (29)

One reason for the resilience of the tutorial (apart of course from the financial underpinning) is the absence of any student pressure for change, and this raises an important general issue. One tutor, a former Oxford student, who had also previously taught in a civic university, described the way that when he was a student he was obscurely dissatisfied with the teaching but unable to challenge it:

> The tutorial was projected on personal terms, and that I think is what stopped me being able to criticize it. It's partly set up in terms of loyalty and identification. There's a lot of transference. It's more than a professional level in that sense. So you tolerate things. For example, when I was a student I don't think I was ever given a bibliography, I don't think I was ever given a question to write on, it was all terribly laid back. 'What are you going to work on next week?' And you'd say 'Spenser' and they'd say 'Fine'. The CNAA would close down Oxford now, straight away. (28)

What he says applies in fact to all university institutions. They are all powerfully shielded from criticism – whether from CNAA or student. Students have a vested interest in confirming their original choices as being well-founded, because this is the basis of their own social status and they have in fact no other experience to compare their current one with. This is the interest of getting lecturers to reflect on their own student days. They report that they were satisfied but are amazed in retrospect that they put up with what they did: 'What a terrible waste of opportunity. But that's with hindsight. I loved it. We pretty well accepted anything.' (8) 'I was too stupid to think of anything else really. It didn't occur to me that there were other ways of doing things.' (57)

Seminars

In civic universities the tutorial system has mutated into a sort of parallel seminar system: there may be seminars associated with a particular topic and led by the lecturer but there will also be 'tutorials' in which a tutor will negotiate topics with the student group. The group will, however, be much larger than the Oxford twosome and is more like a seminar.

In Newcastle this particular dual system is being phased out in favour of a modular system, where the teaching will be done by an individual or small team responsible for lectures and seminars on that topic. There is pressure in Cardiff to move in the same direction. Stirling has a lecture-linked 'tutorial' system in the first year with quite large groups but thereafter the seminar is the main mode. Given, then, a certain disaffection with lectures, given that the Oxbridge tutorial is, whatever its merits and demerits, too extravagant for anywhere except Oxbridge, all the hopes of teachers and students end up being carried by the seminar and the group.

This seems to me to be inevitable. This is where the subject's basic institutional justification must be found. I can read books perfectly well outside the institution; if I am to be within the institution it must be in order to discuss my reading of those books with others – peers or experts. Given that, by definition, my reading will have been private and idiosyncratic, my need and desire is to negotiate that reading with others and thereby to learn more about the text which occasioned the reading, about myself, about others, and about my relation to all that. Listening to lectures will not achieve this because the lecture is one person's reading and there is no negotiation.

The problems with the seminar are considerable, however. There is some agreement about the upper size for a group: 'Twelve maximum. Jesus got it right.' (13) But today Jesus would be taking fees-only disciples and franchising. Seminars in Newcastle can have 30 or 40 students. I had accounts of classes in Cardiff with 30 in rooms for 20, with people sitting on the floor: 'They say, "Can't we move to another room?" I say, "There isn't another room."' (15)[1]

> There are are simply too many people: they tend to split so that five or six make most of the running and the rest form a silent audience around them. And with 38 you cannot ask them to start preparing seminar papers. If they all speak for a minute that's the end of the class. (53)

However good a tutor might be at leading a discussion in a group of eight, that ability does not transfer to a group of 38. Even without this difficulty there are still considerable problems and tutors and students are quite perplexed: 'I still find seminars a bit bizarre, taking them or taking part in them.' (59)

Jaques (1984) sums up various student views on the seminar and concludes: 'Potentially, seminars provide a stimulus that is difficult to match.

In practice the dynamics of the group and the tutor's handling of it make this an unsatisfactory experience for many students.' He suggests, in rather a defeatist way, that 'mere mortals might be better advised to try alternative means' (Jaques 1984: 102). The question for English is what this alternative way might be, given the nature of the task and subject matter.

The communicative context is considerably more complex for the tutor than it is in the lecture or the tutorial. The tutor's power to control is very much less, if only because the ritual 'any questions?' offer which is never taken up in lectures is very likely to be taken up in a seminar:

> In lectures you are in control, you limit what you say, and if there's an area you don't want to go into you don't mention it. Seminars, you can't do that, so the preparation required for seminars is more demanding. You can give a lecture on a novel that you haven't read for a year or two; you've got your notes, you've got your running headings, you've got your quotations, you refresh your memory the night before on the quotations. You can't do that with a seminar, you have to really re-read the books every couple of years, because, sure as fate, someone's going to ask you a question that you haven't anticipated. (8)

The tutor here sees the role as that of the expert, responding to questions with extempore monologues. Where tutors see the role as getting students to engage in discussion with each other they feel even less in control:

> I'm a person who doesn't put his money where his mouth is. I firmly believe in the value of discussion, but I'm lousy at organizing discussion between students. Between students and me yes, but between student and student, which I think is more valuable, no. I've lost courage, I don't do it, I don't get students to talk any more. (4)

And this frustration is shared by students: 'Perhaps I was naive. I expected more in-depth discussion.' (70)

The seminar must be a discussion. If the group is very large, in the absence of any special large group techniques or what Punter (1986: 219) calls 'methodological instruction', only a fraction of the group will participate and this causes problems, since the group splits into articulate and inarticulate along pre-determined lines. But, whatever the group size, the basic question remains, and it is the basic question about the subject. *What should we talk about?* The 'default' answer is the 'Cambridge English' one: 'the text'. A typical seminar in English (and I sat in on several) is one in which tutors and students actually look at a short text and comment on it in terms of what it means and how it conveys that meaning. A student gave a description of this kind of seminar:

> Usually the student [presenter] talks about ten minutes and says the poet published one, two, three, four books and gives a tiny bit of biography and then into the poem, and everyone wanders around

thinking all sorts of things for ages about it and then we shuffle on to the next one. (69)

This form seems fairly relaxing for all concerned. However, as the student implies, it can appear rather inconsequential.

There is an alternative, practised by critical theory tutors. They are not prepared to be relaxed, or to allow the assumptions behind Cambridge English to go cosily unchallenged. Their concept of a seminar is much more bracing: it is a battleground.

> We should all stop expecting them to have an easy time. Let's have the bruising. Let's have the fights. I really would perhaps be cruel and grit my teeth and say, well if you are 18 and you are from a sheltered background and you are female, and went to a female school, and you are not very forthcoming, well you are going to have to go through this experience of bruising encounter, and we hope it'll do you some good. (15)

In this battleground view of the seminar, argument is certainly encouraged, and the leader is ready to take on all comers: 'I like being on the spot, I like it when students answer back, I hate it when they just accept what you have to say.' (42) The tutor will set up two rival views of the text and encourage students to fight it out. But it is not a question of the student's own view of the text: 'No, I don't want their ghastly personal responses.' (17)

Some students find this invigorating, but others resist very strongly in the name of a radically different value system:

> I find it very, very aggressive. I don't come across anyone who would encourage me to pick up a book and read it just for the pleasure of it. I can't imagine any of them reading *Kubla Khan* or the *Deserted Village* to their ten-year-old children. It's all academic and intellectual, I don't really sense any love of it. (92)

This mismatch is fundamental. It is the one that Protherough (1989: 30) discovered in his survey: 'Pleasure and enjoyment' were ranked first by students and by all the groups surveyed, except university lecturers, who put this item fifth ('development of critical ability' was first). Punter (1986: 217) sums it up very well:

> There is only a very distant correlation between the nature of the psychological investment effected in fictions by people between the ages of 14 and 18, which has much to do with the vicarious experiencing of alternative selves and ways of being, and with the evasion of aspects of familial authority, and that kind of investment which is presumed by English departments, which has more to do with induction into various largely unstated authority structures through the dual medium of text and faculty member.

Lecturers recognize how reluctant to leave trenches the troops are and how vulnerable:

> We say 'Please ask any questions you want to,' but of course what they see is a grey-haired man who is probably quite frightening, and they think, 'Well I'll probably be better off saying nothing because he'll probably make me look foolish.' I've had many what appear to be success stories where people blossom in the situation. But to be honest, I've had a number of cases of both female and male students who have been driven into their shells almost to the point of breakdown. (15)

Silence, which is the enemy in the tutorial ('When he stops saying something I have to say something, whether I want to or not' (23)) is also the bane of the seminar. There are all sorts of reasons for silence: 'fear it won't be academic enough'; shyness about speaking English when it is not your language; 'not being confident about the text'; 'a group of 20 is intimidating'; the need for physical stimulus ('The only word she ever said was when her chair collapsed' (97)).

There are those, frequently mature students, who are prepared to speak. The common outcome of this is pairing between the tutor and the talkative students but the talkers themselves are often uncomfortable.

> I should just keep my mouth shut, because I wonder whether I intimidate other people. There's one guy who says nothing unless he's asked, and I keep thinking maybe if I hadn't answered he would have. But you feel as if there's this gap and other people think she's the one with the big mouth, she'll do it, or you think well if I don't do it no one will, and it's going to be really embarrassing and the tutor's going to think nobody cares about the subject, nobody's read it, nobody's interested. Maybe I should just do it. (60)

Jack gives a vivid picture of what may be going through a student's mind as he or she moves from silence to speech. He also shows that, like the lecture, the seminar is theatrical – though there is a bigger cast:

> I am actually very shy and very quiet. The first year, I didn't say hardly anything. Then the second year I'd get very passionate. You'd get out there and you'd realize 'Oh my God. I'm on stage. Get me off.' 'Sorry kid, you're out on your own'. You can get past your shyness by being very eager. If something grabs you then that will have you out there. (87)

All this gives some idea of the pressure upon the tutor. On the one hand the critical success factor is clearly general participation. But there is a great deal conspiring to prevent this, mainly fear of appearing foolish or domineering, fear of embarrassing or being embarrassed. Students naturally expect a tutor to solve these problems: 'Seminars really do depend upon the tutor.' (107) But in the same way that the student tutorial role interferes with the seminar role at Oxford, so, in other places, the staff lecturer role interferes with the seminar-leader role. It is very difficult to be Laurence Olivier at nine in the morning and Carl Rogers at ten.

> Some like seminars to be mini-lectures. Some listen, but then don't take the point, just continue with their own train of thought. It's infuriating, because you don't know the book well enough to go on the offensive against them. (68)

And if you are constructed as the expert, the one who knows, it is very difficult to deal with contrary views:

> We didn't say much because we didn't know much about it, and when we did say something we were usually wrong. 'Where have you got this idea from?' 'Out of my own head.' 'Well it's not right.' We were stabbing in the dark really. (106)

> He disagreed completely, and it wasn't that he disagreed and said well you can have your own opinion, he said, 'You're wrong.' I'd never come across such an attitude of closure in my life before. I was just too stunned to say anything, and too busy contemplating whether I should stay here at all, so I didn't really bother arguing it. (107)

The result here yet again is silence. Silence is the student's main weapon in the battle, which I see as being mainly about the mismatch referred to above.

All this sounds rather depressing and reinforces Jaques's comments quoted above. Is there a solution? The basic question is, *what shall we talk about?* There are various answers: we can do practical criticism of the text on the table or we can do structural analysis or we can discuss differing theoretical positions in an adversarial way. What none of these approaches satisfies is the desire to discuss these texts in a way which is somehow consonant with the way they were read.

In an English seminar the text will arouse feelings, will perhaps have been chosen for that reason, and these feelings will be different according to the age, class, race or sex of the members of the group. In that situation there are things which it would be difficult if not impossible to say. So the more potential for discussion there is, the less discussion there is. The problem can be simply put: 'We don't know how to talk about feelings. That's probably the most important thing. But it's difficult to talk about feelings.' (13)

One solution for the seminar is for the tutor to acknowledge that the text will evoke a variety of strong feelings and develop the skills to work with those feelings, including transforming the given group of strangers into a group where there is more trust than fear, which involves some understanding of basic phenomena like projection and the forms of identification. Certain tutors I interviewed have a background in therapy and they tend to be the ones who have developed this analysis and approach to the seminar. Like Dr Heath:

I found myself more and more in seminars listening in to people's quite primitive gut response to things, then working them out more critically, what people are silent about in texts, what they can't really talk about because somehow it's not there to be talked about critically. Some forms of psychoanalytic thinking allow one to hang on to that precognitive response. (51)

There is here a careful delineation of role. Dealing with a student's feelings about a text is not the same as doing therapy with a student: 'You certainly don't do psychoanalysis in the class, you don't use the text to deal with that student's problem publicly.' Yet this tutor is aware of working in an institution where there are 9,500 students and two part-time counsellors. The boundaries must be hard to keep. Another tutor with a background in therapy includes as part of the Romantic Poetry course a dreamwork seminar: 'They talk about their own dreams in class. I'm spilling it over into the personal experience of the student.' (44)

We are looking at the core of the seminar problem and therefore the core of the problem of teaching English within an institution. The material of study is potentially explosive. To defuse it by treating it technically or historically (objectively) is to make day-to-day institutional work easier but it is also to remove part of the essential affective motivation for the activity. So the energy goes. In a lecture this is not noticeable but in a seminar 'there is no escape'. To work with it needs particular skills. But whereas a therapist can learn about the client's past, the tutor has no way of learning about the student's.

Here is an account of an incident in a seminar. It is unusual only because it is an account, because the student explained to me what usually remains unexplained. Barbara is a second-year student for whom 'English is a very life-changing kind of course. Sometimes, in a particular life situation, you read a book and it's like your situation.' This is what happened in the seminar (she calls it a 'tutorial'):

Last semester a friend of mine tried to kill himself. The next English tutorial I went to we were discussing *The Sound and the Fury* by William Faulkner in which a character kills himself, and I found myself getting more and more upset and sitting, shaking in this tutorial. As I was walking out at the end the tutor said 'Are you all right?' and I just burst into floods of tears and had to go off and cry and cry and I actually missed the next tutorial because I knew it would be about the same book and I couldn't face coping with that.

The student wept in the seminar but no reference was made to this by the tutor or the other students and she remained until the end. The tutor was aware and after the session (outside the academic boundary) acknowledged that she had been aware (not every tutor would have been). But she never discovered the reason for the tears nor for the following week's absence. Should the tutor have commented during the session? Could the link between the experience and the book have been worked with? Barbara thinks not:

> I think she knew why I wasn't at the next tutorial. But I think she made a wise decision in not asking me why I was upset. That was a bit too personal really for me to bring up in a tutorial, because I think if I had I might well have just started crying and I couldn't really have come up with a good intellectual point about it because I was too involved. But where you might well hit a medium point, coming back to this thing about the balance between emotion and intellect, it's sometimes the case that you'll read a book and it's about a situation that you've been in, and you're not now feeling so strongly about it that you couldn't discuss it, so you might actually be able to say, 'Well this has happened to me.' If you're trying to understand a character, and somebody might say, 'I don't understand this character, I think she's really stupid', and you might find yourself leaping to that character's defence because you once did something like that. (66)

There is a clear distinction here between group therapy and a literary seminar and it would certainly have been inappropriate for the tutor to intervene. But this incident illustrates the fact that in any seminar there can be a dozen individuals with emotional relations to the text of varying strengths. It also points to a very real middle-ground where text and experience can meet and merge.

These tutors (and this student) are, to quote a (dissenting) lecturer, 'seeing the subject in terms of an immediate personal interaction. The text in your own life history. To engage with literature is a form of therapy.' (43) I have sympathy myself with this approach to teaching literature but I believe it may be necessary to reframe the notion of 'therapy' itself: extracting it from the medical model and inserting it into the educational model. This does, it seems to me, integrate or seek to integrate the private reading experience and the public interpersonal negotiation. Ultimately it also integrates the unconscious. In theory terms it gives support to the reader (student) in the author–text–reader triangle. But I am aware that there are dangers in this method which are not present in others. In any case, the current selection mechanism for posts in English departments in higher education uses one criterion only – intellectual, cognitive capacity – and it is pure chance if individuals already have or develop in addition the kind of non-cognitive awareness and group skills that this approach requires.

There are other teaching developments which are less subject to caution and which would be easier to disseminate. PNL has responded to the challenge of large seminar groups in English by developing other techniques:[2]

> Our teaching is moving towards student-centred learning, students working in groups. You are saying, 'Try to identify the issue that you

want to bring to a general discussion.' We've had a lot of work done on that recently. It's gained a lot of momentum. A lot of people practise it. (43)

Mrs George represents this approach well:

I don't know when I twigged I didn't have to know everything. When I started teaching I didn't dare let anyone say anything in case they asked me something I couldn't answer. Then one day, I'd been teaching four or five years, I was doing a class on a modern novel, and I hadn't finished reading it, I said to the group, 'I'm sorry, I haven't finished this,' and they said 'Good, we haven't either, can we just concentrate on sections 1 and 2?' We had a wonderful seminar. So I started to experiment in saying to students, 'I don't understand this,' and I thought, 'That's how you teach, you debate what you don't know, and it takes all the fear out of it.' Then it was a question of observing what I was doing, seeing what the results were. I was using my teaching all the time as an experimental block, where I could try things and get feedback. I taught myself how to teach by watching what I was doing and the results I got. I got so fascinated by that that I didn't want to go off doing research, because that would take too much time. I was interested in how you could get people to learn. (41)

Mrs George was able to use an organization which was also concerned with action research into English teaching – DUET[3] – to give her support for her own experiments and to influence her colleagues and the institution: 'I got DUET to come here because the students started pressing for different kinds of seminars. That got up to the Directorate who saw it as a means of getting student-centred learning, less staff and more students being taught.' (41) As a result of the DUET influence, she and her playwright colleague, Dr O'Flaherty, developed creative writing courses in conjunction with the literary courses.

One of Mrs George's seminars was devoted to T. S. Eliot. The students had been given background material and asked to read *The Waste Land*, concentrating on 'The Fire Sermon'. The tutor came in, to the students' surprise, in the role of Eliot (bowler and cane) and spoke an introduction, derived from Eliot's own critical statements: 'Good afternoon. My name's Eliot. My friends call me Tom. Your tutor tells me you have gathered here today to talk about my poem *The Waste Land* and she has invited me to say a few words of introduction.' This introduction ended with 'Eliot' offering a task: 'It would make an old ghost happy to see his Fire Sermon dramatized. It would split very well into three acts, performed by three groups of players. So this is the task I leave you with and I look forward to seeing your performance in one hour's time.' Mrs George/Eliot then left the students and only returned to see the performances: one group dealt with fragmentation and multiple narrative voices, using what they called 'spoken *a cappella*'; another mimed; the third, the 'Rhine Maidens', used speech and action and were concerned with rhythm and music. They got together informally after the seminar to discuss what had been learned and to produce a poster advertising the performance.

This activity is a very long way from all the traditional forms we have been considering. It does address very directly the question of sharing a private reading but without the difficulties associated with personal disclosure. There are considerable advantages for staff in this way of working:

> One new member of staff last year was close to a nervous breakdown. She couldn't stand the pressure. This is where the new teaching techniques have been an enormous help. I go into a classroom, I give them an exercise, and for ten minutes I can meditate if I want to. Whereas in the old days I had to give information for an hour, and I ended up exhausted. (44)

It is unusual for a department to have adopted these methods. Where individuals are aware of possible technical solutions to the seminar problem and attempt to put them into practice they frequently feel unsupported: 'It's not all that easy to run these groups and since no one else has done it I've not always been encouraged.' (3) The most common attitude is probably scepticism: 'I have mixed feelings about some of the so called radical ways of teaching because you can't assume they come to you with a body of texts beneath their belt.' (2)

Assessment

Students choose the subject, and then the institution where they will study it and become for ever English People. By choosing the institution they also choose the method by which their achievement will be assessed. My sample of institutions includes the extremes: Stirling, where there are no traditional examinations at all, and Oxford, where the paroxysm of finals still rules. In between are various mixtures of coursework and three-hour examinations: Cardiff and PNL have options which are examined by portfolios of essays or by dissertations (the University of Wales has a rule limiting coursework to 50 per cent of the total assessment). Newcastle also has a mix. The issue of coursework versus formal examination is one which arouses some of the strongest feelings, not least in the Department for Education, whose hostility to coursework in schools is deep and getting deeper, just as teachers and examination boards are becoming more convinced of its merits (the AEB A level has 50 per cent coursework and open book examinations).[4]

Opponents of coursework cite the dangers of plagiarism, or of students receiving assistance from others. They claim that ability to undergo the stress of examinations is a powerful selection device, giving important information to employers. Proponents point to the superior quality of coursework compared with that produced in examination conditions, and to the reduction of stress, to the greater reliability of coursework (there is more of it) and to the fact that it encourages 'deep learning' rather than the surface learning of memorization (Marton and Entwhistle 1984). They point to the artificiality of examinations and the way that no examiner would dream of writing an article in those conditions. I suspect that, for opponents, a strong but not usually articulated objection to coursework is that it is much more time-consuming for staff. Not only is there a lot more to read but it requires a whole framework of deadlines, penalties for late submission, drafting of dire warnings about plagiarism, etc. Staff at Stirling are strong supporters of the system but describe wearily the burden of the marking and the cross-marking of 'two or three hundred scripts per person per semester'. There is of course the matter of tradition and ritual. Coursework weakens both. And in the world of British education any complex technical issue seems to be hijacked and made into a tradition versus revolution affair. The fundamental difference here again concerns framing. The traditional three-hour examination is strongly framed institutionally, that is it is like nothing else on earth, whereas the process of sitting down in a room, as I am now, surrounded by material, and organizing one's work while drinking coffee and occasionally answering the telephone is recognizably the sort of thing that normal people outside the institution actually do. Coursework assessment is another example of reducing the gap between the private, non-institutional activity of the subject and the public, institutional form, and it is clear that there is strong resistance to this reduction and great attachment to strong framing.

As with lectures, students have mixed feelings about examinations and coursework. Coursework requires a totally different attitude to work and to time-management: 'I think I actually work better under pressure in an exam. I'm hopeless at making myself sit down and write. In an exam you have to.' (93) On the whole, however, coursework is a powerful attraction for students. It seems to be the principal reason for choosing Stirling, and at PNL, where there is 75 per cent coursework, the assessment method even distorts the option system within the faculty, since students are reluctant to choose the examination options.

Underlying all this is the basic question of choice and selection. All systems offer choice and students in every system are permanently selecting. Nowhere in higher education is there the equivalent of the set texts at A level or the French *Agrégation*. The subject matter is always the whole of English literature (which means literature in English and can include other media). It is always a question of what (tiny) proportion of this vast area will be studied and examined. In every institution, except Oxford, students construct this curriculum from a list of options and choose essay topics from those options. As with coursework, this entails complex administration, since some options will be over-subscribed, and others under-subscribed, and the aim is to have all the teachers gainfully employed.

Where there are options, the examination system is relatively simple, since students know what they will be expected to write about. The teacher will have set the paper, and someone who has chosen an option on T. S. doesn't expect to be asked to write about George. In Oxford, although there is some movement towards two of the eight papers being coursework, the traditional examination dominates and the vast majority of people doing the teaching have no say in the construction or the marking of the examination. Things are therefore more convoluted because the gap between reality (the small number of authors and texts one has actually read, the even smaller fraction one can remember) and rhetoric (the syllabus from *Beowulf* on) is greater. Professor Jones, a Cambridge professor who taught for years at Oxford, says the solution is 'ritual cheating'. 'Cheating' seems to mean that the student must appear to match the rhetoric, and show that he or she has 'read everything', whereas this cannot be the case. One example is the student who prepares a very esoteric poem and writes about that in the hope that the examiner will think that this is an indication of very wide reading, whereas the student may not have read the basic texts. In the same way, the examination paper with 50 questions on it makes it look as if the student could answer any of them and is making a choice according to taste or whim. In reality the student has prepared four topics and will do three. As David put it: 'I like the thought that with an Oxford degree I'll be able to bluff my way through any particular period. You touch on everything more or less.' (76)

The final exams are a rite of passage, and like all such rituals produce great anxiety combined with excitement, occasional scars and a suggestion of sado-masochism. It is interesting to note here again the private/public issue: students who live out of college do not feel anything like the same stress as those who live in, because the latter are, so to speak, doubly institutionalized. Paul moved out in the second term, and was preparing normally, but he went into college just before the exams and came out shaking: 'Every year there are people whose finals mess them up for a good portion of their life. There are people who just don't cope with that pressure.' (75a)

The pressure not just to succeed but also to be the best is very strong, both for the student and for the college, and this adds to the stress: 'They say, "If you are not going to get a first take a year off and come back and get a first". It's very much pitched towards finals. Colleges, governing bodies, tutors, are very concerned about this. The famous Norrington table [the publication which rates the colleges by results] isn't a fiction.' (78)

Stirling, at the other end of the spectrum, has its own problems with stress. Since students' essays determine their degree it becomes very important to get good marks in them. One way is to choose options with tutors who mark generously and avoid tutors who give low marks: 'One tutor in particular is known as a very hard marker and were I actually to be assigned him as a tutor I might well pretend to have timetable clashes and things.' (66)

In general, it is important to know what the marker's criteria are. This is particularly difficult at Oxford (except, as we shall see, that you can be pretty sure that mastery of the terminology of critical theory is not one of them). In Newcastle it is uncertain:

> There are people going into exams doing very intense practical critic-ism, but there are other people who are good at other forms of criticism, and you don't know who are marking your exams, and there may be members of staff who are maybe not so much in sym-pathy with those forms of criticism. (96)

Even in Stirling, it is quite difficult to know what the tutors' views are, and to what extent you can successfully oppose them. There are different opinions about this. The cynical: 'You'd like to think that as long as it's well argued, even if you disagree with the tutor it's alright. But if you think that, you live in a naive world. Even if it's a student disagreeing they'd feel unhappy about a rival view.' (68) The trusting: 'If you state what you're going to do, and then do it well, they'll give you a good grade, even if you don't agree with what they actually might think the text's about.' (60)

Success goes, as Miller and Parlett (1974) have shown, to the 'cue-seekers'.

> I've always been able to swallow my pride, and go along and say okay, what did I do wrong, help me. Tell me I'm not as thick as I think I am. And the people who suffer are the people who can't go along and say 'Help me'. (61)

'I'm wondering what actually happens to them'

How do the staff see the students in the teaching situation? The voices most critical of students come not from Oxford or the PNL but from Stirling and the civic universities, and the most frequent complaint con-cerns passivity:

> Much too docile and submissive. They let me get away with the most extraordinary things. (7)

> Very intimidated, hard to teach, inert. Bright, very pleasant, they're just politically dead, frightened of thinking independently. They think teacher's right. (1)

> What shocks me is the relativism as a principle that the students have. One of my students said 'Of course I never make value judgements'. (3)

Staff make distinctions among the students. The good are very good but

> There is a whole pack of students who make their way through it, but they've never got the book with them, they haven't read the plays, they've seen the video. (20)

Some are very bright. Some of them though – you can't hide all of your prejudices – I wouldn't give them a grant. The intake is broader and more lax than in other subjects, it is a soft option. The poor ones write down what they are told, no mental alacrity. (16)

Staff make an effort to think positively:

When you get to a certain age it seems to me you can go in two directions and both of them are irrational and there's evidence for both positions. You can either think the world is getting worse or you can think that the world's a better place. That's got something to do with having three children. It would be shitting on my children if I took the apocalyptic view. (6)

There is doubt about the effect of the whole teaching activity:

They come in as good students and they go out as good students. I'm wondering what actually happens to them. (3)

Teaching English is officially a commitment to pluralism. Most of us are in fact getting our own point of view across, and having our own point of view given back to us. (19)

Teaching? You get on with things and you can do your job but you know there's no gaiety in it, there's no creativity in it. (13)

I think I'd like them to continue paying my salary, let me use the photocopier and get on with my research. (16)

Yet, as we have seen, there are alternatives to the traditional forms of teaching and assessing. There are lectures that are role-plays, essays that are creative writing, poems that become performances. Teaching can be creative and can address the tensions between thinking and feeling, between personal experience and textual knowledge. But staff seem to find great difficulty in escaping from the traditional forms. My feeling, having discussed these issues of teaching and learning with staff and students, is that both groups are grappling with difficult problems connected with the nature of the subject. It is true that the problems of the seminar, the tutorial, the lecture confront all university lecturers and that students of all disciplines have to deal with the task of leaving home. It is true that English lecturers are not any less well prepared for the teaching role than their colleagues. But at the heart of English there seems to be a doubt about the subject itself. Reading is possible. Writing is possible. But in isolation, not in communication. And teaching is communication. Teaching does not emerge naturally from the activity: 'One comes to see that teaching literature may be something almost as different from reading, studying, enjoying and writing it as working in a bank.' (22)

If it were really as different as this it might be easier to accept, but there is the sense that integration should be possible:

I've always tried to marry the writing and teaching. I've not succeeded very well. It's very difficult to do both but it is possible. It's
not simply doing two jobs like window cleaning and bus driving, it
is actually the same job. Robert Frost talks of making your vocation
your avocation and your avocation your vocation. (13)

To fail to integrate, to acknowledge that you cannot bring the subject into
the institution, may in some cases mean that you have to leave the institution:

I beat the feeling down because I'm still in the job. To give degrees
in literature, I think it may be a nonsense. I think it's a very, very real
problem, and it's one of the unspoken problems of literature departments. We can't speak of it, because it means the death of the
degree. So I'm getting out because I've lost faith in the subject. Not
in the students, or in the act of teaching, I enjoy it immensely. But
I've a responsibility to get my students through the exams, and it's
like two separate acts. If I want to pursue the sort of approach I
want to pursue, most of the time they wouldn't get through their
examinations. (51)

The majority of staff and students, teachers and taught, will go through
their careers – short for the student, long for the staff – dealing as best they
can with the doubts and the lack of integration. They will compromise
with the institution, gaining as much as possible from the belonging –
degrees, salaries, photocopiers, sabbaticals – while keeping personal loss
as low as possible. This may mean – for staff and students – taking as few
risks as possible in teaching situations. At worst, this results in 'inert'
students who pass through unchanged and staff who lose faith or despair
of making connections. My belief is that a greater understanding of the
issues we have considered in this chapter, particularly those concerning the
power of the traditional forms, could considerably enhance the experience
of students and staff and the effectiveness of the institution.

Lectures, seminars, tutorials, essays – these are forms, but so are the
institutions where they are enacted. It is these institutional forms we will
consider next, concentrating on the long-term occupants of the institution
– the staff – and on their experience of the job.

five

Life in an institution

La réforme des institutions vient trop tard, lorsque le coeur des peuples est brisé.
(Georges Bernanos, 1938, *Les grands cimetières sous la lune*)

Getting in

Most students spend three years in the institution before moving on and out. But the student of English who gets a first has the opportunity to stay longer, to stay perhaps for life. For that, he or she usually needs to persuade the British Academy to give a research scholarship. In 1991 there were 750 of these for all disciplines. There is no subject quota, and, according to Anthony Kenny, President of the British Academy, there were 'an enormous number of first-class degree candidates applying for and getting awards in English' (in Birkett and Kelly 1992: 28). In the United States this would mean entry into graduate school and the start of professional training as a university teacher. Here it can simply mean postponing a career choice. It does not necessarily signify a burning desire for life-membership of the institution:

> I wanted to get into the film industry, but that seemed to be in a state of terminal decline. I didn't have enough maths to be an architect, so I went into research, primarily to postpone making a decision. But once I was in it, well, ten years drifted by and I got a fellowship. (29)

> I didn't get into it, it got into me. I stayed on to do research, I had no career ambitions. No job prospects, nothing, just obsessive reading. (20)

It is also a wish to continue to choose one's work pattern:

> I like to be able to start work when I want to and finish when I want. Spend two hours in the middle of the day shopping, or lunch. Then

work till three in the morning. The only way I can do that is by being something academic and English is the thing that I do. (111)

At the age of 12, Dr Linsey asked her English teacher: 'Do you think I could be a university lecturer?' The teacher replied, warily: 'I think you should concentrate on your O levels.' (58) Such precocity is unusual. Mostly, opting to do research does not mean a vocation for university teaching: 'It was a negative choice, not a vocational thing. I just felt that my first degree didn't meet all the needs it should have met.' (96) Dr Jameson had actually finished his thesis and was teaching in a cramming school before it dawned on him that he could be a university teacher. What happens is that the committed and skilled reader and writer gets to 'stay close to literature' and carries on reading and writing without much soul-searching and with a lot of pleasure: 'It was more of the same really. It's just that you have more time. Most of it was pleasure. Especially the manuscripts. It's like being let loose in a sweetshop – a childish sense of wonder and greed.' (59) 'I tootled along as before.' (28) 'I just settled in to seat 83 in the Bodleian and got on with it.' (57)

The PhD student will need a subject. The process is often presented as being routine: 'Okay, start looking for a twentieth-century novelist who has written in English and who hasn't been written about a thousand times.' (65) The reality, as I discovered in *Language People* (p. 88), is more complex. The range of what can be done under the umbrella 'English' is very wide and to choose an author or a theme from that vast array is a powerful statement of identity: 'These things occur to one later. I can now see that Conrad's outsider status, the themes of isolation, alienation . . . Being Scottish was probably more important than I ever recognized.'

The actual process of doing the research is very variable. It seems wisest not to assume you will get much supervision, especially in Oxford and Cambridge where the experience of supervision is sometimes described as 'hopeless' or 'surreal':

> I had enormous difficulties. It was just completely hopeless. He had a desk covered with so many books that you couldn't see it at all, and he was so shy he could hardly say anything, and most of what he did say I didn't understand. So really for the whole time I was actually quite worried about whether I was doing something which was unacceptable. (9)

This respondent did indeed fail his PhD initially. Others lost their way during this period as life caught up with them. I had glimpses of how the thesis can be in competition with relationships, so that only when the relationship ends can the thesis be written; in one case it was the academic relationship with the actual supervisor, which is an interesting twist:

> It took me ages to get the degree, I lost all sense of direction. I used to go and sit in cafés all day, and do bits of writing. I had this supervisor who was a very strong personality, New York, Jewish.

When she went back to the States I finished my doctorate. I just sat down and wrote it.

The degree of involvement in the institution at this stage depends to a large extent on how much teaching the graduate student gets to do. An Oxford post-graduate whose first degree was not from Oxford can be very isolated: 'I don't do any teaching. They rely on people who have been undergraduates here. My contact with Oxford is remarkably small. The collegiate system is irrelevant for graduates.' (73) And, in general, post-graduates in the British system are marginal, less integrated than under-graduates or staff (Whiston and Geiger 1992: 148).

For others, teaching is a first step into a profession – a remunerated activity involving others and distinct from the continuation of private student work. It can also eventually lead to a permanent job, especially at Oxford. Indeed, at Oxford it is, it seems, the *only* way: 'It's hard to think of jobs going to people who have no previous experience here.' (24) 'I wish we interviewed more people we don't know for jobs. We tend to say "X or Y are around. Let's have a look at them." There is a sense here of the queue. If people hang around long enough, they'll get something.' (25) But 'long enough' can be very long and involve considerable peregrinations from one temporary job to another:

> To tell you a little metaphor of my existence. My supervisor sent me a letter to New College. They crossed that out and wrote St Hugh's who crossed that out and wrote Wadham who crossed that out and wrote Corpus Christi who crossed that out and wrote Lincoln, who crossed that out and sent it here.

This kind of academic labour is no sinecure:

> You get paid much less and you do much more work. As a Fellow I now make three times as much money for a job which has less hours. Also the very real stress and strain of not knowing what you are going to be doing next year. (27)

Dr Clay was determined not to go through this process: 'I had no intention of lowering my dignity like that. Wild horses would not have kept me around grovelling.' But he was anxious: 'My fourth year at Oxford was full of fear that I was going to be unemployed; endless interviews for research fellowships. I was getting jumpy and paranoid, feeling that a job was just outside my grasp.' (54)

Outside Oxford, it is less likely that the temporary teacher will land the permanent job; to have to apply for your own job when it is advertised is particularly stressful and can have long-lasting effects:

> I had a lot of difficulty getting my academic job, and I think that affected me quite deeply, I was on temporary contracts, and a fellow-ship, I was beginning to think I would not get a job. Eventually I did get offered a job here after four years. I started out with a difficult relation with this department, the sense of being exploited by it. (58)

I accepted a one-year contract on the understanding that it would be made permanent, but then the professor who'd made that promise got a job elsewhere and I suddenly realized that there were four people on the campus . . . It really was quite sinister. Everyone had their little team. They wanted them appointed, and they would quarrel and juggle the appointments panel. So I was left at the end of that without a job. I was so cross with that experience that I was very difficult to interview and if anyone condescended to me I would be aggressive. It was quite fun. It did enable me to say the sort of things that people normally only say in Kingsley Amis novels. (45)

The getting of the permanent job is a matter of strategy and good fortune combined. When a department has a traditional map of knowledge certain territories become vacant when the occupant moves on, so a department may need a Chaucerian, and if that is what you are and other things are equal, you may get the job. Dr Clay gave a vivid account of how single-minded his generation can be when it comes to job-seeking:

I set about creating a CV that would make me as employable as I could be. I ran a conference, I organized a publication from that conference. I was sub-dean. I carefully did those things so that when the CV was written it would look as if I was an all-round man. I got the job because my face seemed to fit, and I was what the department wanted. I knew about theory but didn't appear to be an obsessive, trendy theorist. I was immersed in deconstruction when I came back from America. I reined that in, knowingly. (54)

Doing the job

Teaching

Once in the job the researcher/writer becomes a researcher/writer/teacher/administrator, and this can be a real baptism of fire, made worse by the tendency of permanent staff to off-load tedious administrative tasks on to the newcomer: 'Administration is a real pain. I'm getting landed with it because I'm the youngest and I'm female. That's pissing me off.' But the biggest demands are made by teaching:

I think it ridiculous that in my first job I had as much teaching as people who had been in it 20 years. Last year I had no summer holiday. I was working every weekend. (54)

When I came here I didn't have time to think, I was working six, seven days a week. (46)

In the majority of cases, none of these researchers will have had any training for the teaching role: they will prepare and deliver their lectures, run their seminars, mark their essays, calling on whatever they have internalized as good practice from their own experience. Assiduous occupation of Seat 83 at the Bodleian will not have contributed anything. Some institutions provide training (not many, not much), but the paradox (as with study skills for students) is that the new lecturers are too busy to attend. These courses are often like swimming lessons offered when you are going down for the third time. The most valuable support comes from colleagues, particularly colleagues of the same age and sex. A recently appointed woman:

> It's still quite nerve-wracking. I'm exhausted. I lose sleep from anxiety. The reason I've been able to cope is that the staff have been so good to me. Jane that I share a room with came at the same time, so we give each other support. I've never been in such a supportive environment. (48)

There is an interesting gender difference: two young male lecturers give each other support less directly, through *badinage*: one will say to the students, 'Ah well, Dr Smith is taking over next week, there's going to be an intellectual falling off', paradoxically, implying a bond of trust between them.

When the pay cheque comes in there is a sense of mismatch between the achievement and the reward – expressed readily by parents who compare their offsprings' lives: 'My mother's very sorry for me. She sees that I've spent all this time studying and I'm not getting anything for it.' (48)

Clearly the range of first job experiences is considerable, but a lecturer, now towards the end of his career, sums it up like this: 'For me the job has got better, because I know more about what I have to do and I am allowed to do it, but for young people coming into the profession now conditions are dreadful. They are exploited, manipulated.' (13) Newcomers and old-stagers have, therefore, very different experiences of teaching. But institutionally they are in the same situation. Overtly with polytechnics, much more ambivalently with universities, the central institutional task is teaching. A department which has a superabundance of undergraduates whom it is prepared to teach will, if its research rating is poor, be made to feel inadequate but it will not close down and no teachers will be made redundant. A department of scholars which does not attract students is in serious trouble unless it receives substantial outside funds, and unless somehow the institution feels it can use that group solely for prestige purposes. And yet, paradoxically, the teaching role in universities is extremely insubstantial and the unhappiest people, it seems to me, are those who are essentially educationalists. One of the most unpopular things to do in a university is to think reflexively about education, and hence education departments are perhaps the most unpopular departments of all.[1]

Dr Soper was appointed to a strange post – half in education, half in English. It seems to have been a disaster. His view is that 'the universities are not interested at all in the teaching–learning process, only in the product'. He says he has suffered for more than 20 years from the marginalization of teaching and the reluctance of colleagues to discuss educational questions or to share any teaching experience:

> We don't talk about these processes. We don't attempt to measure what we're doing one against the other. It's a big problem but one that we've never addressed for 20 years so it's most unlikely that we'll do it now. The only attempt that was made foundered almost immediately because the person couldn't convince other colleagues that any change was possible or desirable. (3)

Given the isolation of each teacher and the absence of support and quality control, nothing, he says, prevents good teachers lapsing into the mechanical. A colleague illustrates this:

> I'm getting very tired and I've not got much creativity. I used to think of myself as quite a good teacher. I don't think of myself as a good teacher now. Spoon-feeding is less creatively taxing. It's a cop-out if I was honest. It's easy to do something relatively mechanical, and there's a part of me that's despairing. (4)

In *Language People* I suggested that this might be because of the university teacher's need to make a very clear boundary between low-status school *teachers* and high-status university *lecturers*. Anything which revealed commonality was rejected: anything which underlined difference was accepted. Since not much lecturing takes place in primary schools (though the Policy Studies Unit is working on that), lecturing is good; since a lot of pair-work and story-writing goes on in primary schools, these things are not good. My French colleagues have since given me a good barbaric term for this phenomenon, '*secondarisation*': what this means is that virtually any alternative to the two higher education forms, the transmission model and the good-students-do-it-themselves model, is seen as making the university lecturer look like a secondary school teacher and therefore as status-threatening.

Dr Clay, who has just started a permanent job, illustrates the vehemence with which this status distinction is maintained:

> I would rather have been a lawyer than a schoolteacher. That's why I resent this idea of throwing teaching-only contracts at us. It sickens me. I wanted to be a university lecturer. I was snotty enough not even to apply to polys for jobs, because research was what I wanted to do. (54)

One of my respondents, Professor Patterson, was involved in 1968 in an attempt to set up a specifically British Marxist practice of literary study in English, 'Marx plus Leavis'. The embryonic school was broken up by the university after a violent and public fight (Patterson calls it a 'witch-hunt'). The question here is whether the university was reacting to the Marxism or to the libertarian pedagogy and it seems that the greatest hostility was directed at the latter.

It could be, however, that the resistance to teaching comes from a feeling that teaching as conceived by Dr Soper is impossible in the institution. What if all students acted like Simon, a mature student in PNL? 'I do make a pain of myself. They're being paid for it. I just drop in. If I've got a question I'll go and ask it.' (81) In one sense students do all think like this: they may not be prepared to knock on doors so readily, but they all see the need for group discussion. 'More tutorials or seminars, that's what I do the work for. It's quite easy to go into lectures, take notes down and never look at them again.' (93) Teachers too see the danger of lectures without seminars: 'Lectures change as a result of seminars. Remove seminars, and you get inferior lectures. As far as the Government is concerned I can video mine once and walk away, can't I?' (20)

This is where the relevant disciplines for our discussion are arithmetic, astronomy, and biology: if the only techniques available are the lecture, the tutorial, the tutor-led seminar and private study; if student numbers increase, if staff numbers do not, and if tenured staff have administrative tasks decentralized on to them; if the time the earth takes to revolve remains constant; if no dramatic modifications are made to biological clocks; it follows that there must be less and less actual 'teaching'.

It is possible to modify one of the conditions by introducing a new element – tutorials and group teaching done by post-graduates or short-term staff, variously described as 'teaching assistants', 'tutorial fellows' or, at Oxford, 'supernumerary fellows' [sic]. For less than £20, a university in 1992 can get a seminar group taken and essays marked by a post-graduate student. Such a student told me he does two hours a week, 'which can easily occupy 30 hours' preparation and marking'. Lecturers view this trend with dismay:

> More and more, the only teaching undergraduates will get will be from post-graduates, not experienced teachers, not experienced researchers, not from people with children. You can't have a university taught by 24-year-old post-graduates, especially when they are teaching more and more mature students. Post-graduates are well-intentioned, but they don't have a professional responsibility for what they are doing. No CV, no formal interview, they are just taken on. You simply grab them because you have to have the teachers while the academic staff are busy doing administration. We are not being freed for research, we are being freed for administration. When I was a post-graduate there was no question of letting us loose on undergraduates in that way. There is a point where standards will be threatened. They are threatened. (20)

Here are some specifics from another respondent:

> There's £16,000 for post-graduate teaching. The whole of the first years for half their seven-hour time are taught by post-graduates, and half of the second year the same. Six of the twenty or so third-year classes are taught for half their time by post-graduates. It isn't good that we should be so dependent on post-graduates, because when the

students want to know how best to work the system they really ought to have an old horse to look in the mouth of. (19)

If patients only ever see the nurse because the consultant is always away at a committee or a conference, they may have cause to complain about the hospital.

It is not, however, just a question of pedagogy; it is also a question of concern for personal growth and development, what Dr Soper, the educationalist, calls 'nurturing'. Schools accept this as part of their mission: universities are therefore reluctant and prefer the narrower notion of knowledge acquisition. As we have seen, passivity and silence can be the consequences of a situation rather than student personality traits. That situation can be the actual teaching form – lecture, seminar, tutorial, assessment – with its power relations, or it can be the institution itself and the way it sees itself in relation to students.

For staff, the main task that students have is academic learning. Yet students are coping with other important life tasks at the same time.[2] Students tend to think that staff are out of touch with this reality. A first-year student:

> They say 'Fill in that form, fill in this,' and 'Oh, by the way, here's a couple of books.' So you start to read that book, and you say, 'My God, I've never seen anything like it,' then you go home and discover that you have to cook for yourself. I work and I am student rep. I've got washing to do and shopping, and at the end of this you think 'If I've got any time left I'll sleep.' I work 15 to 20 hours a week, I have to, the average for a room in London is £45, £60 a month travel . . . (88)

A final-year student reflects on her first year experience and illustrates how, for first-year students in particular, 'leaving home' is a task more urgent than the academic one:

> The first term was the worst time I've ever had in my life, I didn't make friends, I stayed in my room, I didn't go out for six weeks. I was used to having friends all around me and I knew absolutely no one. It was horrible. It's always taken me a long time to get friendly with people, but here I have learned to make friends. (94)[3]

If this transition is not successfully managed the whole experience may be wasted. Mary thinks that this may be her case:

> I don't suppose I've benefited from the course very much at all. I don't think it's altered me. In the first year I resisted it, mainly because it shakes all your stability, and I wasn't very sure about being here in the first place. I found it very hard to deal with it. (92)

This issue of forming and joining social groups is important for all students. But in English it mirrors the opposition of private and public which, as we have seen, is specific to the subject.

One might expect that the Oxford college would be precisely the place where this process would be worked out most ideally. In fact this seems not to be the case. The students do not know the other six or seven people doing English in their college very well because there are no groups or seminars. Even less do they know the people doing English in another college; they glimpse them at lectures and in exams. The sense of a group is lacking. They even work in their own rooms rather than libraries. The university itself does little to assist integration:

> The whole idea of people finding their own way and things being necessarily difficult has a lot of currency in Oxford and in English studies. (71)

There is some scepticism about the whole college ethos:

> If you buy into the myth of the colleges, then you're family, but it's not a family, because in some sense the idea of the family is unconditional and it's not unconditional. It's very conditional. The college always says there are safety nets but really there are so many people in the college, and the contact between college and students is so academically orientated, unless you are already confident and aware enough to know where to go for help ... (75a)

In contrast, PNL offers support. A word which I heard very frequently was 'comfortable'. 'When I came here I just liked the feel of the place.' (86) 'It seemed a very comfortable place to study. It's not a grand building, it's very much within the community.' (89). The students who have the most difficulty are those who have come straight from school, though they too adapt:

> In our fiction seminar there's a group of four or five ladies, late twenties, early thirties. They've all got children, they've all done degrees or they've been out to work. At the other side of the classroom there sits me and three of my friends. They always dominate every seminar. We do feel a bit frightened of them. We do try and join in the discussions but they don't let us get a word in edgeways. We feel very naive. They're old, and they think they know it all, and we're just little children, but as we get confidence in our own abilities we'll get to stand up to them more. (91)

A 20-year-old first-year student:

> It's as if they are saying, we are making it as easy as we can for you, and we are wrapping you in cotton wool, and eventually you will stand on your feet. It's as friendly as they could possibly make it. (88)

So this student, unlike Mary above, is able to develop:

> You couldn't not change. There are views that I wouldn't compromise, probably about my own sexuality, but my academic views in the light of feminism or Marxism or whatever, those will certainly change. (88)

Research

The research and publishing aspect of the job is intermittent. A newly appointed lecturer will be looking for a niche but there may be a long period when publishing is difficult or impossible, followed perhaps by a spate, followed perhaps by a drought. Dr Ford: 'I found the thing I wanted to do fairly late in academic life. Up until then I was a bit of a lost soul.' (52) Dr Grant: 'I am heavily involved in a lot of things which I would have loved to have had in my twenties, which I didn't get. I get up at six o'clock in the morning to do it, and I'm constantly fighting for bits of time.' (16)

The strange thing about the university teacher role is the extent to which it is both bureaucratized and freelance. Certainly the reluctance to say 'No' to proposals is typical of freelance people – self-employed consultants or actors – though the motivation for the university teacher is not financial survival since the monthly salary cheque sees to that. Among compulsive researchers there is the fear that you won't be asked again if you say 'No' to work; there is competition with other sub-groups; there is a sense of moral obligation:

> I think I must be mad. I fear I may drive myself into the ground. On the other hand, with the grace of God I'll get it done, at the same time knowing it probably doesn't add up to very much. I don't totally believe what I do. I think it's all rather weird and strange. At the same time I believe with total intensity that I will beaver away at it and not have much of a social life and all the rest of it. It's a funny contradiction. But, having had the opportunity to do this for 40 years (and part of me wishes I'd done something else) I would like at the end to feel I didn't waste it. (16)

Others, as we shall see in Chapter 7, have a very different motivation: the combative desire to change the discipline. On the whole, these have the least problems with publishing their work because they are in touch with controversial issues of general concern. Dr Clay sent his thesis to a publisher:

> They said, 'Forget it'. So I phoned up and said, 'I know it's not all that commercial, but the chapters are on politics, gender and colonialism', and she said 'Ah, that's much more interesting, would you care to recast the book so that it's about colonialism and gender?' (54)

For more traditional researchers, or those who cannot easily recast their work thus, publishing can be hard:

> Faculty demands you have something to show, but . . . [one] University Press (whom I would gladly see bombed to the ground), don't seem to realize that it makes any difference whether your book comes out this year or next. I need the book in my hand *now*. (31)

Oxford, as always, is *sui generis*. A don can be involved in producing a magazine for schools, like *The English Review*, which circulates 10,000 copies and has 50,000 readers, or writing for *The Sunday Times*, or being a Booker Prize judge. 'We've got this reputation for being elitist; in fact it's not true, the opposite. I reckon the culture is in trouble if the common reader goes. The last couple of years *The English Review* has interfered with my research, but I regard it as a more important mission.' They live double lives, writing for the 'common reader' but also doing scholarship:

> Ideally you should be able to do both. It would show that you've got a foot in both camps. Being a Booker Prize judge, for example, you won't be seen as enjoying yourself at the firm's expense. It wouldn't be acceptable to talk about your research, you would keep quiet about that. You might suddenly stun them all by producing an enormous history of the Byzantine Empire, but they wouldn't have known you were doing it. (23)

The clear assumption in polytechnics is that you are paid to teach and administer, and if you do research it is in order to get promotion to principal lecturer or to get a job somewhere else. In reality, the same thing applies in universities: publication means promotion; no publication means no promotion and a life of teaching and administration, though not necessarily more of these than the researcher. The difference between polytechnics and universities is that no stigma attaches to the non-researcher in the polytechnic, whereas now the non-researcher in a university, however good a teacher or administrator and whatever his or her current responsibility or previous output, is constantly reminded of the contract to produce research, constantly required to present and re-present pie-in-the-sky projects as if they were real. This is one of the obscurities which the removal of the binary divide and the universities' research money will undoubtedly clarify. Professor Martin Harris, Vice Chancellor and Chair of the CVCP/UFC subcommittee on research indicators, had this to say recently:

> It may well be that in higher education we need two career routes that are somewhat more independent than they have been in the past . . . Is it not the case that we need in universities people who see their careers as successful teachers – who are appointed on that basis and who are then recognised, rewarded, promoted and in every way given equivalent opportunities to those who are teacher-researchers or in fact simply researchers? We have got a core of staff who are teacher-researchers who have basically all the benefits, and an increasing number of short-term contract researchers, instructors and whatnot. It may be that that is no longer a tenable situation . . . We've got to address the issue and make sure that we appoint, motivate and reward people for doing what they were appointed to do and not something else. To appoint somebody to teach and then throw them out because they don't do research seems to me outrageous.
>
> (In Birkett and Kelly 1992: 23)

Unless and until the role is clarified in this way university staff remain, in theory, 'teacher-researchers'. Some are, in practice, teacher-administrators. But there is a sub-group of English People who are writers, for whom writing is the core activity. As we saw in Chapter 3, some may be creative writers using the institutional framework for security. They are finding this position less and less tenable: 'The last couple of years I've been so busy academically that I'm not getting nearly enough time for my own imaginative life. I'm feeling bad about that.' (8) And they dream of miraculous escape: 'I live in the hope of winning the equivalent of the football pools. I'd give up teaching and get on with writing.' (22) The majority are academic writers. But writing is still for them the core, rather than an occasional activity which complements teaching and administration:

> I think of the business of writing as the heart of the whole thing. I don't think I would mind if I never taught again if I could go on doing the research and the writing. The most rewarding thing in my life is completing an article or even a review. (7)

Like most writers, they describe the activity as a kind of sweet, all-consuming, unhealthy torment:

> Writing is very painful. It's the toughest thing. But at the end of the day when you produce four or five pages, the satisfaction of doing that is enormous. It's an exhausting, time-consuming business. I promise myself I'll pack it up at a certain point. It's an unhealthy lifestyle, too much smoking, drinking, plus not being around to see the children that much. It clearly would have been better for family life if I'd not done so much writing. (12)

The difficulty is fitting this kind of intensity into the institutional framework which requires a range of activity:

> Some people argue that those who do a lot of writing and write well tend to be the best teachers, because they're keeping up, they're thinking about the subject, and the fruits of their research go into their teaching anyway. I'm not sure it works out that way. I think it's a quite different equation. If you write a lot then most likely you are not putting in the amount of reading and preparation and time with the students. So I think there is a real clash there. (12)

Research is for universities a major requirement but it is not institutionalized in the same way as teaching and administration. The institution expects it to be done in the margins by ambitious, committed individuals. The fact that there is such a thing as sabbatical 'leave' I find evidence for this, as is the fact that it is always possible to get teaching materials typed, but rarely, if ever, an article. Yet research is also the one thing universities feel they can measure. In the same way that you only teach what you can examine, so you attach institutional importance to what you can measure even if this is the most institutionally remote activity. But all this is currently in a very confused state, as universities compete desperately for premier league status. This makes it look as if they are prepared to see teaching as earning the money that pays for the research that earns the rating. People with teaching-only contracts will be support staff for the researchers. But, as Martin Harris said, there may be an advantage in a contract which does not require people to do something they cannot do (or which specifies at certain times of their career what their precise commitment is).

The Apollo group

Most English People live their working lives as members of quite small groups which, like families, remain very constant over many years, and which, again like families, can be dominated by absent members, including the long dead. These groups may be organized in larger groups – English literature may be paired with English language or other entities in a school of some kind – and individuals may belong to various worldwide 'invisible colleges'. But basically the core sentient group is the department.

As far as I can see, there are no empirical studies of these groups as groups, and I am in no position to remedy this since my research has been based on individual interviews and attendance at a very small number of departmental gatherings. If we want to understand more about how disciplines function as institutional subjects, we will need to observe more departmental groups (we will also need to observe more actual teaching situations).

Such research could do worse than start from hypotheses produced by Belbin's experiments at Henley (Belbin 1981). He and his colleagues investigated management teams by forming groups and getting the groups to compete using a business game called 'Teamopoly'. A university department, it seems to me, is very similar to one of the 'Apollo' teams he describes (Chapter 2). At one stage he and his colleagues created a team which was made up of all the cleverest people attending the course, so much so that other participants complained of unfairness: 'When very clever people are put together in a group, there is no disguising the fact.' They stopped complaining when it was discovered that these so-called 'Apollo' teams almost always did very badly. 'It amazed many Henley members that companies comprising such clever people could collectively perform so poorly.' Observation of the Apollo team's activity showed why this was so:

> The Apollo team members had spent a large part of their time engaged in abortive debate, trying to persuade the other members of the team to adopt their own particular well-stated point of view. No one seemed to convert another or be converted. On the other hand, each seemed to have a flair for spotting the weak points in the other's argument. There was, not surprisingly, no coherence in the decisions that the team reached – or was forced to reach – and several pressing

and necessary jobs were totally neglected. The eventual failure of the company, in finishing last in the exercise, was marked by mutual recriminations. Altogether the Apollo company of supposed super-talent proved an astonishing disappointment ... Apollo companies usually ran true to type – difficult to manage, prone to destructive debate, and in difficulties with decision-making. Members of these companies acted along lines that they favoured personally, without taking account of what fellow company members were doing. This at least circumvented the blockages caused by collective indecision, but unco-ordinated action is only slightly better than taking no action at all. What one member did was undermined, usually unintentionally, by the actions of another. The lack of coherent team work nullified the gains of individual effort or brilliance. Apollo companies were frequently in cash-flow problems ... due to the competing strategic demands for whatever cash the company had.

(Belbin 1981: 10–11)

Belbin sums up the Apollo team as being characterized by 'socially satisfying but anarchic autonomy'. I would be surprised if this description did not ring bells for university teachers of English. Compare this account of Oxford:

No one has got the power to change it, not even a professor. You can't get a collective decision. I once said to an entrance candidate, 'You must realize that English tutors are a law unto themselves', and my colleague who was sitting in the other chair said, 'No, no, they are an anarchy unto themselves.' (29)

Belbin attributes this competitive individualism to the education system, of which university teachers are, of course, the ultimate product:

Those who, at school, are 'top of the class' ... are continually being judged in terms of their scholastic pre-eminence. To come second is to fail. Beating the next man is the name of the game. Difficult problems excite the greatest rivalry, and so destroy the bonds of mutual co-operation and complementary functioning upon which the success of a team ultimately depends. In other words, over-concentration on coming top of the class provides an unconscious training in anti-team work.

(Belbin 1981: 13)

He also invokes as part of the failure of the Apollo team the emphasis on 'critical thinking'. Critics are not good team members. The Apollo team also performed poorly as a team because it did not have the range of types which teams need.[4] They have high critical intelligence (as measured by the CTA test), are dominated by 'shapers' ('seeking to impose some shape or pattern on group discussion and on the outcome of group activities') and, being clever, 'over-rate cleverness' (Belbin 1981: 168, 59, 17). The situation is perpetuated by what Belbin calls 'elective homogeneity': the group will recruit in its own image.

Another eminent management specialist, Charles Hampden-Turner, worked with senior academics at a conference. He concluded:

> There is something both exciting and appalling in working with academics and politicians instead of business people. The former are in so many ways more articulate, succinct and impressive in what they have to say . . . But at another level, one begins to realize how polarized the best of rhetoric becomes. To be articulate in the sense of sharpening ideas and communicating them forcefully leads inexorably to an *entrapment within one's own rhetoric*. It is almost as if language was entertaining in proportion to the irreconcilability of the ideas expressed. There is a fatal cleverness . . . which dooms some of the best and brightest minds to an eternity of sterile jousting and a total inability to resolve their differences . . . One wonders how great a drag on our capacity to create wealth is the Western tradition of *flamboyant individualism* in which the purpose of life is the theatrical presentation of a unique personality, and to be different is far more important than to be reconciled.
>
> (Hampden-Turner 1990: 210)

The quotations in this book demonstrate the extent to which this applies to English People. Indeed they may be the most flamboyantly individualistic of all: 'Oxford dons would sell their souls for idiosyncracy. They would far rather be thought eccentric than clever.' (23) They may also be the most capable rhetoricians. I even wonder whether I have not been seduced out of my anthropologist role into giving excessive prominence to respondents like Professor Dover (15), simply because of the provocative theatricality of their rhetoric. Professor Dover is not 'typical', indeed he is unique, but he does represent what is valued, what makes for success: fluency and rebelliousness. My interviews give me copious evidence that English People were and are rebellious and individualistic and very unhappy with the institutional concept of role: '*Mr Chairman*, I'd rather die than say that. I've never said *Mr Dean*, never.' (16) If they are in the university it is because they wanted to avoid bureaucratic structures: 'I chose to enter a university because I didn't want to end up in that sort of Civil Service tagged and boxed kind of world.' (53) They are uneasy with anything that involves cooperation. If they have to emerge from solitary research and teaching, they may prefer a task which, however painful, does not entail negotiation and collaboration. Dr Grant did the faculty timetable: 'It hurt me so much doing it but I'd rather do that than try and cope with lots of difficult people.' Conflicts like double-booked rooms can produce fury: 'University teachers are not obliged to work together very much, so when they do work together they've got no practice.' The result is: 'You can walk into the place being a decent human being in the morning and come out in the afternoon a flaming asshole.' (13)

The solution to this is to avoid as much as possible having to operate as a team. A mixture of core courses and options, or better still, a modularized course entirely made of options, absolves the group from having to decide its priorities, from having common goals. Research also requires no team sanction, and the invisible college offers refuge: 'You're a member of a larger international community. I used to feel, when times were bad, at least there are people in the world who think I'm all right.' (15) This lack of team-work means that even the sharing of teaching and administration tends to be done privately, not publicly. A key administrative job – the faculty timetable – was proposed to Dr Grant in the car park, and he agreed to do it because he felt he owed the previous incumbent something.

Recent changes have had the effect of making all these avoidance strategies less effective and individuals are being forced to negotiate more. This is undoubtedly a cause of increased dissatisfaction:

> Previously there were differences, but they never surfaced, because everyone got on with their own things, devised a course, taught and examined it. Now the differences are much more apparent, and the fissiparity greater. (12)

Professor Edgeworth makes a connection between all this hostility and the problem of the cohesion of the discipline:

> I think one reason why departmental politics are so stormy and difficult, is that a lot of people don't have any clear sense of professional purpose, so they take out their quarrels with themselves on other people. There is a lot of professionalized neurosis in English literature. You get these very unreal faculty wars, the Cambridge thing was an example of that. There's an awful lot of free-floating resentment. A lot of misdirected or unfocused radical energies which don't find an adequate object or outlet and turn into internecine warfare. (12)

Let me end this section on a note of hope. A younger member of a department, recently appointed:

> I don't like to be in opposition to people. I see myself as a bridge-builder. So, being someone who believes in history and chronology and the Renaissance, and being someone who believes in theory and feminism and politics, I hope I can be something of a bridge there. (54)

Leadership

Civic universities: Power and authority

For some, it was as if I had made a rude noise or a joke. 'Write, "At this point, one of my respondents dissolved into helpless laughter." When you say "leadership", my mind goes blank. A vacancy occurs.' (17) 'I've never thought much about it – what do you mean? It's so far outside my horizons, I don't take it into consideration.' (12) 'There is none, absolutely none.' (20) 'I don't think there is any leadership.' (13) I'm suspicious of it I suppose.' (15) 'That's not an idea I'd ever thought about really, I hardly understand it.' (24)

Some of these quotations are from senior professors, and here is a dramatic difference between the university and the people Belbin and Hampden-Turner work with: it would be impossible in industry to be one of the most highly paid members of an organization and yet to have no leadership function or to deny any understanding of that function. In general, whereas for every other aspect of this study I merely had to tune in to the sophisticated thinking which my respondents had already done, in the area of organization and management, I felt they had never given this much attention. One of my respondents admitted this and drew conclusions:

> There is no serious analysis of the institutional or academic structures of universities. That kind of self-consciousness has been very slow to develop in British universities. That's why we're sitting targets for any government organization that wants to pick us off. (2)

Professor Leigh is responsible for running a post-graduate degree, but what she does in that section she does not see as leadership: 'It's skating around obstacles. It's like a domestic situation, I don't call that leadership.' (17) Leadership for her is associated with power, and that means money, and only the head of school has that sort of power. She did once get what she wanted, she said, by banging on the principal's desk. For her, the distinction between authority and power[5] does not exist: 'I think it's all power really. I'm not sure there are any legitimate sorts.'

Since there is no legitimate authority, it follows that there should be no leaders: 'We shouldn't be needing them. This stupid arrangement that there is a head of department who is supposed to be a leader. We are all grown-up.' On reflection, there is one leader she admires: 'I read Biggles avidly all my childhood. He was a leader.' *Biggles, thou shouldst be living at this hour.* But he is not. So there can be no representation: 'I think X would like to see himself as spokesperson for a whole generation, but many people including me would say, "You're not speaking for me, baby." Even his nearest and dearest would not allow him to speak for us.'

The hostility to authority is amazingly strong. Dr Soper has memories of a previous head of department and his senior colleagues, many years ago: 'The people who were there to give us a model were unspeakable in their awfulness. They were tsars. It was a kind of living death. They were saurian.' There is the same idea that leaders infantilize:

> He was like the Big Daddy and everyone rushed up to him with their little potties saying 'Look'. It was totally infantalizing. He allowed them to do their own thing. He didn't care as long as he was leading the power of patronage, the money bags. (3)

Professor Dover remembers 'a period when we had macho leaders of men laying the law down from the head of the table'. Now, he says, there is 'a series of chairpersons who are amenable and answerable to the department as a democratic body'. He prefers this, 'with all its inefficiency'.

The basic issues are brought into focus, as always, at times of crisis: a crisis in this context means a new appointment. One of my sample institutions had appointed a new professor and a year after that was making a new junior appointment. The first thing to notice is that the professor was not appointed to be head of department, a job which was already being done by a non-professorial member of staff. So here status and authority are oddly at variance and this dissonance is seen as 'democratic'. In theory, the elected head of department (it could be a lecturer) has the authority to allocate duties to the professor and in a meeting the professor's vote counts for no more than anyone else's.

Basically then, the conflict is between a collegiate concept where decisions are taken by majority vote and implemented by a chair who is the servant of the group, and one where senior people consult but act executively. The department feel there is a move towards the executive model and that that decreases their control.

The whole thing is made more confusing by the recent creation of schools – agglomerations of departments. A school is a cost centre, and central management relates to the school. The departments have traditional identities and operate in a collegiate way, with elected heads, but these elected heads are not recognized by the university and this is a particularly acute problem when there is an appointment to be made. The head of department is elected, but the appointment committee is nominated and what counts here is status: 'He's going to be on every single committee, and he's going to be making sure he picks all the people who get the jobs. And I guarantee he'll employ one of those boring, old-fashioned scholars. It'll be over his dead body if there's a feminist appointed.'

The question of jobs is crucial. It already was in 1908, when Cornford said there were two kinds of jobs, 'My Jobs and Your Jobs':

> My Jobs are public-spirited proposals which happen (much to my regret) to involve the advancement of a personal friend, or (still more to my regret), of myself. Your Jobs are insidious intrigues, for the advancement of yourself and your friends, speciously disguised as public-spirited proposals.
>
> (Cornford 1908: 22)

I was told of one department in 1978 which created a new post for a medievalist when there were already three on the staff. The professor at that time was a medievalist: 'It was Professor X empire-building.' Where groups are small and jobs for life, any appointment will alter the balance of the group, and a senior appointment will alter it radically (or conservatively, as the case may be). More abstractly, an appointment forces the group to define itself and to say where it sees the discipline going, in ways that it normally takes pains to avoid. In this particular case, there was a strong desire on the part of some members of the department to have a feminist and a theory person. After a vote in a staff meeting the phrase 'an interest in women's studies' was included in the advertisement, but the radicals still saw this as a tactical ploy by the conservatives: the actual short-listing and appointing committee could ignore candidates who had responded to this signal. In fact, in spite of my respondent's fears, the department did appoint a 'theoretically informed feminist' and there are no reports of dead bodies. This could be more evidence for my suspicion that authority is less malevolent or powerful than is really the case (though it has to be said I do not know all the details of the appointment). The whole question of university appointments is one which deserves closer study and I hope to publish some research on this topic in the near future.

While the rebellious, anti-authority feelings are very strong with regard to non-elected leaders and management in general, there is appreciation of elected leaders:

> Dr X has been a magnificent head of department, ridiculously careful to listen to what everyone has to say, and sensible. She doesn't have axes to grind, or play games. She gets sick and tired of being leaned on by people who want forms filled in and want her to tell them what teaching they are doing at the end of the week. (54)

It seems clear from this comment that what people look for is a chairman (in Belbin's terms even) and also a mother-figure, someone who will handle the troublesome aspects of life for them. What they do not want is a father-figure.

There is another definition of leadership which concerns relations across the boundary with other groups: 'Leadership would mean that someone defended your contribution to the outside world and recognized it.' (20) But this sense of the leader as spokesperson does not seem very common. Basically an English department wants someone to deal with irksome administrative matters and paperwork, chair meetings and maintain the balance of forces so that the department remains 'a civilized place'. What is not wanted is any pro-active leadership. One newly appointed professor and head of department took the modest initiative of using sub-groups in a departmental meeting: 'We were all sent off in groups to discuss papers, but it was met with obvious undercover derision and he's never done it since. He was startled by the weight of opposition to any notion of change.' (3)

From the way that the leadership role is seen, one senses they would also quite like a therapist: 'You just sit there and take endless human problems and trouble as far as I can see.' (16) 'I've never gone down so far that I was clinically depressed . . . if I didn't function as a cog in the wheel the institution would reject me. You couldn't go to your head of department and say "Look I'm depressed, I'm going through a hard time, drinking too much."' (13) The job of leader is generally seen as extremely unattractive.

Here is a rare bit of empathy: 'The principal and the head of school are in impossible positions because there are so many demands being made and brick-bats from all directions. It's why I'm glad I've kept out of administration [*sic*].' (12) There is awareness that, unlike what would happen in industry, there is little financial compensation for taking on a leadership role, and your research will be hindered:

> I'm not sure I'd want it. It's going to take me away from something that I love doing and what I'm good at doing and leave me with something I don't like doing so much, and I'm not so good at probably. If the professorial salary was about twice what it is it would be different. My hunch is that a lot of people think that a Chair is not as attractive as it used to be. (8)

The distinction between elected leaders and non-elected seems to be that the former see themselves as administrators or as chairpersons with no obligation to have star quality in other activities such as research or teaching, whereas the non-elected (professors) see themselves as needing to be a model, to shine at all aspects of the job: in practice not so much teaching, which is relatively unimportant, but research. At Oxford the medieval 'group' has a leader 'who is a manager and calls meetings and chairs them; he is the person you turn to,' (31) but English as a whole has no leader 'because such a person would have to be a star, but also sympathetic to the medieval, and such a person doesn't exist.' (31) The star or pin-up metaphor is common. 'The major figures are like pin-ups.' (24) Professor Weston says you must be 'like Olivier at the National Theatre. Show you can do it. Be yourself a productive scholar and a good teacher, lecturer.' (50)

Professor Wagstaff is head of a large school. He has a 'huge amount' of administration and other commitments:

> If I take a week's holiday in the middle of the long vacation I have so much mail on my desk that I can't see over the top of it. And there's nobody else who can do it. It isn't stuff that can be done by somebody else. It is stuff that is referred through me requiring my decision or signature. It is just phenomenal. Committee work is quite bad as well, and there are activities which try to raise the profile of the department or the college or the subject. It is incumbent on me to know influential people. (18)

He rejected the idea that the main part of the role was financial control: 'That's not leadership, that's accountancy'. For him, as for Professor Weston, the important thing is modelling, particularly the research activity. University leadership has more in common with sport, where the captain is expected to be a performer, than with the army, say, where generals do not usually pull triggers. As is the case with Belbin's successful 'Chairmen', he has to be good but not necessarily the best:

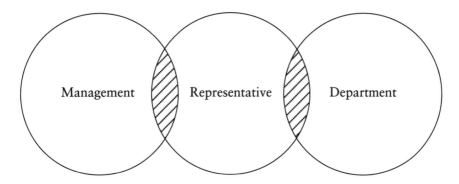

Figure 5.1

I don't think that my publications are as intellectually stimulating as those of my colleagues, but I feel it would be a cheek to go urging other people to do research if there was no evidence of me doing any myself. One must demonstrate, and go on demonstrating, that one can do it.

This aspect concerns his relations inwards, with the departmental group; it is unlikely that the university management is very concerned about his publications. For the outside world he speaks a different language: in particular the language of finance. The fact that he can and does gives him (and therefore the school) prestige in the eyes of senior management. But to be able to speak this language is to be suspect in the eyes of the members of the school. This is the classic position of the representative, who has to be 'bilingual' and maintain credibility within two groups which otherwise have no shared membership (Figure 5.1).

When he says 'I can't speak our language to them out there', the 'our' is necessarily ambiguous since its meaning depends on which circle he is standing in at the time; like the word, the leader is a shifter. His position is in fact more complex still and he needs several languages for *intra-group use*:

English always has been many different things, and the only way you can lead a group as complex as I've got is by seeming to each of them to identify very strongly with their needs. I have imaginatively to make the identification, it's not false. I have to convince people that I am identifying with the interests of computer grammar, sociolinguistics, TEFL, medieval.

Like Belbin's 'Chairman', he is not strongly identified with any particular sub-group. His problem is, he says, that the sub-groups themselves 'hate each other's guts, in all sorts of combinations.' His solution is

to make them run so fast that they don't notice who they are running next to. If they are still, they all turn on each other and tear each other's throats, but if they are all going for the horizon, da dum da dum da dum, they haven't got time to turn and bite each other. I manage that by taking a hundred new students every year, by expansion and development.

Professor Weston (who is not a head of department) can afford to believe that 'you have to make your views clear. I do believe there is a canon, that the canon should be prioritized in our work.' But to the extent that he represents the department on committees (by virtue of status), he has the same need to speak the languages of different sub-groups (in his case this is a euphemism for telling lies):

> If you have colleagues working on things that you don't believe in, you simply have to lie. If asked 'Do you support Dr X's work on black lesbian novelists?' you say 'Yes, of course I do, wonderful work.' The basic trade-unionism of the departmental structure requires you to, otherwise other departments will all say, 'English is tearing itself apart.' I'm perfectly capable of lying on behalf of my colleagues.

Professor Wagstaff and Professor Weston both seemed to me to be thriving. On the other hand, an elected leader of a school sub-unit can be very unhappy, with strong feelings of hostility to the university management which is perceived as deliberately obscurantist. Dr Leroy: 'Look at the way they present the figures. It's so that the plebs can't understand. They use abbreviations as an obvious device for keeping the plebs, us, in ignorance. [Then a touch of paranoia] I am glad you're only quoting me by number.' (19) He is mainly concerned to escape: 'I do try to understand the latest thing that is being thrown at us, but often I can't. I shan't be sorry to pack that up. It isn't what I came in for. They bloody well ought to pay administrators to do all that.'

There is, it seems to me, a simple explanation for Dr Leroy's dissatisfaction: a head of school has authority; that is, he or she is given legitimated responsibility by the management. He or she also has power (in the sense of personal power, his or her own scholarly status, and in the sense of a certain amount of financial power). The chair of the sub-section has little authority and even less power (this is probably why he or she was elected in the first place). What has happened in universities is a confusion of the collegiate and the hierarchical which makes life difficult for everyone. It is not that these two processes – vertical and horizontal – do not coexist in every organization; it is that *in universities the current horizontal one looks exactly like the former vertical one and the current vertical one commands no assent.* University management is complicated not so much by the presence of two groups – managers from the vice-chancellor down, and academics from the professor down – since this 'us and them' situation is familiar to all organizations, and the UN expert in the field has similar feelings about Geneva as does the lecturer about central management, but rather by the hybrid situation (perceived nevertheless as the ideal) of individuals being both academics and managers. People feel there are two clear tribes, but some people temporarily have to join the administrative tribe and this is not congenial:

> The people who run universities are the people who tend to be hierarchical, and who want to be in the company of other hierarchical people, with a fairly strictly set up world, white shirt and tie and a suit. But they are not actually doing the same things that the rest of us are doing at all. There are times you think, 'I'm going to have to do this for the good of my career,' you get a sinking feeling. No one admits to being a joyous administrator, but I think there are quite a lot of people around here who quite like that, who don't want to do research any more. That's fair enough, but they are a different tribe to me. (53)

This is an unusual tolerance. The view that English academics have of the administrative tribe is usually more hostile. There is dislike of 'the whole ghastly institutional framework' (22) and a belief that management is self-serving. Heads of school are seen as fellow academics here; they are not, in this view, perceived by the 'real' management as real managers (this gives a good illustration of how the whole system is dominated in an almost Laingian way by the views people have of other people's views of other people):

> There is no leadership. The term has gone out of fashion. We have management. It's not aimed at servicing teaching or research. Management operates in a closed world. It has its own mission. It has no interaction with the academic world, it's a separate phenomenon. It's been its project to separate itself off. We are rather a nuisance. Students and management – that would be fine. It's the staff that are the inconvenience in the system. They would like to get casual staff that they could get rid of when they wanted to. Management has nothing to do with human relationships. Those disappeared long ago. Heads of departments are not regarded as managers, and not recognized as such by the management. (20)

Management is seen as 'useless':

> It may be a tight economically run place, but they are unimaginative and not very intellectual. Some time ago when I suggested giving an honorary degree to a writer who has since won the Nobel Prize, there was no question of giving it to this writer because they were going to give it to a local builder. (53)

Oxford and PNL: Traum und Wirklichkeit[6]

What I have written so far applies mainly (though not exclusively, as far as the reflections on the Apollo syndrome are concerned) to 'civic' universities:

Newcastle, Cardiff and Stirling. There are differences between these institutions: Cardiff seems to be particularly hostile to management and many of the quotations above are from Cardiff people. This is mainly, I feel, because of the after-effects of the traumatic merger between UCC and UWIST in 1988, which left the institution as a kind of post-Jarratt flagship. It is striking how long-lasting the effects of institutional trauma can be: memory of the disruption of the Queen's visit is still fresh in Stirling; and at PNL they still talk of the Harrington affair.

To a greater or lesser extent, however, what I have said about leadership and the clash between the collegiate and the hierarchical, academics and management, is true for all three institutions. If one thinks of leadership as *Why?*, management as *What?* (without much concern for why), and administration as *Who, When, Where?* (with not much concern for why or what), it is clear that there is not much leadership, and that the corporateness that comes from all members of an organization knowing the answer to Why? is therefore singularly lacking. In the absence of this, greater attention to What? appears intrusive, and everything ends up seeming administration: Who, When, Where? or – crucially perhaps – How much, and How many?

Oxford and the Polytechnic of North London are institutions which are very different – dramatically from each other, but significantly also from the other three, where leadership is in a transitional or hybrid state, midway between the extremes represented institutionally by Oxford and the PNL.

Oxford

The whole question of leadership which preoccupies the civic universities is almost an irrelevance at Oxford. There is hierarchy – the Junior Fellow serves the tea at meetings, there are delicate nuances about who can park where and when, who can have guests where and when – but no one has anything like the role of Professor Wagstaff. This is, by definition, virtually undiluted collegiality.

The tutorial system and Anglo-Saxon are practices which people at Oxford find hard to defend but even harder to change. The possibility of change is closely linked to the nature of the structure: catastrophe theory tells us that centralized monoliths seem immobile, can suddenly collapse, whereas organic structures survive. La Fontaine, catastrophe theorist *avant la lettre*, said the same thing in the fable *Le Chêne et le Roseau*. For many, Oxford is the oak, but in fact I see this institution as the reed: *Je plie et ne romps pas*. There is a sense of uncentred perdurability. Individuals trying to explain to me how the university system worked in Oxford commonly referred to Kafka and to Dickens's Circumlocution Office in *Little Dorrit*. A post-graduate: 'It's a Kafkaesque situation. I'm constantly putting forward proposals to a committee I don't know. I met the guy who was blocking it, and he said it wasn't his decision. So there was the sense of constant deferral.' (73)

Dr Stone did her first degree at Oxford but had her first job in a provincial university, where she learned the ropes. She could not have done this in Oxford:

There I had space, AUT, Senate, University Court. I saw how power works and how to manage power. I couldn't have learned that here. Oxford is more mysterious, Byzantine. A strange and fragmented system. (25)

A key to this is the relationship between the colleges and the university. Poorer colleges need the university (rather as poorer countries need the European Community, or poorer regions need Italy, the state). The rich colleges in their group will pass on the students they reject, who may be better than those who applied to the poorer colleges. The university also channels funds, rather as the EC helps the Mezzogiorno. In fact for everyone, the college is necessary, the university contingent. College life is another desirable and much imitated feature of the Oxbridge experience. Some of my respondents were ready to demystify the notion of High Table conversation between nuclear physicists and medieval historians:

It's not the done thing to talk about your subject very intensely, except with other members of the subject. If you sit next to someone at lunch and start telling them about textual strategies in Old Norse poetry, they look at you slightly anxiously and start edging away. I'm always struck by the incredible ordinariness of the conversations we seem to have in the SCR. I had a conversation the other day about the relative merits of upright and horizontal vacuum cleaners. I used to be a chamber maid in a Norwegian hotel and I had very strong views on that. People who move from here to go to other universities say how nice it is to spend most of your time talking to people who know where you're coming from, as distinct from making small talk with physicists. (31)

Women and North Americans seem particularly hostile: 'It felt as if everyone thought they were really at boarding school still. Very male.' (53) 'Belonging to an Oxford SCR has got to be hell on earth. *Huis Clos*.' (74) One tutor told me he might accept a chair elsewhere because he missed the intellectual contact he had previously in his provincial university.

Even if these views are jaundiced and the college does give opportunities for cross-disciplinary discussion absent elsewhere, the fact that the subject specialist is isolated in ways not possible elsewhere remains:

People say to me in other universities, 'Is poor Eagleton still so isolated?' and I have to explain that every English tutor I've met is isolated, because there is no faculty. Being on your own is the condition of a tutor. The whole consequence of the collegiate system is that you don't have someone else on your subject, you are it. It's quite hard to generate real professionalism in these circumstances. In fact Eagleton has a much more effective collective around him, so he was less isolated. He also knew what he was doing. He had a group and a theory. (26)

From the tutor's point of view, the college–university split is enacted at the most basic level: two pay cheques, one from the college, one from the university, though there are supernumerary Fellows who are employed on renewable contracts solely by the college and who neither lecture nor examine for the university. Each college is relatively autonomous, even in the matter of appointments, so leadership with respect to subject planning becomes impossible, since the needs and wishes of the college may be at variance with the needs and wishes of the faculty. There is a power struggle between the two. Faculty is entitled to have two 'advisers' on each committee and there is fierce competition to be one of these advisers because they can manipulate the situation by saying that only one or two people on the short-list are up to the faculty standard and may get the necessary faculty lectureship. But rich colleges can ignore even this.

> What you have got to do is plan for the future. In five years we want to be here, in ten years we might like to be here, and then think about the kind of recruitment. It's impossible to get the colleges to accept that. The faculty might have a plan, but the majority of appointments are college appointments. (25)

The faculty, which is the institutional representative of the subject at Oxford, describes itself in the hand-out as existing in name only: 'The board meets, takes minutes, but does not circulate them, so it is impossible to know what goes on.' (28) The overall effect is to make any changes in the structure extremely difficult. Discussions seem to lead to decisions to take no action or to contradict a previous decision to take action. I was told of a vote for a change in the exam syllabus and then a vote against a change in the exam structure which would have made the change in the syllabus possible: 'The operation of the structure here is enormously monumental and slow grinding and reactionary. It's terribly hard to get anything changed.' (24)

One would expect the radicals at Oxford to be frustrated by this, and of course they are; but there is also an awareness of a paradox. Because Oxford is feudal, pre-bourgeois and anti-bureaucratic, there are aspects which are appealing to anti-bourgeois, anti-bureaucratic people. Professor Thomas:

> It is the reverse of a bureaucratic system. You make it up as you go along. Everything at Oxford is *ad hoc, ad hominem*. It's the seductive aspect of the system – it's anti-system. It makes it depend on the people involved, and the ad-hocery can be very attractive. (23)

As in the civic universities, 'democratic' is defined as collegial. There is a strange sense in which an Oxford college is a rare example of functioning communism: 'In certain ways the colleges are very democratic. Everything is decided by the fellowship. It's like a little commune, exactly what Marx thought.' (23) The feudal and the socialist come together, having excluded the bourgeois epoch. Oxford has not had its bourgeois revolution.

> Its enormous privilege and wealth means that it can produce structures which are attractive in themselves but which are part of an elite institution. The enormous arrogance means that it can tolerate absolutely anything. They elected me, a Marxist, because they thought it would be amusing. (23)

For people in other institutions, bombarded by questionnaires and directives, Oxford must seem like a dream:

> The personal way that it's all conducted does mean that there is a whole tier of bureaucracy missing. As someone said to me when I came here, 'colleges don't die'. It means you are very insulated. You never see a DES directive, if you didn't read the *THES* you wouldn't know. (28)

This is clearly the escapist aspect of dreaming, and yet even critics recognized the power and even the essential value of the dream, when opposed to what they see as the dehumanizing, constricting aspects of the real in its bureaucratic forms. Dr Draper left a provincial university for Oxford three years ago:

> A lot of the advantages of being here are things you have to remind yourself of. There is this sense that the institution is bigger than all of us. There isn't a cynicism about the institution that you get elsewhere. You do have this sense that we'll be here tomorrow. In other universities you have the sense that the place might quite literally not be there tomorrow. You might be amalgamated with another department next week. If department X goes, it'll be you next. In Y the arts faculty was always under threat and held in low esteem by the rest of the university, whereas this is an arts-dominated university, or at least they are in balance. So it feels very different. It's very refreshing after ten years of being told you are rubbish. Someone's got to believe in it somewhere. (28)

Here the dream is opposed to cynicism and associated with belief in the arts, in the same way that, as we saw, the subject English represents a vision of people as more than producers and consumers.

Oxford reminds us that rational organizational analysis alone will not enable us to understand the meaning of institutions for those inside or outside them. In the *Traum und Wirklichkeit* dilemma, Oxford is on the side of *Traum*. The spires are not so much dreaming as dream: dream and desire. Ryle (1949: 17) used the fact that you couldn't direct the foreigner to the 'university' as an example of a 'categorical mistake', but it is more than that – the university is a creation of the mind, not much affected by lower-order changes of personnel: 'It might be possible to dethrone Yale by buying in but that wouldn't happen here. If you transferred the whole Oxbridge faculty to Cardiff, it wouldn't work.' (20)

It is not affected either by performance indicators. Oxford is not saved by works but by grace. Whether the tutorial, Anglo-Saxon or the college system do or do not meet pedagogical objectives, whether Dr Lake is right in her claim that the English Faculty is 'an intellectual disgrace' and 'doesn't hold a candle to the Faculty of English in, say, Cornell or Columbia, or Duke', (27) all this is irrelevant. An outsider puts it like this:

> It's an enclosed world that really does have power. A major institu-
> tion of political and cultural authority. Despite what they actually do
> (and much of what happens at Oxford is quite irrelevant) it still has
> that cachet. It can then take over the game, the game that's being
> played elsewhere. (8)

Power and authority are used here as synonyms, but we can use them more precisely and say that everything about Oxford is about *power* (cachet, the seal of a king; money earned by freelance artists outside insti- tutions) and very little about *authority*. The whole effort is devoted not to being the best at a specified task, in comparison with others, according to public criteria, but to being seen as in another league:

> Oxford is a dream, desire. Remove that innate cultural superiority
> and you have to compete on professional terms with Cardiff or PNL.
> You can't afford that, and you can't admit that there may be people
> out there with a valid opinion about your status, the quality of edu-
> cation that you dispense, the quality of the research that you perform.
> You can never allow there to be out there an audience which has a
> right to an opinion, because you are unquestionably Oxford. The
> radical group is saying, 'we have to think about where we stand with
> respect to the rest of the world, we have got to think about this
> subject', and that is heresy. The idea that there is a rest of the world
> to which one is answerable in any way. If one can change this, it
> will have a proportionately larger influence than changing other
> institutions. (27)

This other league cannot be just Ivy. It has to be a league of one.[7] But surely there have to be comparisons between Oxford and the rest of the world's leagues? Sceptics believe not: 'The five rating [for research] is a joke. The people who do the judging are themselves Oxbridge products, they are not going to denigrate their own past.' (27)

The aim seems to be to have influence in the world without being in the world:

> There are people here who couldn't very safely be let loose north of
> Banbury. It's like a monastery. It systematically disables you from
> living outside it. But you gain vicarious power and pleasure by pro-
> ducing the ruling class. (23)

Oxford mirrors Britain. Britain as the dream, striving not to compete but to be in a different league; not everyday goods but the Queen mother, Formula One racing cars, Concorde, the Falklands . . . striving even, as we shall see in Chapter 9, to have a 'special relationship' with the USA.

The question is whether the historical fact of political continuity in Oxford and in Britain is now to be a source of strength or a contributing factor of decline. It is possible for parts of the system to be somehow bracketed off and to carry on behalf of the whole system certain aspirations and values: these values are projected on to the fragment, and this process of projection is what I have called the dream. It is possible for the rest of the totality to value, even revere, the fragment and to contribute in various ways to its preservation. This is exactly what has happened with the Royal Family until very recently. But the dream must be known as a dream; desire must eventually be gratified and the reality principle given its due. Dreams can not be more lovely than the flesh, because the dream is an essential aspect of life, not a substitute for life. It is a means of imagining change and adaptation, not defending against them.

PNL

PNL is *Wirklichkeit* with a vengeance. You take the Northern Line to Kentish Town or, if the escalators are not working there, to Camden Town. Either way you walk down Kentish Town Road, which has an excellent bookshop and good salt-beef sandwiches, but is very light on lawns and spires and heavy on lorries, double-decker buses and beaten-up telephone kiosks. Entry into this particular citadel is not easy: you have to convince a security guard that you are legitimate. Being older does not automatically confer legitimacy at the door as it might elsewhere, since post-adolescents seem a minority. My first meeting is with the Head of the School of Literary and Media studies. He has a small office to himself; everyone else shares. He is a Cambridge graduate and still lives near there: 'I go back for odd days and I wander around and I think: this is wonderful, but . . .'. The 'but' concerns the very concept of higher education:

> I have grave reservations about the British higher education system or the university sector of it – the traditional Oxbridge ivory tower, or the campus university in the sixties. It's a period when you take young people out of society, take them apart, into an artificial context, preparing them for future leadership roles, which they re-enter society to fulfil. The institution should be integrated with the life of society and that's what the poly is. Its very much towards one end of the spectrum and Oxbridge may be at the other end. (40)

The PNL is at the other end of the spectrum in another sense – wealth. Staff and students are under no illusions about their working conditions: they find the institution 'excessively underfunded and very badly treated as an institution'. (48) Compared to Oxford, which has 'peace, stillness, a beautiful library, time', PNL has 'overcrowding, noise, too much teaching'.

(44) A student compares: 'Things that most universities take for granted like common-rooms, we just don't have them. The canteen is a horrible environment.' (90) Yet in spite of what they see as inadequate resources, the staff say they feel 'comfortable' and, in classical management terms, this is because, as the Head of School says, 'PNL has a much clearer definition of what we are about than most other institutions.'

What this means is that they can do what no university department can do: write an advertisement for a new job which is defined extremely precisely. The result is that they appoint people who believe that some miracle has happened to them:

> I knew the moment I walked into the place that it was absolutely right. They asked me all the right questions. I didn't have any problems answering, I felt comfortable here. (48)

> I am incredibly lucky to have got this job. I was thinking of going to the States. I didn't see much hope in this country. The job was advertised as full-time lecturer in discourse. They wanted someone with a specialism in psychoanalysis, post-modernism and/or linguistics. I'd never seen a job like it before, it's a very rare opportunity. The other jobs I was putting in for, they were interested in theory, but it had to be in that straight line of English in terms of your qualifications. I teach on the poetics of fiction, discourse, introduction to poetry, the MA on theories of representation, the psychoanalysis option, semiotics. I'm co-teaching with someone from Philosophy a course on theories of the subject, and I'm teaching Hegel and *Rameau's Nephew* by Diderot. It's wonderful. I didn't think I'd ever get a job that would allow me to do this. (42)

The appointments are made not on the basis of research, as in a university, but on the professional criterion of teaching ability. The fact that this respondent had been a mature student and was therefore more likely to understand the students was a plus:

> They didn't want someone who had gone to school, university, research. I'd been in the real world. They didn't hold it against me that I hadn't finished the PhD. You wouldn't get a job in this department if you couldn't teach, however much you'd published. The interview was a whole day, we had to give a ten-minute presentation, I decided not to talk about theory, which the others did, but to talk about teaching, and that was what they wanted. That worked.

Purity is not a requirement: on the contrary, a hybrid background seems to be appreciated. Dr Black had a first degree in history of ideas, having dropped English in the first year, then did an MA on theory, a dissertation on psychoanalysis, then a PhD on psychoanalysis and a particular author. One can imagine that such appointees are going to feel a great deal of solidarity with the department and the institution. 'I just feel they want me to be there. They want me to teach what I'm teaching.' More crucial still is the fact that these appointments have been made at all: PNL, like other polytechnics, does have a more reasonable proportion of young women staff.

The polytechnic is similar to universities in some ways: the individualism, for example – 'We never really talk to each other about academic matters. There is a lot of respect for each other, but we tend to leave each other alone' (44) – and the value attached to freedom. But there is one dramatic difference. PNL, like Oxford, does not suffer from the confusion between the two organizational modes, collegiality and hierarchy, which, as we saw, causes such difficulty in universities. The dilemma has been resolved – but in the direction of hierarchy. PNL has line management. The current Head of School was asked to become course tutor in 1982, and convinced the polytechnic (a university would not have been convinced) that if he was going to be a manager he needed professional training. He was released between 1982 and 1986 to do a diploma in management studies, and later an MA in higher education. The diploma was conducted in the polytechnic and was, he says, the more valuable since the MA was based on the university system 'and the polys are so in advance of most universities'. He now sees himself as a manager. He is executive. He may consult the department but he is not mandated:

> The old collegiate structure didn't work at all. Members of the community wanted their input into a decision, but didn't feel bound by it, or responsible to it. I am sometimes at odds with the school. Some people want to bind me or the Dean to a collective view. Any manager, given that you are dealing with a highly educated group of people, would be unwise not to weigh the advice from them carefully. But I'm going to be held responsible for the decision and they are not. At the end of the day I would have to instruct them, and if they don't carry out the instruction, they are in breach of contract. I am instructed and I might have to instruct them. I am happy with this system, but I don't know if they are. (40)

He is in a vertical reporting line: 'My line manager is the Dean. I have to set my objectives for the year with her. They will be reviewed. There's no alternative, you've got to have good management. The worse scenario would be to have this sort of structure and to have bad management.' Here is a revealing exchange:

– Do you see yourself as a manager?
– Yes, I have to.
– And that is not a dirty word in the PNL?
– Oh, it is a dirty word.

The answer to the question of whether the staff are happy with the situation is that they are not. PNL teachers are teachers before being PNL teachers, and their hostility to management is strong: 'I get so angry about those idiots at the top of the poly. They haven't a clue about what we are doing. Even the Dean seems to have gone over to the managerial side. "How are we going to make more money?"' What is missing is appreciation from management:

> In English we care about education and about students. All we ever get from those above is 'Yes, but we have got to be more economical.' English is the leanest operation, really bare bones, no luxuries whatsoever. They don't care about our commitment, nobody ever comes and says, 'This English degree really works well.' PNL has got a terrific reputation. Sussex says that the PNL students are the best post-graduates they have, but no one ever says that.

Dr O'Flaherty mentioned two leaders, one he perceived as looking after him, the other 'trying to squeeze out an extra drop'. Clearly the leaders themselves are under pressure to do both, but staff are convinced that squeezing takes precedence over stroking.

Above all, they resent giving up the control represented by the collegial model. To be consulted is not enough. It is seen as 'genuflecting to democracy'. (46) There is a sense, they say, of being 'on the receiving end': 'We have monthly meetings at the school but people say "What's the use of them?"' (46)

> We are being told, 'It [franchising] will take place. Tough'. That's a change. We used to discuss things. Make our decisions, send them up, now they come down. 'Discuss this, it's going ahead anyway.' So we've stopped going to meetings. (46)

The Head of School is aware of this, but feels that the staff do not realize how far up the squeezing goes: 'People don't realize the constraints with which senior management operate. They see the Director as the boss, they tend to think he can do as he likes.'

The picture of staff morale at PNL does not sound very different from that at Cardiff – the university in my sample which has gone closest to the line-management Jarratt model – yet I think it is different, because there is much more common ground ideologically, a much better age pyramid and gender balance among staff and students, a clearer, more public sense of the institution's mission (the Why? question) and a more precise, public definition of work. Dr O'Flaherty, on his grade, has not more than 18 and not less than 16 student contact hours a week. A principal lecturer does two hours less. Research time is deducted from that (in hours). Being in charge of examinations or the timetable means another hour off teaching.

The point is not that the PNL staff are not being squeezed, not having to negotiate with management, but that the rules of engagement are much more 'front-stage'. There are fewer deals done in the car park. This does not actually resolve the problem of leading Apollo groups, nor does it address the 'expansion in contraction' problem directly, but there is a clear, visible and non-contradictory framework in which people can work, with whatever skills they can muster, at the management problems.

Some people in universities recognize this, especially if they have had experience on the CNAA. Professor Leigh is apocalyptic about universities:

> It's polytechnics where the real breakthrough has happened. Universities will have to take account of that. Universities have got away with so much. I am on the CNAA and we rigorously scrutinize. When you think what goes on here. Of course those people won't shift. Why should they? There's no pressure, no motive to shift. So I think universities, in the end they'll just die. Lyotard says the epoch of the university is over anyway. Universities are the last to change, and lazy, just plain lazy. (17)

Dr Wilton sees them as more vulnerable than polytechnics:

> They encourage individualism. Any form of solidarity is really a compromise. That's why they can be easily divided. Polytechnics are harder to pick off. They have a more proletarian sense of their own solidarity. (2)

PNL students are also questioning the power of the dream:

> My degree from the PNL will be just as weighty as one from a university. There seems to be a certain backlash going on at the moment against elitism. The university as a whole is seen by a lot of people as elitist, whereas polytechnics aren't. I think a degree is a degree, and I would expect that people in the big wide world are astute enough to be able to realize that. (89)

The job today

The actual nature of the job and the way a university teacher experiences it is surprisingly unresearched. We have nothing more than popular ideas about 'cushy jobs' or 'loss of morale'. This chapter and the previous one have attempted to describe these men and women in their chosen subject and career, in the university, their chosen institution, exercising leadership, experiencing power and authority, working with colleagues and students. In conclusion, let me attempt to give more specific evidence about the way English People in universities, the recently arrived, the established and the soon-to-leave, feel about the job today.

Some of the feelings expressed to me are not really specific to English People at all, nor even to university people perhaps. They are feelings that human beings have as they live their lives and narrate those lives to an interviewer. The gap between the original aspiration and the achievement, the 'road not taken': 'I'd have been much happier as a crazy sixth-form teacher somewhere. I wanted to teach real things to real people.' (3) The sense of the futility of success: 'You get to pack and unpack your suitcase

and go on long and uncomfortable journeys. And that's the reward. So
when you're stepping off the tarmac on Tokyo Airport wondering, "What
the hell am I doing? This is absurd", that's your reward.' (15) The fear of
nullity: 'Time is passing. What have I got to show for it?' (22) The fear
of retirement: 'Is there a life after retirement? I don't look forward to
retirement.' (6)

Some aspects are specific. Part of the reason English People came into
the job was to perpetuate a certain notion of work, but that notion itself
has its down-side, and is in any case threatened. The down-side of freedom
from the boundaries is guilt and depression:

> One of the things that you do have in university teaching is quite a
> lot of latitude to plan your work and do as you see fit. One of the
> results of that is that the whole thing can become obsessional. It lacks
> mental health. If you are flying an airliner you get in your plane and
> you do your job. Jobs that have a lot of mental health are ones that
> you can start and finish and walk away from. This is a job where you
> can always be feeling guilty because you haven't read *Moby Dick* for
> ten years or something like that. Certainly there have been times
> when I have been putting in far too many hours, being obsessional
> about it. But you are also very vulnerable to depression as well. It is
> kind of manic depressive, anything where you've got that kind of
> latitude. I've certainly been going through a bad patch for the last
> year or so, and I can see now looking back that I have been really
> depressed. I've done nothing but cope for the last year. It's a physical
> thing as well. It certainly has to do with your domestic life, and
> everything. What's been going on in our institution has made life
> more difficult. (13)

> I always feel guilt, and inadequacy, and vulnerability. If I stand still
> I'm guilty. (16)

> The guilt – there's always something else you should have done in-
> stead of what you actually did. (20)

In order to write a book, we divide and section: work and the institution
here (relevant); home and family there (not relevant). But individuals at
any moment experience all the sections at once – career, physical health,
domestic life, the institutional or political situation. The boundary between
work and family life is a particularly fraught. Here is a confession with a
striking coda:

> What suffers in this system is family life. My wife spends a lot of time
> complaining. She says I'm neglecting the children and so on, and has
> been very unhappy with it. That is what has suffered, to be perfectly
> honest. Any less determined woman would have undoubtedly have
> ended it in divorce. She says, 'I don't know why these guys get
> married, there's no time.' So something has to give somewhere. What

I suppose sustains me is a great love and belief in the subject. If I
didn't have that it would be hopeless. I've never really had doubts,
or lost that love, but if I did I would be in trouble, because we have
these terrible conditions and high demands that can't be met. But not
many people here have committed suicide. (29)

Dr Stone runs an MPhil with seven students. She has nine doctorate
students. She does a lot of thesis examining. She has 14 hours undergraduate teaching contractually. She is senior tutor:

– What effect does that have on family life?
– What family life? Next question. (25)

There is a sense of conflict which may be peculiar to the caring professions and proverbial cobblers:

What the university wants is not family people, although it values the
gifts we bring. It wants your total commitment and time. The ideal
teacher is one who brings to the work the sympathy they don't show
their own family. The university demands a great deal, it gives back
a reasonable salary but not much more than that. (20)

Finally, there is the government and what is perceived as the attack on
universities. Dr Clay has just got his first job, and compares himself with
his colleagues, some of whom 'fell into jobs in the sixties'. 'For me and my
contemporaries at Oxford there was one job a decade, and you fought
bitterly over it.'

I find it very irritating. We were being told that we had to publish,
we don't work hard enough, when I have worked my arse off for the
last seven years with this single goal in mind of getting this job and
doing it right. I couldn't have worked any harder. I would have
collapsed, and to be told by Kenneth Clarke that you're basically an
idle bugger . . . (54)

The situation is made difficult by public perception: 'Friends point out
that I'm in a very well-paid job. I'm not overworked and if I choose not
to do any writing I would be distinctly underworked, and they see the
writing as just an ego trip anyway, so you are liable to feel absurd if you
complain.' (12)

How seriously should one take the complaints of English People in the
institution? When Dr Packer says, 'The system is killing me. There's too
much teaching, too much admin, too much research, too much everything,' (20) is this the whingeing of someone who is finally being required
to pay the price of joining an institution or a genuine *cri de coeur*? And,
given the subject, is it possible to work while having feelings like this,
justified or unjustified? Many think not:

I toy with the idea, certainly when the house is paid for, of shaking
the dust off my feet. I'd be very sorry to lose out on the teaching, but

all this extra administration. That's crazy. I'm helpless in the face of it. It's the helplessness that's intensely angry-making. (19)

Six months ago I thought I might survive 20 years. I am beginning to think I might have to readjust that. A lot of academics will go. They have to have a new style academic, a set of people who don't know the old ways. (20)

I am waiting for that green exit light above the door. I haven't come across anyone who wouldn't quit now if he got the money. That's a desperate situation for a university. (21)

But not everyone feels like this. As we have seen, PNL, in spite of its limited resources and fears about increased student numbers, gives its staff considerable job satisfaction. The problem may be specific to the 'civic' universities and it may be a transitional one.

As I write, the newspapers are full of advertisements with drawings of dead parrots, illustrating this or that 'defunct poly' which has resurrected as a university. The ending of the formal distinction means we can put the problem simply: how are *universities* to be managed so that the institutional experience of large numbers of clever people is satisfying, both for themselves and for the society that foots the bill? The answer for the universities may well be to imitate the polytechnic style of leadership. But the question will remain for all institutions: how can both dream and reality be given due recognition and due weight? This is the dilemma for the university and it may be that the subject English has this as its 'specialized work task' on behalf of the institution and of society.

*part two*_____

Dividing

six

Male/female

Ardhanarisvara, Siva as male and female.
(Government Museum, Madras)

English People are biologically male or female. This rather uncontroversial fact is worth stating because sex and gender are particularly important aspects of the subject. First, the sex balance is not equal: there are more female students than males, but more male staff than female. Second, as we saw in the first chapter, one social movement, feminism, has had a special impact on this particular subject. Third, the gender metaphor, the idea of 'masculine' ways of being, contrasted with 'feminine' ways of being, has considerable explanatory power in English. English is a 'female' subject in the straightforward sense that there is a preponderance of female students, but it is also a 'feminine' subject in ways which are less straightforward and which we will need to explore.

Balance

In universities, women represent roughly two of every three undergraduates, one of every two post-graduates, three of every ten full-time staff members. Of the hundred university professors of English, 15 are women.[1] In Polytechnics and Colleges the proportion of female students is higher: three out of four students are women.[2] However, the proportion of women staff is also higher, and nearer a balance – four out of ten are women.[3]

The figures are eloquent. They show a subject which is predominantly female in its clientele but which (especially in universities) has been successfully professionalized by males. The contrast with another humanities subject – history – is striking. In university history departments, while the staff is even more male (eight out of ten, 94 per cent of the professors) there are also rather more male than female undergraduates.[4] The situation for English today is, in its proportions, no different from the situation when the subject was created: Quiller-Couch began his lectures 'Gentlemen' but most of his students were women.

Why is this, and what are the consequences?

We have already considered the question of subject choice. To choose English is to deny, provisionally at least, a view of life and of education which puts career, consumption, material success and upward mobility first. It represents the bike against the BMW. It is easier for women to do this than men. Women's upward mobility has historically been dependent on marriage, and the option of full-time homemaking, even in the 1990s, is still realistic. A woman student: 'Guys are more expected to go into business. There's more pressure on men than women to be successful, and studying English is not considered successful, so I think it's just not a male subject.' (61)

English thus becomes an eminently suitable subject for the prospective wives of practical, materially successful men. At one level, like women themselves, the subject is constructed, both in the world and in the university, as a necessary mitigation of instrumental male activity. While male activity remains basic, it is acknowledged not to be everything, and that which it is not – the ineffable, the magical – art is and women are. There is indeed a powerful myth which has women either validating and recompensing male activity (especially after combat with other men),[5] or invalidating it by proposing a radically different project: this is indeed men's traditional fear of women – they will be distracted from their project of making war or money or writing successful books.

For women to choose English then is to go with the social grain. For men to choose English is a very different matter. It is a rejection of the powerful male injunction to enter the world of work; it is a movement away from the male-only group:

> I didn't like the atmosphere in this all-boys grammar school. Then I went to a comprehensive school and it was a much more natural environment, much less aggressive. In the grammar school the younger, weaker ones tended to get picked on, and everyone tended to be in gangs. The comprehensive was mixed, that made an awful lot of difference, the girls seemed to be a civilizing influence. (97)

It also reverses the difficult move which boys (unlike girls) have to make, away from the female, away from the mother.

Relating

Men and women have then made the same choice but the meaning of that choice is radically different for the two sexes. The relationships between English People are affected by this gender difference. In Chapter 5 we considered the relations between staff and students. The complete picture needs to include the relation between the sexes in a four-cell matrix (Figure 6.1). If staff are 'older' (O) and students 'younger' (Y) we have the following relationships: YM–YM; YM–YF; YF–YF; YM–OF; YM–OM; YF–OF; YF–OM; OF–OM; OM–OM; OF–OF.

I do not claim to have systematically investigated all these possibilities. In particular, I do not have much interview data concerning students' feelings about staff in gender terms nor about the most common relationship of all, that between young women. Furthermore, even this schema is a simplification since it assumes age and status are congruent: the reality includes mature male/female students being taught by much younger female/male lecturers. In general, to obtain this kind of data would have necessitated a different research technique, specifically group and intergroup work with appropriate (i.e. male and female) group leaders. All I can do is to offer the data I have and give an impressionistic picture of this aspect of the experience of English People, hoping that subsequent studies may deal with the whole complex picture more systematically.

YM–YM/YM–YF

This is significant, particularly with regard to young men from all-male public schools. Public school boys are making quite a transgressive choice

	Male	Female
Older		
Younger		

Figure 6.1

in doing English and it is not surprising that they have particular difficulty coming to terms with the transition to a feminine discipline and a mixed environment:

> Those colleges that have large numbers of boys from private schools who are seeing women in the same organization for the first time, are the ones that have the most immature attitudes and the biggest problems about harassment and so on in the JCR. (31)

In the eyes of, say, engineering students, male English students live the life of Riley. A male student reports: 'They say, "You're lucky, you've got six hours work a week and more girls than you can handle".' (99) And there is an interesting contradiction here, in that male-dominated subjects see male English students as effeminate, 'sissy' (as Babbitt put it), compared to their own 'hard', 'pushing' subject-identity but still fantasize them as pashas. This says something about the life of predominantly male groups and their attitude to women (as I write the attitudes of the police are being scrutinized in this respect). Members of all-male groups make sorties to find women but do not expect to work with them, and they respond to everyday access as the hunter might respond to a back garden suddenly over-run by rabbits.

The male English student is matter-of-fact about it: 'I get on just as well with the girls on the course as the boys. If you hang around with just one sex it gets monotonous. You just tend to get more laddish and do more stupid things.' (99) This is a position which seems to be shared by the young women:

> The people who go out to the pub on a Saturday night, drink ten pints and do all sorts of horrible things to each other, I don't consider them 'real men'. I think I meet men who are slightly more sensitive in English. (103)

YF–OM/YF–OF (OM–OM)

In teaching situations, given the statistics quoted above, women under-graduates can hardly avoid male teachers. And even at post-graduate level there may be difficulties in finding a woman supervisor. There is clearly a demand: 'I chose a woman supervisor. It would have been harder for me to work with a man.' (71) This demand creates difficulties for women staff. It is one of the practical disadvantages of the imbalance. Dr Paisley:

> With so few women in the department it makes all sorts of 'invisible-work' demands – advising women students, pastoral work . . . Women are overwhelmed by women students wanting to talk to them about problems, or following them around, having elected them as mentors, or choosing their options and choosing them as dissertation supervisors – because they all want to do something on Margaret Atwood or Charlotte Brontë. (53)

From the male tutor's point of view the teaching situation seems pleasurable enough. ('There is an unavoidable frisson always present in an exchange with the opposite sex.' (6)) But one respondent offered an interesting hypothesis about the effects of this on the relations between male tutors (OM–OM):

> There is an added pleasure for men teaching young women. It's benign, but it's benign power. Maybe teachers are unpleasant to each other because each teacher is a pasha with his harem and is incensed by the presence of other pashas and their harem. And this is no easier for being unrecognized. (22)

And another commented:

> There's something very odd about us middle-aged men teaching classes which are more than 50 per cent young, nubile girls. We've only got two women in our department. We can't change our sex, but the imbalance is absolutely appalling. (4)

YM–OF

The relation between young male students and female lecturers is rarer and my evidence is scant, but I have the feeling that this relation is especially difficult. I was given one account of an incident in a lecture which is significant mainly for the light it throws on the difficulties both sides have when the expected power relations are reversed and when, as in this case, the woman is prepared to break another taboo and make the issue available for discussion in a here-and-now way:

> I tried to use the question period to illustrate those dynamics: 'So I have power, I am a woman, let's see what this does.' A student at the end of a 50-minute lecture on feminism referred to a comment I had made about pen and penis and I responded to this by saying that in making this remark he was putting his penis in the middle of the room for all to discuss. This was greeted with outrage by all the men students in the room. I had figuratively emasculated this boy in front of everyone, and that was unforgivable. The previous day, Professor M [male] had lectured to them and had humiliated three students in his deft way and they lapped it up. (27)

She understates her impact perhaps, when she says, 'Incidents like that give me a sense that I'm disturbing something out there. It may have to do with masculinity.'

OF–OF

In most institutions women staff are in such a minority that the relations they have with other women are a matter of chance based on individual likes and dislikes or specialisms. One feminist told me that she was in fact closer to her younger male colleagues than her women colleagues, and found the male students less resistant to feminism than the females (she also saw the reason for this in both cases: 'It's less of a core issue for them' (58)). In a much more balanced department like PNL the relations between women staff are more revealing of general processes:

> Consciously I like men just as much, but the bonding doesn't seem to happen. I think it's to do with the teaching that's being done. A lot of the innovations are being done by women. There is a sense of the women as a group and the men as a group. I try to work against that, but it's quite hard, because the women are so good to you. (48)

OM–OF

Male–female staff relations seem difficult, which is not surprising given the statistics I quoted at the start of this chapter. Women academics, particularly senior ones, are conscious of being professionally dominated by male power in the university:

> In theory, there's nothing to stop you joining the others on the roof but in practice a glass ceiling prevents the women getting up there. Almost nobody with any real power in the university is female. It's

a male-oriented kind of university. I went to the Senate dinner. There were 116 people there, and a dozen women, a great phalanx of dinner suits. It makes you realize how few women have got any degree of clout at all. (53)

There may also be other reasons, specific to English and connected with the male choice of this subject. The original motivation of male lecturers was similar to that of the male (and female) students – postponing career choice, avoiding classification and so on. But they were more ambitious, more competitive than the majority of the pupils and students, then and now. To be a male student of English, temporarily absolved from the demands of the male world, an enthusiastic reader, writer, actor or poet, to be in rebellion against expectations, that is one thing. To join an essentially feminine discipline for life is another. The response may well be to adopt masculine working patterns – long hours, clear boundaries, male pursuits, travel – and to seek leadership roles and institutional, professional success. Dr Hamish describes such a person:

I compare myself with X, who is very dynamic and at the centre of things, and an absolute workaholic. I don't feel like that about academic life. He lives for the subject. I live for a variety of things – music and painting, linguistics, teaching. My career could have been totally different from what it's been, but I don't think his could. He's got his goals, his ambition. (14)

For many years, English departments were not very different from other male groups, with the sole difference that there were large numbers of subordinate young females around. The (relative) rise of women has challenged this. A female professor analyses her male colleagues in rather an unflattering way and gives some idea of what gender relations must be in some staff groups. First, she describes, by contrast, her own (female) attitude to the subject, which is essentially 'cavalier', self-indulgent, pleasure-seeking, adoring: 'always, always Shakespeare, it's always been Shakespeare, it's still Shakespeare – and Stratford-upon-Avon. I'm a woman so I'm allowed to be self-indulgent. Self-indulgence is all right for women.' Then she describes her male colleagues, who are, she says

a fractious lot, very intense, and tormented, and hostile and paranoid, and I think it's because 80 per cent of their students are women, and I think they think this a girly subject. They are drawn to it or they wouldn't be doing it, but at the same time they despise themselves for it, because it's not masculine. It's not hard and phallic, and rational and analytical. Someone like X can't afford to be effeminate. He'd rather die. So he hates that bit of himself that responds. It's the only way I can account for the venom which seems to be turned on against literature in general and Shakespeare in particular by a particular bunch of theorists. I hold them in a certain contempt, I have to say, arrogant creature that I am. Perhaps they are just bored or disappointed. They were golden boys, they were top of their grammar schools, their year in university or whatever, they got their firsts, and somehow the world was their oyster, they were just wonderful, and they were going to do such things, and somehow nothing you did can live up to that dream. It may be that women, and maybe the young now, don't have that dream, they don't have that ideal version of themselves which they have constantly to live up to. Men have such an investment in mastery and success. I can't escape being a woman and no one expects women to do anything very much. I think it's because of never having been a golden boy that I can value the ride more than my image as a rider. (17)

I do not have any comparable analysis of women colleagues by men (apart from some comments on feminism which I shall report later). However, it would be wrong to see women staff as banding together in a anti-male, separatist way. 'Women's studies' is an interesting example of an opportunity for separatism which some women actually resist. Dr May was appointed to teach women's studies but switched to English. Women's studies, she feels, denies the problem of difference, whereas English faces it:

I found English more sensitive to race and gender than women's studies. In women's studies it was more entrenched. In English, people are prepared to talk about difference. I like men a lot, and I wasn't happy with the situation where I had a group of 25 women every day. English is a way you can put gender issues on the table but you don't have to be exclusive about it. (48)

YM–YF–OM

I have described these relationships so far in binary terms. In order to show that the reality is more complex I shall give an example of a triangular relation which shows male/female and young/old operating together. My respondent is MCR president, a female post-graduate. She joins with the young, male JCR president in negotiations with the SCR president who is, in his dealings with the JCR president, 'nasty and very violent'. She is the mediator between the young man and the older man:

I was the one who said, 'Well Professor, I don't really think the JCR president is trying to so and so', and I turned to the JCR president and said, 'It's not that he hates you.' I was doing this female helping role. I was the one who kept them from tearing one another's throats out. And I couldn't sleep for three weeks and thought, 'Why do they have to fight?' and they were going home and sleeping quite soundly, because this was their job. (111)

There is something archetypal about this. What emerges is the pairing of the men (albeit in fight mode – shades of Oedipus and D. H. Lawrence) across the age boundary rather than the pairing of the young people across the gender boundary.

Feminism

Feminism is organized political and intellectual response to aspects of this reality. The popular press is convinced that the feminists have completely taken over. A. N. Wilson in the *Evening Standard* (4 February 1992: 17), referring to a survey by Tim Cook of Kingston Polytechnic, asserts that 'the pendulum has swung in a direction which is harmful and lunatic . . . It is evidently thought to be more important to turn out politically correct feminists, male and female, than it is to turn out graduates who are well-versed in the great classics of English literature.'

He is referring to two pressures which are undoubtedly real, though not to this rampantly successful extent: the pressure for syllabus change (female writers, women's studies) and pressure to appoint more women. The situation seems to be that the younger men have accepted both these aspirations. Older men either sit on the fence or are aggressively dismissive. The argument of the latter tends to be that feminism is bad but (contrary to the A. N. Wilson view) passée:

> I am bothered now by the desire on the part of feminists, to establish an alternative canon, which means the graduates of English emerge ignorant of the essential works. I am worried about that, people like Catherine Belsey and Terence Hawkes seem to be in favour of a notion that Barbara Cartland, if handled with the right sorts of post-Marxist, post-structural techniques, displays to you things about your culture. I deplore that. It's a misuse of undergraduates' time, and to have senior people telling undergraduates to use their time in that way seems deplorable . . . Anyway, I think feminism is on the retreat. One of the challenges is, are you allowed to manipulate the institution to appoint more people like yourself, and there are so many horror stories coming over from American universities, that senior people in British universities are beginning to close ranks, and say we can't have any more of this. (50)

The view that feminism has somehow run its course is not confined to unreconstructed males. One of Oxford's feminists is grateful to feminism but would like to distance herself:

> It's not nearly as central as it was. That's a matter of fashionability and academic pragmatics. In the early eighties there was an assumption that if you were a woman in academia you were not only a feminist but working in feminist issues, and that publishers went, 'Please, please, I'll give you a cheque and let you write something.' I don't want to have a label put around my neck now, 'One of Oxford's feminists'. It's not the focus of my work, and that is a problem,

because women are in a minority at Oxford, and there's a terrible temptation to feel that you ought to be paying allegiance to the ideological beliefs that got you where you are. But I do a lot of teaching in it. It's not consciousness-raising. It's after that. They've had their consciousness raised and I'm saying 'Hey, it's not as simple as that. It's not enough just to be interested in women or to be one.' (25)

Is it in fact the case that women students have had their consciousness raised?

The basic feminist thesis that what seems 'natural' is constructed comes as a welcome revelation to many, especially to mature students:

It's totally empowering, because as a woman you are used to being told what to do, what to read, what to watch, what to wear, how to think. It gives you tools to realize that this is not a natural state of affairs. (89)

Male tutors are also convinced that 'the female students are all feminists now'. But they wonder whether this is not just another example of their passivity: 'Whether you see that as acquiescence or rebellion is a moot point. In a lot of cases they're just doing what they're told.' (16)

In fact, I found, particularly among young women students, a considerable resistance to 'doing what they're told' by older feminist women – lecturers or students. Many of these students have not had their consciousness raised and do not want it raised, thank you very much:

In our seminar there's a very feminist student. She's quite a bit older, with two children and she was talking about women's magazines. She was saying how wrong they are. I just don't agree with that. I'm not a feminist, I'm quite proud to be called Miss instead of Ms. I thought why ban ladies' magazines? I do like the recipes in them, I do try them out. And the beauty pages don't offend me at all. I don't see why people get so worked up about it. (91)

Here is a more extreme statement from a young woman:

I think that feminism is an abnormality, people who are against what to me seems natural. What's natural, and this may be my working-class background, is the man going to work, and the woman looking after the house and children. Even though I came to university I never intended to have a career. It's slightly changed but I still want to marry and have children and give up my job. (92)

This response is not confined to the young: a mature woman student claims that 'the lectures on feminism upset some of the mature students' and that she hears them saying 'but I like my husband to be the boss . . . but I like to have the door opened for me'. (70) There is a great deal of inner conflict:

I want to be a good feminist but so much of my life has been made easier by smiling nicely. It's a conflict. I'm working with it all the time and it bothers me. I think now there are differences between the sexes and it's not just that I've been culturally conditioned. I do think differently from men. (111)

This is a particular example of the general problem of teaching in this subject. Learning here means not just seeing more things but seeing things differently. Where the consensus no longer exists, where there are various ways of seeing, rather than one dominant perspective, staff sub-groups (feminists in this instance) will wish to advance that way of seeing. Inevitably there will be conflict and dissent and the question is how that conflict is handled within the general context of staff–student power relations. Raymond resents the effect of feminism on the syllabus and complains that the principle of selection is not literary quality:

I read *The Color Purple*, I thought it was appalling. The Virago classics, I've read some of those, they are absolutely awful. They are published because they are feminist, not because they are of any quality. Last year we were given eleven texts, nine of which were written by women, a huge reading list of critics, all of which were women. We were told not to use a dictionary of literary terms because there was a much better one written by a woman. (90)

But he claims cynically to be able to write a successful feminist essay for a feminist tutor. Doubtless other students are writing eulogies of Shelley for Shelley admirers. The feminist question is just one example of the intractable problem we looked at in the previous chapter: how may students express their own views, independently of staff views, while being judged by staff and while staff determine the syllabus?

Graff (1987: 260), while not grappling with the examination problem, does offer a useful analysis of the teaching dilemma as it applies specifically to feminism. His conclusion is that the controversy Raymond points to ('quality' versus 'political' in the syllabus) should be brought into the classroom and made part of the subject matter. Students should be exposed to the controversies between their teachers, and not only to the results of those controversies. This sounds very much like the battleground model of the seminar we looked at in Chapter 5. It is consonant with Graff's overall position, which is that, in the absence of any consensus, the subject can only be argument between competing groups and that the defence-mechanisms which groups have created in order to avoid confrontation have produced 'patterned isolation' and an absence of the learning that would come from 'diverse groups talking to or about one another'.

Further valuable evidence is provided by the unusually open reflections on the problems of teaching 'feminist' courses provided by Peter Humm and Jan Montefiore, separate contributors to Brooker and Humm (1989). What their chapters demonstrate is that feminism is very closely connected to interdisciplinarity (in practice to the breaking down of traditional disciplinary boundaries), to the 'rise of the reader' (and the demise of the Reader) and to participative pedagogy 'derived from the women's movement'. Both Montefiore and Humm struggle with what Humm calls the 'paradox of my lecturing on the need for more democratic and open ways of learning'. Montefiore defends the lecture in the name of the necessary authority of the teacher, while insisting that students need to be free to disagree with their teacher. Seminars, she says, tend to become 'impromptu lectures by me' or practical criticism sessions, and she recognizes frankly that there can be 'a great deal of silent resentment and anger in the classroom'. Both are, because of the nature of their approach, asking 'how effective are the teaching methods that remain hidden within the sanctuary of the seminar and lecture room', and dealing with the masculine–feminine difference in the shape of the authority–acceptance opposition.

Masculine/feminine

So far I have described English as a female subject dominated by males but with the minority group female staff representing a strong opposition. To talk about men and women as different groups having different numerical size and different powers within an institutional setting is uncontroversial, especially since this particular distinction (unlike young/old, black/white, English/foreign) is clear-cut and visible.

The problem arises with the adjectives. I have said that English is a 'feminine' subject. What does this mean? What is 'feminine' behaviour? One could answer trivially 'what biological females do', but we usually want to be able to say that males have a 'feminine' side (and females a 'masculine' side). For example, Dr Hamish, who made a comparison with workaholic X, is male but I would want to say that his position was 'feminine' compared to X's, which is 'masculine'. When we do this we are referring to behaviour we see as typical of males and saying that in this instance and in this respect the man is behaving in ways we associate with women.

'Most women are more emotional than most men, most men are more cognitive than most women': even to make statements like these positions emotional men and cognitive women as somehow aberrant. To state it makes it seem also as if the distinction is 'natural' when we know that such behaviour patterns are learned through social conditions of which public statements like this are part, so that such statements are coercive and self-fulfilling. It also implies that an individual is at all times and in all situations 'masculine' or 'feminine', 'cognitive' or 'emotional'.

The consequence of these scruples is a strong pressure not to talk about sex difference at all – no men and women, only people. The very fact of referring to sex difference is sexist (as the fact of referring to colour difference is racist). Humm reports a student resisting distinguishing texts written by males from texts written by females because 'she did not want to separate and label people in this way'. I think this is a mistake. There are massive and observable non-physical differences between men and women and saying they are socially produced does not make them go away. In practice, as Culler (1983: 49) points out, feminists who would deny any distinctive identity to woman (he refers to Spivak and 'the most radical French feminists') 'always have moments when they speak as women'. They appeal 'to a condition or an experience deemed more basic than the theoretical position it is used to justify'. In other words the constructed identity is constructed (or deconstructed) *from a given*. As Sartre put it, we are free to make something out of what we have already been made into. This means that the gender metaphor, precisely because it is so inextricably linked with such a powerful binary mechanism, can and does illuminate. It could be that we should jettison it in favour of something apparently less confusing – right brain/left brain, for example. I think this would be to sacrifice associative richness for an illusory clarity. To call one set of characteristics feminine and another masculine is not to be prescriptive or stereotypical. It is to tap into a basic human experience and to offer a description of the reality of a situation which is a compound of the given and the constructed. A reflection like the following is interesting as a serious account of a lecturer's experience coupled with qualms about stating it:

> I think that women are often extremely sensitive about literature. They do seem in some ways more interested in personal relations, or at least that is part of their cultural inheritance – to be made to think they are whether or not they are in any essential way. (6)

I am prepared to take the risk of saying that English is a feminine subject to the extent that its roots are in relationship, creativity, imagination, emotion, subjectivity, responsiveness, receptivity, the non-instrumental, the transcendent; that its mode is analogical. But it is also a masculine subject, concerned with action, with logic, with mastery, with control and analysis, with objective consensual truth, with theory and argument; that it is digital. I think statements like these can be useful if we see that such categories represent two human tendencies, present in every human being (and every discipline) but unequally developed. Subjects are distinguished by the extent to which they favour one aspect or the other, and whether the subject choice is consonant or not with the current stereotype. The overall aim must be to release people from these stereotypes or to assist the integration of the masculine and the feminine. Put crudely, human beings need to think and to feel. But an aim may also be to develop one particular side. If this were not the case, education would consist in directing students to those subjects that they were worst at – bookworms to physical education for their pectorals, and body-builders to metaphysical poetry. In reality, while education, especially in the early stages, aims at some kind of balance, the whole process of choice consists in finding what we are best at and developing that specialized strength while protecting or concealing one's weakness. Subjects can be judged by how well they meet these competing needs of specialization and integration.

Individuals can be observed using the subject in order to develop and to resist splitting. So, when Virginia, at a very early age, is taken to the library, where the children's books are divided into boys' books and girls' books, and sees that the boys' books are 'far more exciting' and goes for them, she is clearly avoiding the split that is offered. When Dr Black does a post-graduate theory degree in Sussex she is also offered a split: 'These men from Oxbridge were saying "Psychoanalysis is for the girls, Marxism for the boys".' She tried to resist this but her interest, she says, was in Lacan: 'Lacan speaks to me as a woman.' Dr Linsey says she is a Marxist, but she has the complete works of Freud on her shelves, not those of Marx. Women focus on their own specific, specialized concerns, what 'speaks to them'. Integration may be a luxury. But at least here the specialization is in the direction of personal development. The problem for female students may be that the subject and the presence of males reinforce the splitting, which is also an alienation. Dr Lake:

> I've just taught a class 50/50 men and women, and there was no difference. I guarantee that in two years time the women will have learned to be silent and the men will go on talking. Women are picking up all society's strictures, about who talks and who doesn't. (27)

So males, it might be said, are behaving in counter-stereotype ways by doing the subject English and are achieving a better integration than women, who are forced either into specialization or conformity.

The subject offers, in both its material and its institutional enactment, an opportunity to explore reflexively these tensions around gender. In the next chapter we will look at the effect of theory and consider the way it can be seen to represent a masculine incursion into the feminine subject of English.

*seven*_____

Theory

They should never have let us in. (15)

The rise of theory

I attempted in Chapter 1 to set out my understanding of the origins of the discipline. While it is tempting to speak of a succession of named periods or movements, following one another and being magically mapped on to the succession of chapters, the reality is more complex and, above all, less linear. There is a great deal of reproduction in Bourdieu's sense: some of my respondents were sent by their schoolteachers to colleges where they, the teachers, had been students themselves; most people teaching in Oxford now, I was told, 'were trained in the sixties by people who themselves were trained in Oxford in the thirties'. (27) We need to think, then, of a set of oppositions which underlie the subject at any time. The balance of strength changes with the generations but, in a highly traditional, decentred education system like the British one, species rarely become wholly extinct and victories are never total.

Nevertheless, in the 1970s something happened. Of course, something happened in the 1920s too. Something is always happening. I single out what happened in the 1970s because of its relation to today. Twenty years is how long it takes for an academic to go from untenured iconoclast to jet-set professor. The members of staff I interviewed include individuals who were instrumental in launching 'theory' in the 1970s; people whose professional boats were alarmingly rocked by this new wave; and others who had, and still have, safe harbours in which to gently bob. All the students I spoke to are having their current experience of English determined by teachers of one type or another. This chapter attempts to describe the effect on 1990s English People of 1970s theory and of the dramatic weakening of the border controls between English and social science disciplines, linguistics and philosophy. It also describes the contribution theory has made to the masculinization of English.

My interview sample includes an eminent professor, an angry young lecturer, a turbulent undergraduate and a cocky schoolboy from Birmingham. All these are the same person. And other persons in my sample are similarly multiple. So I do have access to the staff and student experience over time, and specifically in the 1950s and 1960s.

For some that meant English before Leavis and 'Cambridge English'. Dr Singer read English at Durham, where there was no alternative view of English on offer: 'At Durham, philology was the name of the game. We would spend two hours a week with the professor on *Beowulf*, and that would be getting the translation, discussing the cruces, going very slowly and minutely through texts.' (57)

Questioning, if it came, came late. Professor Patterson remembers, after finals in 1954, 'writing a huge indictment of English literature [teaching] as it was then [in Scotland] – how it never came near the present, how received judgements by people long dead were endorsed unthinkingly ...the dispiriting curriculum, the droning lectures'. (55) Patterson also illustrates how students like himself, who thus tardily distanced themselves from the dominant ethos, were able to do so by almost chance encounters – a conversation in a political meeting, a *Scrutiny* article found in a library.

The Leavisites

Leavis

For people like these, Leavis was the key to the prison door. While conducting my interviews I became more and more astonished at the place occupied by Leavis in the folk history of English People. Either *bête noire* – 'monstrous', 'pretentious', 'mean-minded' (7) – or revered idol, his name evoked and still evokes amazingly strong feelings. Even those with whom he eventually quarrelled (and they are many) still assert his genius and apologize for his shortcomings. Patterson left Scotland and went to do research in Cambridge on the strength of Leavis's critical writing: 'His wonderful sense of how words worked. To me that was criticism – sensuous, oppositional.' (55)

The impression I get of Leavis and the Leavisites from my respondents is complex, not to say contradictory. The contradiction as I see it is between the way he is represented as an elitist and a traditionalist and the affirmation of his profoundly oppositional position. Leavis was an outsider – a townsman in a town where university despised the town, mocked in Cambridge for his Cambridge accent, a local grammar school boy, albeit from a special grammar school, Perse. It is odd that views that remained heretical should have been treated subsequently as if they were establishment, although the phenomenon seems to be common in education: a particular radical position – 'real books', 'progressive teaching', 'pupil-centred learning', 'feminism', even, as we saw in the previous chapter – which remains a minority position gets treated as a bogey by the establishment. Leavis himself put it characteristically:

It is not noble when you are bent on perpetuating an orthodoxy that
has long been in possession, to point to the heretic who has survived,
somehow, as the establishment you are bravely displacing.

(In Walsh 1980: 10)

'How we are to live'

Leaving (reluctantly) aside the paradoxes of the man and the movement,
it is still reasonable to state that for decades the one-word answer to the
question of what was the dominant ethos in most departments of English
would have been 'Leavisite'. Stirling was presented to me as having been
'massively Leavisite', Newcastle too; Cardiff had a *Scrutiny* contributor,
a Leavis disciple; the professor at Bristol was an associate of Leavis; Cambridge was Cambridge (Oxford, of course, was different – 'not only pre-
theoretical but pre-critical' (23) – and PNL was a glint in Tony Crosland's
eye). What exactly was this 'Leavisite' consensus?

There was general agreement about the canon as the knowledge base:
'There was an understanding that if you hadn't studied figures like Chaucer,
Shakespeare and Spenser, you hadn't studied the subject.' (50) The canon
could change (unlike in classics) but the criteria for inclusion were fixed.
They had to do with complexity and seriousness as against gentility: 'As
critics we felt ourselves to be missionaries of seriousness . . . Jane Austen
was shallow, George Eliot was rich.' (55) 'Complex texts, related to real
experience, were better than things that were sentimental . . . discriminating
between books according to whether they were morally healthy or not.'
(16) The belief was that studying English would make people more moral
and would enable them to lead better lives amid the pressures of the
modern world. English was *redemptive*. When you press them, this is what
many older teachers believe today (the allusions to the *Book of Common
Prayer* are significant):

> I feel that that through the study of literature I'm at least aware of
> my sins of omission or commission. I suppose by extension I must
> believe that the bank manager who's faced with seven kinds of
> malpractice . . . someone who's read *Middlemarch*, who's gone through
> Lydgate's experience, who's come to that moment of having to vote
> and who votes imperceptibly as it were, against his conscience be-
> cause of a kind of financial pressure on him, I would have to believe
> that somebody who has read that novel, for whom the experience has
> been a serious one, that that must make some kind of difference.
> When you press me, and when I have to tease it out, it is redemptive,
> ultimately, yes. At the centre of it all is a feeling that if it doesn't
> make some kind of difference to the way that you actually live your
> life then it would be a frivolous sort of activity. (6)

The Leavisite view, then, can be put very simply: 'I see it as a subject about
how we live, how we are to live.' (13) 'The question was, what does it
mean to be human – the meaning of existence. You were given the answer
at the same time, to be human is to study English Literature.' (1)

It seems clear now that the Leavisite approach was about professional-ization, demonstrating that this activity was not frivolous or dilettante but fundamental.

'Close reading'

The other dominant aspect of the consensus was close reading as a core skill – like life-drawing for an artist. It meant privileging the text over knowledge about the text or the author: 'Close reading is crucial. If you can't do the close reading then you can't do the other things . . . Leavis was awfully good at it.' (5) Close reading aimed at an objective statement – about the text and about the subjective response. It was emancipatory in that it was a skill (reading texts and observing oneself as a reader of texts) that did not depend on inborn or inbred sensitivity to beauty. Richards seems to have been genuinely experimental – curious about the variety of student response in what now seems a remarkably modern way, though, as Eagleton (1983: 15) points out, he did not take the next step, which would have been to look at the common features of the protocols and see them as social and class signs. Dixon (1991: 104) reports on the way Richards and his colleagues (including Forbes and Leavis at the time) were prepared to accept a plurality of readings, from each other and from students. Dixon defends Richards against recent detractors (Baldick, Graff and others), saying that they attack Richards 'without showing the slightest interest in investigating for themselves what readers are doing'. And he claims that 'no one attempted to take this type of investigation further, then or later'. This may be to ignore recent reader-response work, and particularly the work of Bleich (1978, 1988) but it does point to a dispar-ity between 'practical criticism', as conceived and practised by Richards, and 'close reading' as practised by followers (and as derived from classics). In most classrooms the author of the passage was given and close reading was designed to confirm the value of the already valued text: 'It was very much "This is a nice poem, why is it nice?"' (42) Studying a poem was rather like doing a physics experiment: you do not expect Ohm's Law to be invalidated in the third form nor do you expect to have to compare it critically with Evans's Law of the misplaced integer. So, in practice, sen-sitivity was necessary as an entrance qualification. The close reader who failed to find a beautiful poem beautiful or to be moved by it, to love it, was incompetent in ways other than purely technical. Here is a hostile caricature of the process: 'English, as it was then taught, became a sensi-bility game. "Look how sensitive I am," says the teacher. "I can respond to the poem in this way and I can see how wonderful it is. And notice how all my wonderful emotions are pouring out of me. Can you be as sensitive as I am?"' (15)

So outside the experimental situation created by Richards there was a temptation to fake responses, to be rhapsodic about what you were expected to be rhapsodic about, rather than what you were really moved by, or rather than admitting that you were moved by nothing. The scientific acceptance of response, however 'immature', as data to be analysed, which was to a certain extent present in Cambridge English at the start, did not survive becoming the standard classroom technique, with predictable results:

> If you were a wily lad from the Midlands on the make then yes, you could be as sensitive as anyone, if it was going to get you a job. I was being sensitive all the time, but I flatter myself that sensitivity was something I never did feel. I couldn't understand what everyone was going on about, the beauty of Shelley or Wordsworth. (15)

It seems as if Leavis should be absolved from the sensitivity-seeking. If anything, he seems to have been more interested in ideas and moral and social issues than in aesthetic experience. But this was not true of the Leavisites: 'The Leavisites did harm to Leavis. He seemed much tougher than they seemed to be. There was a whole side of Leavis's pupils who were old aesthetes. Ideas were anathema to them.' (3) And this meant that close reading came to exclude ideas, again with predictable results: 'I just found the way it was practised incredibly boring. I'd heard about history of ideas and the way that it integrated the cultural, social and political perspective, and I thought that's so much more interesting.' (42)

So there were tensions and there was hypocrisy and there was narrowness, but nevertheless this particular practice functioned for years, precisely because, like any practice, it represented a viable compromise between individual sincerity and conformist social requirements (particularly examination requirements, since it met the need for examination questions admirably). Provided no one probed the genuineness of the responses too closely, provided no American asked awkward theoretical questions about criteria for judgement, useful teaching work could be done: powerful texts could be introduced to students and they could learn to be better readers of those texts and (who knows?) perhaps better people. There might be some 'insincerity' but this kind of mimicry may be inevitable in the early stages of learning. Meanwhile, salaries were earned honestly, qualifications obtained, readings produced and pupils, as we saw in Chapter 3, enabled to circumvent the purely factual.

The grammar school boys

Into this innocent china shop a quarter of a century ago came the grammar school boys: sons of immigrants – Irish, Greek . . . – or from the Celtic fringe, or at least non-metropolitan and non-RP. Dad was working class or lower middle class, a building worker, clerk, publican. They were spoiling for a fight. In some ways they were like the rebellious, non-conformist secondary modern boys described by Hargreaves in *Life in School* (Hammersley and Woods 1984: Chapter 11). But they were very bright and ambitious. Their chosen metaphor was war:

I wanted to change the subject of English, to explode it, to destroy it. I've always felt combative about the subject. That [publication] was my machine-gun. English was and is a battlefield. English is where I want to do the damage. This is the front line. (15)

I enjoy being oppositional. (55)

It's nice to be a Shakespearian because that's the battleground. (54)

Socially, the enemy was Oxbridge. Mostly the battle was conducted with long-range guns, though Terry Eagleton was behind the lines:

I can remember faculty meetings twenty years ago when Terry stood up and you could see the indulgent smiles on every face while he did his 'leftish spiel'. It wasn't a comfortable thing for him to do. (24)

Intellectually, the enemy was the dominant critical pedagogical practice, not so much Oxford, which was seen as intellectually irrelevant, but Cambridge and the Leavisites. Leavis, who in retrospect seems to have so much in common with these young men (even to the rugby-playing), ended up being one of their prime targets. He shares their combative, anti-establishment position, but he is also elitist and, as the famous exchange with Welleck showed, intuitive, whereas the young theorists were motivated by resentment of secretive elites. They were against any system which was not democratic, whose workings were invisible, so that a person could make a judgement which was recognized as 'superior' without being required to show how that judgement was arrived at (making the invisible visible had also been Richards's project). 'Sensitivity' was thus the target for hostility, because, while in theory you could learn it, in practice you were either born with it or you faked it: 'Terry [Eagleton] describes it as the wine-tasting school of criticism. Sniff, "Oh, this is good, a fine nutty flavour." ' (27)

So the theorists were committed to questioning premises. They adopted the basic oppositional strategy of showing that the natural is constructed, the given has a history. They sought to make strange. They looked for alternatives to 'sensitivity' or personal empathy, good taste, response to beauty, all of which were seen as mystifications perpetrated by the dominant elite, people who had read *The Faerie Queene* at home by the age of 12, people who did not need the institution. Although they were oppositional and anti-establishment they were nevertheless fundamentally pro-institution and pro-profession.

This attack on a dominant position was powerful. Arguments were directed at weakly defended, taken for granted positions, and they were conducted in an abrasive style, reminiscent of Leavis, but shocking to Leavisites:

I'm shocked by the lack of courtesy. Critical theory people are derisive of traditional ways. There is more gentlemanliness about the traditionalists. The other side make dishonest debating points. (22)

I've read the letters X publishes in journals – extraordinarily belligerent, arrogant utterances. (7)

The other shocking aspect is the fervour. Again, the last accusation anyone
would put against Leavis or Arnold was that they lacked fervour. Professor
Bishop asked about Leavis, 'Why does the animosity go on?' and gave the
answer: 'I think it's people don't want to be taken quite so seriously.' The
theorists, like Leavis, were hostile to an upper-class, dilettante, epicurean
attitude to literature and to life, the attitude of those who could afford to
be that relaxed and amateur.

> We were reading an essay by Eagleton and we noticed, the students
> and I, how Arnoldian he was in his moral fervour, and there seemed
> something particularly English about that. It's an upper-class thing,
> hostility to moral fervour. (58)

Some see English literature as having been written to challenge, not
strengthen, the status quo and they see the institutionalization of it as a
hi-jacking both of it and of the experience of reading, or, more subtly, of
privileging a conservative reading of texts: 'Until quite recently texts were
taught as if they endorsed the status quo, whereas my first experience
[reading Shelley in public school] was that they did the opposite.' (7)
Another way of putting it would be to say that the university has been
engaged in a process of *neutralization* or damage-limitation. The potentially subversive aspects of literature and of the institutionalization of
literature have been held in check.

The assumption of the grammar school boys (based on their own experience) was that intuitive response to literature was either fake or something which denoted inherent aristocratic superiority and which could be
used to exclude. Paradoxically, in spite of the fervour, the theorists are
attempting the move from valuing feeling (sensitivity), to valuing thinking;
from receptivity, the intuiting of shared feelings, empathizing with authors
and other readers, to penetrating questioning and challenging; from the
Cavalier pleasure principle and swooning consent, to the Roundhead notion
of work and the struggle to master hard texts. In my shorthand, from the
feminine to the masculine. This is of course a shift towards their own
masculine strengths and away from the feminine which seems to underlie
the initial choice:

> A particular position is in fact simply a development of personal
> strengths, and the protection of personal weaknesses. So in the last
> analysis the people who are into theory are good at philosophy, good
> at thinking, good at argument, and not so good at enjoying books;
> and the people who are good at enjoying books, response, expressing
> feelings, are actually not so good at argument. (13)

This move towards the intellectual is a move against the British tradition, especially the taboo surrounding any meta-communication. To reflect

about what you are doing is to run the risk of destroying something. Until very recently the dominant modern form of meta-communication about society has been Marxist. I referred in Chapter 1 to Anderson's view that Britain conspicuously lacked a totalizing approach to society, and that literary criticism in the shape of Leavis was providing it. I expressed some scepticism about that,[1] but one could certainly argue that literary theory in the subsequent generation has been the nearest thing Britain has to an analytical, critical, reflexive view of culture and society, that literary theorists are the nearest we have to intellectuals in a society which is suspicious of them.

So the grammar school boys became that very un-English thing, intellectuals. But the materials had to be imported. They were imported from France (I say from France rather than from the French because the French themselves have done their share of importing: Kristeva came from Bulgaria, Todorov from Russia; Derrida and Althusser were both born in Algiers, and Cixous had a German mother and was brought up in Oran). The theorists brought over the boundary both continental thinking and social science thinking and popularized them by publishing clear, readable, critical accounts. They were inter-cultural couriers (in ways that language people were not). It is interesting also to see the extent to which theory did not travel direct – Calais–Dover – but via the USA. One of the leading figures in the establishment of theory was not at all interested in French or France at school but was fascinated by America. He went to North America as a post-graduate and by chance discovered linguistics and Lévi-Strauss:

> In the sixties language meant philology. Everyone laughed at the relevance of linguistics. The same for structural anthropology. No one in England had heard of Lévi-Strauss. The British thought he made jeans. (15)

Overall this was again a powerful move, directed at yet another weakness of the establishment position, its monoglot insularity (once again Leavis, fluent in French and competent in Italian, himself escapes this censure). The position, 'I can't understand it and it's foreign, and I think it's ridiculous,' is not one which serious academics wish to be saddled with. Yet very often, willy-nilly, they did find themselves in this position.

Women and theory

My narrative is that a feminine, accepting subject, based largely on tacit agreement not to issue uncomfortable challenges at a cognitive level, was attacked by lower-class males intent on imposing masculine values. Yet this seems to be contradicted by the fact that feminism is a highly visible part of literary theory.

As I tried to demonstrate in Chapter 6, the homology between feminine and female, masculine and male, is not total. There is no reason why some women should not be at one with the men whom I have described; in the same way there will be men who do not share this masculine way of being and these values. The motivation for the grammar school boys was the sense of being excluded and oppressed, and this is clearly the basis for feminist revolt, so that there is an obvious alliance. As I also suggested in Chapter 6, the aim, for men and women, is integration and whereas men may be doing quite well on that score by making the choice of a feminine subject in the first place, women are being prevented from developing masculine traits. Dr Stone had been in a job for a few years:

> I felt something was missing. I went to the University Teachers of English Conference in Bristol, then to the first LTP Conference. I realized what was missing was theory. I put on a course on critical theory to get myself sorted out. (25)

> I wasn't particularly brilliant in the first two years at university. The language wasn't one that appealed to me, an impressionistic language. At the end of my undergraduate career I discovered Marxist criticism and everything began to become clear for me. I knew what I'd been lacking before in terms of being able to conceptualize the process of reading and understanding a text. (58)

Theory, for women, may be a way of avoiding splitting. Here is a good example. Professor Leigh is a theorist and a feminist:

> Theory may be a way of getting out from under the indulgence of English. I love it but I still have this uneasy feeling that just straight English is an indulgence. It doesn't belong to a university. It's pure pleasure and I oughtn't to be paid for it. It's a conflict but I've resolved it by doing theory and applying it to literature. So I've every excuse for doing whatever I want to do, but then I can theorize it. And that makes it okay. (17)

But the theory is still used in a 'feminine' way, not for mastery of the text but for its rebirth: 'Every time I see a new bit of theory I see a new way of bringing another text alive.' (17) And women are more likely to admit to feelings about literary texts – and theoretical ones – feelings which they do not have to fake:

> They [French theorists] are incredibly sexy. It's their Frenchness. Anyone who has been an au pair girl in France will be absolutely dazzled by anyone who turns up in an oatmeal cashmere sweater and starts talking in this wonderful Maurice Chevalier accent about exotic things that you can half understand.

This is a very different discourse to that of her male colleagues, whose relationship on the whole does not involve any feeling about France, and who prefer the critique of the decently detached to the enthusiasm of the joyfully seduced, and metaphors of war to metaphors of sex.

Not all women are able to integrate as well. Alice is an Australian post-graduate. She was a typical New Critical student:

> It was very much American New Criticism. What I loved in literature was feeling an empathy. When I first read about theory I went into this serious depression. I'll never forget it, it was a real dark night of the soul. The way I was trained I can't use any more. It's changed everything absolutely, and as a result I don't think I want to stay in academia. (111)

What this respondent illustrates is that theory may be simply the exacerbation of the process of institutionalization, the hardening of the boundary. The refusal of theory is resistance to bringing the work across that boundary into the institution:

> As a result of becoming an English Person I have lost the love that I had. As a child I can remember staying up till three or four and not wanting to go to sleep because it was so exciting. I wasn't discriminating at all. And if you learn that you should discriminate, once lots of shoulds start to inform your reading . . . I lost an awful lot of the joy that I had in reading. I'm at a point now that I hardly ever buy books, hardly ever. I've lost the impulse that sent me towards being an English Person in the first place. (111)

Her thesis cannot be written without acknowledging theory and yet she cannot integrate it:

> I read my texts and I've found they are interesting and I have insight, and I know my work is good. It leaves me cold. All the feeling's gone out of it. It's anti-life. I think I will have to get out because more and more I have visions of myself sitting at my computer all day on my own. I think I can't stand that, I'm going to die. I'll have to be free again to experience things in a way that I prefer to experience them. I don't think I am prepared to pay the price, the loneliness. (111)

The price paid for this professionalization is for her too high, the loss too great. It's worth reflecting on the nature of this experience of loss. She doesn't challenge the need to lose innocence, to become aware:

> Sometimes I think to myself, well it's good you should feel like this because at least it shows you are aware. So many people in Oxford are not aware, they are either ideologues, or they say things like 'I don't need theory', but they can't tell me what it is they are doing, they can't give me a methodology. What I resent in those people and I am jealous of is their ability to sail through life and not let it affect them. They are quite sure that what they are doing is okay. It drives me crazy that they are not having the angst, they can sit for hours to

write, and they have dreamless sleep. That's the greatest value that critical theory has – it makes liberal humanists know they are liberal humanists, and not self-transcending beings, who know exactly what is right and what is wrong. Liberal humanism was the great un-labelled. I know now my position is an ideological one, but it's the one I prefer.

But as a self-conscious liberal humanist her objection to theory seems to be along masculine/feminine, thinking/feeling lines. And again, the metaphor is sex:

They are always saying it's about playing, and you get these incred-ibly boring things about the striptease of the text, and I'm thinking 'There's no sex there, there's just no passion in the whole thing.'

Loss seems to be the key notion – loss of innocence, of love, of joy, of impulse, of desire, of empathy. The gain is in awareness, but for her the message of the balance-sheet is clear. Theorists themselves have little sense of loss, and this is a major difference between them and English People like Alice. It may be a difference between male and female English People. It certainly shows how the nature of the subject – feminine/masculine – is deeply linked to the nature of the people in it: a shift in one direction makes it more or less acceptable to certain individuals who may or may not be able to shift in response.

This case could be described as the feminine being driven out by the masculine. A male theorist: 'Theory represents a phallic rigour, it's gender-policing. Theory is deemed to be difficult, challenging, impressions are not sufficient, and that can be conventionally gender-coded.' (74) But again it should be made clear that the feminine could be driven out by the mas-culine even in a situation where all the members of the institution were biologically female.

The impact of theory

Staff

Theorists
The theorists operated through conferences and the publishing of journals and books. Easthope (1988: Appendix 2) gives a lively summary of the conference activity: the Essex conferences from 1977 to 1984 (also Barker *et al.* 1986); the literature/teaching/politics (LTP) conferences; the South-ampton theory and text conferences of 1981–3. The DUET (Development of University English Teaching project) annual six-day workshops began in 1980 and were concerned, among many other things, with the application of theory to teaching (see Broadbent 1981; Punter 1986). Contrast this activity with the traditional University Teachers of English (UTE) con-ference, and its state of 'desiccation' which eventually led to its being

recast as Higher Education Teachers of English (HETE). Journals included general Marxist publications like *New Left Review, Radical Philosophy, Theoretical Practice, Economy and Society*, as well as *Screen, Literature and History* and the *Oxford Literary Review*. Feminism was represented by *MF* and *The Feminist Review*. Since 1987 three new journals have been launched: *Textual Practice, New Formations*, and *Cultural Studies*.

As far as books are concerned the most powerful influence has been the New Accents series, published by Methuen/Routledge, whose role has been very significant. Two individuals – the commissioning editor Janice Price and the series editor Terence Hawkes – can be said to have orchestrated the publishing of theory in Britain.

The organizers of the conferences and the authors of the books were members of a small number of university departments and a much larger number of polytechnic departments.[2] One theory appointment was made to Southampton and this was enough to turn a department without a strong identity into a theory place. A former undergraduate says of his first-year experience there: 'It was like the devil marshalling up all the new recruits in Hell. "You're here to study English, and by God [*sic*] you're going to study English."' (62) By pure chance three people with strong theory interests found themselves in Cardiff and the New Accents series was edited from there.

The effect, over twenty years, has certainly not been to substitute one orthodoxy for another (as we shall see in this section and in the next, which looks at student response) but to do away with consensus. The kind of monolithic world which Dr Singer inhabited in Durham has gone. English departments today are happily or unhappily pluralist. Most are in a state of tension and conflict.

The theorists still see themselves as representing a cause: Professor Leigh was concerned about how my interview material would be used, because journalists had interviewed her and 'it comes out with me looking like a dangerous loony . . . It's the cause. I don't want the position I subscribe to to look like the position of a nutcase.' (17) They can occasionally be observed behaving as a group:

> Terry [Eagleton] has a constellation of people who tend to vote the same way at faculty, and they all tend to agree with each other, (although they all work on very different things) and they all wear leather jackets. You could hear the leather jackets creaking with rage when people said things like, 'Well the students seem to like Anglo-Saxon'. (31)

It is also a fact that the various conferences could not have happened without group collaboration on the part of the organizers and a sense of belonging on the part of the participants. Nevertheless, the idea of a tightly knit theory camp is an illusion – which is not surprising given the basic fight mode which characterizes the protagonists. A theory person, a woman, described an attempt at collaboration at Oxford:

They tried to have a collective of the people interested in theory on the lines of the Women's Studies collective. Someone described it afterwards as a meeting of Mafia leaders. You are all there pretending that you have the same agenda and you don't want to blow the other guy's head off. They managed to put on one lecture session and that's it. There is no way these people can collaborate. The only thing that energized that group is that they could have endless debates with one another, for a student audience, that they could differ in public. (27)

There are sub-groups of one I think, that's what it comes down to. There are larger coalitions but they're pretty unstable. Theory, that monolithic form, is in fact very unstable. (19)

This is not to say there are not very general traits which distinguish theory people – being oppositional, of the left, intellectual (or hostile to British anti-intellectualism), in general against literature seen as autonomous, separate from social phenomena, or from other disciplines. And there is a Roundhead (Leavisite?) belief in giving a too pleasurable Cavalier subject teeth: 'I think in order to justify doing a three-year degree you have to grapple with those things. That's the Protestant work ethic coming out again. Unless there's some kind of teeth in the thing it's not really worth doing.' (57) Yet within the theory camp itself there are dramatic divisions, particularly between a mischievous, provocative wing, Cavalier in its own way, gaily and daily writing death notices – Author, Subject, Humanism, Value, Language, University – and a sober wing invoking the Enlightenment. One of the latter:

Critical theorists who talk about the death of the author are in a very difficult situation when it comes to exam script marking, where you are attributing thoughts and judgements and powers of reasoning, or if they are asked for a list of publications and they say 'It's language speaking through me'. As for the death of the subject that's an extremely drastic thing to say. What happens to the notion of moral accountability if you completely dissolve the subject into language or memory, if you do it Hume's way or Foucault's or Barthes's? Who is it who has the responsibility? (12)

This respondent reminds us that theory is nothing if not self-critical:

There's a particular danger about post-structuralism which is that it throws away so much of what it sees as bad old enlightenment heritage, that it leaves itself no room for critique or for values or integrity. Truth is what it comes down to. The trouble is this tends to polarize debate. If you talk about truth people tend to think you're talking about some unitary, fixed transcendent truth. That's not at all what the Enlightenment philosophers were talking about. They were talking about validity standards and argumentative claims, not some quasi-religious absolute truth. (12)

The opposition
Not everyone was prepared to accept the new paradigm. Some were ready
to be belligerent back:

> In the department I was hanging on to my job by the skin of my
> teeth. I started a little course on literary criticism and one of my
> senior colleagues proposed that it should be closed down immedi-
> ately. He thought it was terrible. He brought that to a departmental
> meeting. They wanted me out. They were terribly upset. Nobody
> wanted us. My God, if they could have got rid of us they would have
> done. (15)

> There's a fight on, and there has been for some time. There are
> battlefields and truces. The current phase of the war started in Cam-
> bridge in 1981, when McCabe did not get a permanent appointment
> at Cambridge, because Ricks and the others took the view that the
> work he had done on Joyce was too theoretical and the liberal
> humanists who had been trained in Cambridge thought that was not
> the direction that Cambridge should go. (50)

The war is permanent and every so often a skirmish makes the headlines. The most recent episode involved an honorary doctorate for Derrida
at Cambridge. There are two armies and each is prepared to be very nasty
to the other, including insulting the other's high command:

> I think Eagleton's an old fraud. The posture he adopted for himself
> would only be possible in Oxford. There he's been in a state of lethal
> opposition all these years while drawing a salary and publishing his
> books, and benefiting from the high profile that Oxford has given
> him. (50)

At one level the conflict is a primitive struggle for power and control
between individuals and groups. Professor Dover is frank about this aspect:

> All I've ever wanted is my chance. When is it my turn? That's what
> I felt about this research selectivity committee. It's assessing research
> in English. How do they choose the people that should be on it? I've
> been teaching English in this country now for over thirty years. I've
> been a professor for over ten years. By the nature of my work I know
> more about what goes on in British English departments than most
> people. Why isn't it my turn to be on that committee? Who chooses
> these people? I don't mind being the only voice speaking for critical
> theory, but there should be a voice, and why isn't it me? We've won
> the war, but the occupying troops are still there. I want them to pack
> up and go home.

But it is not just a question of individuals hanging on to power or long-
ing for it. The groups *represent* interests – material but also ideological.
As always, the struggle is at one and the same time about individual

dominance *and* about general values; the two are inextricable and it is as much a mistake to reduce the whole battle to primitive stag-fights as it is to see it as only lofty argument and debate.

What then does the opposition to theory represent? The conflict is, at one level, left–right, radical–conservative. Conservatives object to overt infusion of politics into literary studies. If it were just ideas, it might be acceptable: 'It's as well they [post-graduates] know about theory, provided they don't combine it with half-baked politics.' (50) But there is a deeper conflict than this, and one which cuts across the right–left opposition. It is peculiar to the subject and it is to do with ways of knowing:

> Theory is staked inevitably on the idea of good argument. The trouble is that those who are against theory wouldn't accept that there is such a thing as having their ideas knocked down. They are appealing to values which claim to stand beyond any sort of theoretical dismissal. So there's an awful lot of mutual bafflement and ill-will generated by the fact that we are talking on different wavelengths. (12)

One group is transmitting on the wavelength of cognitive discourse, the other on the wavelength of intuition. It is an ancient opposition (Hegel distinguished the *Verstand* and the *Vernunft*). These are two distinct ways of knowing and the subject English attempts simultaneously to deal in both. Theory is seen as a threat to the intuitive. The language is that of religious persecution:

> I still believe that a lot can be gained by the intuitive intelligence following its nose. I have a strong resistance to theorizing my position, or declaring what my theory is. I would almost go to the stake for the right to keep my mental independence as I see it. (29)

What is required of the reader and student of literature is a submission which, using one metaphor, could be called feminine but which, using another (and the two discourses often feed on each other), seems religious. There is seduction, accompanied, as in many seductions, by intoxication: 'You have got to be intoxicated even if you sober up afterwards if you want to have any idea what makes the thing worth doing. Open yourself to the reading experience, "bring with you a heart that watches and receives" as Wordsworth says.' And there is submissiveness: 'One submits oneself quite humbly to a master. We are servants of something which is valuable and there is a function to perform in transmitting this love of this valuable thing to other people. It's a priesthood.' (22) The scholar's relation to authors and texts can also seem like religious, discipular service:

> He will die if he's left in those old editions. I think bringing him out in a new edition may give him a new lease of life, and I see no harm in that. He was a great man, and a great writer. This is me being a humble disciple. (16)

'Delight', 'pleasure', 'enthusiasm', 'rhapsodic engagement' – what is being defended is a capacity to have strong feelings. Literature is what develops and enables this feeling capacity. Theory is seen as inimical to this relation with reading:

> Some people are into critical theory because it's a way that they are going to be able to absolve their consciences from reading books. If you could have a little kit which would inject you against literature with a little dose of theory, that would do. (29)

One respondent described how he and a theory person were both involved with a post-graduate student writing a thesis on a foreign author neither of them knew. The theory person was bored by the books; he on the other hand 'disappeared into that world'. He concludes from this: 'I'm interested in literature as a part of human communication, human spiritual illumination. For them, it's a philosophical subject. Literature is grist to the mill.' (13)

I conclude then that the opposition to theory represents resistance to the process of professionalization, which is conceived as essentially cognitive. It represents a defensive fear that one kind of knowledge will destroy the other.

Seismic shock

Individuals have been able to find arguments against theory and perhaps to clarify their own positions in the process. Some, like Professor Duke, were sufficiently established to be indifferent:

> I don't know anything about it. It's like the Jehovah's Witnesses, they come round and they say here is our whatever, and until you know all about it you can't argue. It would take the rest of your life to find out, and you might decide you'd wasted your time anyway, so you say 'Life is short, sorry. That has to go.' (21)

But for those in mid-career this option was not available and theory was a major shock. I shall describe two of these people in some detail. One is from a civic university and is basically a scholar; the other is from a polytechnic and is basically a teacher.

Dr Grant talks of a 'traumatic period': 'It was a seismic shock when Critical Theory came in, a change of paradigm like Puritanism in the seventeenth century.' Ideology and fanaticism can be to the death. Two of his colleagues, a Leavisite and a theorist, 'would have killed each other if they thought they could have got away with it'. His personal response was to read the major figures, to be selective (for Bahktin, against Derrida) but basically to lay low. 'It's death if you show people your neck ... 95 per cent of the people during the Puritan revolution got away unscathed.' He 'found an escape' in 'scholarship and editing of texts'.

When people invent a new language and you can't participate in it, it's only natural to feel awkward and threatened. At the beginning when it was very aggressive in its way of proceeding, it was very difficult to bear. I see it as a punishment. I see them as aggressors towards people like myself. At the time it was happening I felt disorientated, because I did to a degree believe in what I was doing. I did think it had a salutary effect on students as part of the educational system. All that seemed to be threatened. (16)

This was a civic university. Here is another example of the effect of the seismic shock; but in a polytechnic the outcome is different. Mrs George, a committed teacher, was unable to cope with theory and was about to resign. By chance she heard of a DUET workshop which was advertised as offering opportunities to work with theory in an experiential mode. She decided to attend *in extremis*:

When we went over from practical criticism, which I could do, to all these new theories, I was lost. I didn't know what to do, I was in despair, and I was going to give up teaching. A colleague left a pamphlet about a DUET workshop. I looked at this and it was about theory, and I thought, 'I can't do that, I'm terrified', and then I thought, 'Well go to it. If it helps that's fine, if it doesn't you've nothing to lose because you're going to leave teaching anyway.' And I went to that DUET on theory . . . It changed my life. I came back here, and I was over the moon, I was high, because I had suddenly gone through into a whole new realm of stuff and I could use it. The thinking and the feeling came together, and I was able to have the confidence and see which theory appealed to me. The theoretical framework develops out of yourself, it isn't something that's imposed from up there that you've got to learn. (41)

Working through
Mrs George represents a worked-through response to the challenge. This experience took place in a particular department in a particular institution where, as we shall see later in this chapter, things happen fast. In universities we are looking at the subtle interactions within quite small staff groups over long periods of time. A great deal depends on the personalities of the individuals in a department, and on the relative size of the forces. A single theory person in a department is not a threat and may well influence colleagues; a group of people is likely to produce defensive retrenchment.

English People have in fact responded in ways which are not outright rejection. There is bluff ('Most tutors would be able to drop in a phrase about Derrida or Kristeva') but there is also incorporation. Some teachers have distanced themselves from the militant Marxist aspects and responded to the part of theory which is concerned to question premises and beliefs: 'It's made people ask why they are doing what they are doing. The habit of trained suspicion is laudable.' (45) They have seen the limits of their own undergraduate training: 'I wasn't challenged. I supposed that all texts were things that would convey messages to me and all I had to do was learn them all.' (7) They are aware of the power of the argument that the position of not having a stance is in fact a stance: 'One side says you can take it or leave it and the other side says you think you can.' (20) They become more aware of the political: 'I do have political commitment and I'm just not admitting it.' (7)

Some people have seen theory as an aid to communication, a practical teaching and research tool. They are suspicious of the high-profile theory people, seeing them as reproducing the elite 'charmed circle' of the Leavisites. The editor of a successful series for schools says: 'I'm a camp-follower. I'm interested in doing things with it, it's a way of re-examining what you've been doing for twenty years.' (20) And a self-styled 'neo-Leavisite' believes he is now 'a much more helpful reader and therefore helpful teacher. It's carried over into my life in general.' (7) He has responded to theory in a liberal way. When he says of theory, 'that's the image of itself it likes to construct', he is showing the extent to which a certain idea has penetrated. Traditional scholars gratefully accept labels: 'I find that what I do is called by other people now New Historicism, but I didn't know that until I was told.' (7) (I myself must confess to a certain satisfaction on being told by one theorist that my project, this book, was 'Bahktinian': it had not occurred to me previously.) It is possible to use theory to give credibility to your work:

> I'm very much a magpie with modern critical theory. The bits of it that suit me are bits which support this reading and give it credibility. I mean, one of the good things about accepting that everything is discourse is that it seems to me to allow literary critics to start talking about how language constructs our reality and I think that as literary critics we are uniquely trained to draw attention to this. (8)

There is a great deal of honest assessing. How much of a new paradigm can actually be taken in? How much fundamental change is possible for an individual in the last half or third of a career? In the end it comes down to time: 'If I had to choose between reading Derrida and reading new literature, I'd read new literature.' (6)

One aspect of 'working through' involves a new subject-matter: film. The sub-discipline of media and film studies was created by theory. Some regret this and would have liked the new material to have been dealt with by the old methods: 'What happened to film studies in Britain I think is quite sad really. It was colonized by structuralism, post-structuralism, deconstructionists and so on.' (13) But there was no alternative. Dr Ford wrote an article on film for a journal and 'got this very snooty reply from the *Australian Journal of Screen Theory*, saying that they did not publish practical criticism.' (52) The case of Dr Ford is striking. He was instrumental in getting film studies established in his English department, but to teach and write about film meant 'battling to read the criticism in *Screen*':

> It was an interesting experience. It took one a long time to have the confidence to be able to feel that you had mastered the *Screen* position, to turn around and say, 'Look I do think this is intolerant.' Part of our wish here in the books that we have written is to be no less serious but to construct a book that is readable. When I die they can say I published in *Screen* and published in *Movie*. (52)

One could hazard, then, a generalization: that for university English People in mid-career, theory constituted indeed a seismic shock, but many adapted to it, becoming more wary, more questioning. The reality of a phenomenon like this does not take place front-stage where the gladiators fight, but back-stage where individuals decide what they can and cannot live with.

Students

So far we have considered the way that staff have responded to theory in their role of scholars and teachers. As always, the whole picture must include students. As we have seen, the public debate is between (usually male) members of an older generation and this debate is in some ways ritualistic. But change is taking place at the level of intra- and inter-generational exchange. There is also the exchange between secondary and higher education. Undergraduates become teachers and their pupils become undergraduates who then may become teachers. Over a 25-year period there is ample time for this cycle to repeat itself, so that a first-year student today may have been exposed to ideas which are unfamiliar to his or her lecturer: 'Students when they arrive are much more *au fait* with ideas. Students in schools are taught to question things in a way they weren't before.' (28)

I collected some evidence for this from students:

> Professors will say, 'At A level such and such happens,' and I think, 'Not in mine it didn't.' You try telling them this and they don't know. They had to fight against it. X gave a lecture on *Macbeth*. Lots of the points that were made about it were made to me at O level. I'm not saying that my teachers were Critical Theorists, but they certainly weren't saying 'This is a remarkable piece of art and you should learn to appreciate it.' They weren't Leavisite. The theory people are tilting at windmills in a way, and I often get annoyed with them and then I think, well, it's not their fault, I'll be doing it myself in thirty or forty years time. I'll be going on about 'that bloody Mrs Thatcher', and the kids will say, 'What are you on about Dad?' (110)

Nevertheless it must be said on the basis of my interviews that such students are a minority, and lecturers' references to A levels are not as outdated as this student thinks (I reported the view of a chief examiner in Chapter 3 – that A level was 'simple decoding'). Most have done A-level courses which consist of a small number of texts studied intensively in terms of character and plot. They will have produced examination essays, done close reading, and they will have chosen an institution of higher education without any awareness of how theoretical it might be. What determines their experience is the institution; there will be in each place a range of personalities among the students, from cautious to adventurous, from romantic to analytical, from 'masculine' to 'feminine', but it is the institution which will determine whether their experience is good or not. So in this section I will look at the theory question as it affects students, institution by institution.

Oxford
One woman fellow felt Oxford less hostile to theory than her previous provincial university had been, because of the students:

> It's a very student-led place, and if something gets students excited and interested and involved, quite a lot of tutors are generous-spirited enough to think this can't be all bad. (25)

There is a theory option in Oxford. College tutors have mixed feelings about their pupils taking it: all eight from one year from one college took it; the tutor called them lemmings; only two finished it. A student who did finish it was told by his tutor, 'Don't let it upset your period papers because if you do you are going to get nobbled.' And there seems to be a general view among theorists in Oxford that to use theory in finals is dangerous. A resolution of the apparent contradiction between this view and the idea of tutors as 'generous-spirited' is offered by an undergraduate:

> There are very few tutors left who opt out of theory, but the ones who do are all examiners. There are few colleges in which you would have no access to people who are talking about theory but on the other hand there are few ways in which you can introduce that into your finals. (75b)

Another theorist was less jaundiced: 'The examiners have adapted to the language [of theory] or they would be "putting down their own best men".' (23)

The students who take to theory do so because they see it as an opportunity to think:

> I loved it, it was the first time since I'd been here that I'd felt intellectually challenged. You always feel pushed in terms of the amount of the material, but I didn't always feel pushed to do any thinking. I was writing the same essays in similar terms on different authors. (72)

This student is another example of someone who is liberated by theory from a nebulous requirement to respond:

One of the reasons why our tutor didn't want us to do theory was that he felt it blunted our natural response to the text. I've never felt that I had a natural response. I'm not creative in terms of literature, I'm a good analyst, so I work on the text. It's not a romantic experience. I don't identify with characters, I'm very alienated in that sense. (72)

Others, more pragmatically, see it as a way of coping with the reading requirements: 'People like to go into critical theory, because you don't have to read many primary texts.' (77)

Mostly, however, there is massive resistance for reasons which by now are familiar: theory is work, whereas they chose English for pleasure; theory is not related to the text, it's 'hermetically sealed', 'sterile'. They test out their feelings or salve their consciences by going to Terry Eagleton's lectures and this confirms them in the view that it is all remote from their real concern, literature:

I could follow more or less what he was saying, but I found the link to literature tenuous. You learn some interesting stuff about Wittgenstein and Heidegger and Freud, but not so much about Browning. (76)

There are other powerful counter-models in Oxford:

I know next to nothing about it. I have been quite resistant to it, because the bits that I do know about it I don't like. So I'm always very happy when I find certain critics like John Carey here, who are also resistant to it, and who have reasons for being resistant. I believe in the primacy of the author, and the text having a core of meaning. I don't think you can play the games that theorists seem to play with texts. It also ties in with my religious beliefs. Anyone who has a singular world view has to reject an interpretation that sees things as completely relative. (76)

Teachers confirm the extent of student resistance.

I find the first years hugely difficult. They come wanting to learn English. They have only done English at A level, they like reading literature. Any other sort of thinking is foreign to them, more threatening than to American undergraduates whose approach to every class is that it's something new and something challenging. That's what the American notion of a liberal education is about. I found it very difficult to get them to think . . . even about what it was they were doing when they were reading. (74)

Students have a shock . . . especially when they are told about characters. 'You mean you can't be in love with Heathcliff?' (27)

The overall picture at Oxford is one where theory is at most a minor irritant. Provided it remains on the optional theory paper it is compatible with Oxford openness. But it is a virus which must not escape from the option laboratory.

Stirling

Stirling, which was strongly Leavisite, now has a head of department who contributed to the Essex conferences, who was at one time Director of the DUET project, and whose research interest is in psychoanalysis. The staff has one theorist and has just appointed another, a woman. My impression, from my interviews with students, was that, in spite of this, unlike Oxford students they had not had to engage at all with theory. Staff realize this:

> I think we get back as far as method, but I don't think most of the students have any experience of us going back as far as theory because there's only three or four people in the department who would want to perform in that particular intellectual medium and given that all the core courses are substantially classicist and historical there isn't a space at the moment. (9)

There is a genial pluralism:

> If you find the Marxist approach is anathema to you, well then, you'll have a different one later. It all works out in the wash. So I suppose we're producing magpies. You should have some notion of where you are going, but to get there sometimes you need a canoe, sometimes you need a bicycle. (8)

For the students, this translates into a kind of non-committed individualism: 'I don't call myself a Leavisite, I don't call myself an anything-ite. Texts get a "me" reading.' (69) The basic view is that theory would 'muddy the waters'. These clear waters are 'you and the text'. (68)

Cardiff

Cardiff is a special case because of the presence there of a group of high-profile, polemical theory people, and the existence of the Centre for Critical and Cultural Theory. However, it is a large department, and they do not have things their own way. Two extracts will, I hope, give a flavour of how staff and students relate in Cardiff over the question of theory. Students certainly question theory and the senior proponents of it. They are particularly conscious of a contradiction between the espoused belief (pluralism, argument) and the practice (lecturing):

> Critical Theory is a great tool to be used, but lots of the senior people here have got too much faith in it. They espouse this idea 'I hate lectures', but at the same time X gave ten lectures and a lot of it was very contentious, and then at the end said, 'Well, of course you may disagree with me.' I thought why not say this at the beginning, and why not do what others do, give a lecture and then have a couple of seminars, or split up into groups? They could do more to make it less of a soapbox thing. Deconstruction encourages plurality, and yet they're trying to convert people. The younger ones are different, not setting themselves up as demagogues or mandarins. (110)

Here is the view of one of the senior Cardiff theorists on students' response to theory:

> They have a hard time actually, because they come with this great
> certainty. They know they're good at English. They've done very well
> at A level, and then they suddenly find the currency they have doesn't
> buy anything in this new world. Some of them respond very well and
> abandon the old currency, but they are few in number. A lot of them
> remain baffled, and worried, and we say to ourselves, 'Well, it's good
> that they should be baffled.' There is a group of people who resist it.
> Trouble is, they are in no position to resist it. They find allies in the
> department who want to cling to the older ways, but these are inevit-
> ably people who are not in a strong position. In this department the
> people who are in strong positions are all now critical theorists. So
> this group of people who want to resist it, they haven't the weapons
> to resist it. How could they argue against Derrida when they can't
> even spell Derrida? (15)

Newcastle

Newcastle is a department with a strong philology tradition: currently the
Department of English Language and the Department of English Literature
are awkwardly combined in one school. There are young people in their
first job, feminists, and a recently appointed professor from Oxbridge.
Film is studied and there is a creative writing option. The student intake
is highly qualified and there is a large proportion of public school pupils.
There is in Newcastle an attempt to grasp the theory nettle by putting on
a course in the first year. But there is also a lot of practical criticism. A
post-graduate comments: 'The idea is that it can all coexist quite happily
but it doesn't.' (96)

This hybrid situation enables us to gauge how students respond to theory.
I got some positive response:

> Doing an English course you can get too mixed up with analysing
> books and characters and things, whereas with literary theory you
> don't get so immersed in the book itself, you look outside, I really
> like that, I was able to sort out some of the concepts. (99)

> The psychoanalytical bit was interesting. It's all to do with sexuality.
> That's something I'd never done before, we didn't discuss that at
> school. But Marxism, deconstruction, structuralism, it just went over
> your head. (100)

But the reaction was overwhelmingly negative on the whole, and offers
a remarkable demonstration of the enormous resistance to new ways of
learning to learn and to reflexivity in general. Students found the course
'bewildering', 'irrelevant', 'pretentious', 'pointless', 'irritating', 'far-fetched',
'hostile', 'over my head' (*passim*); 'We did semi . . . semi . . . this is how much
it sunk in.' Diane expressed very clearly the resistance and its roots:

Boring. One thing I was good at at school was practical criticism and that came to me easily, so when they started putting names on it, I thought, 'No, I don't like this.' What would I be doing to a poem that I didn't know I was doing? It frightened me. (94)

To tell students selected on the basis of success at one activity that they have to abandon it in favour of something different is indeed to provoke that mixture of fear, resentment and passive resistance which is usually called boredom. And, as at Oxford, the students are reinforced in their resistance by resistant staff:

We had a conversation with our academic tutor last year and none of us could see the point of literary theory. He had a kind of *laissez-faire* attitude to it, and he said, 'Yes, I know, I look at these things but it's a waste of time, I take a liberal humanist approach. All these Marxist feminist things are a waste of time.' So we all just agreed with him because that seemed the right approach. (95)

One statement by a final-year student seemed particularly violent:

That first-year course in Critical Method, I was outraged really. All they seemed to do was to take everything apart, and made it into a science, took all the heart out of it. I would always be very angry after it. I have an insular and sentimental view of literature I think, and it hasn't changed. (92)

And in one sentence the same student sums up a common reaction to theory: 'I'm very sure, and I'll avoid anything that makes me unsure.' However, she goes on to express feelings that I did not hear expressed so strongly by anyone else: 'I hate the department. I don't find anything in common with anybody because of the variance in values. I'm made to feel that mine are inferior.'

It is not surprising that, faced with this degree of resistance and a clash of values as strong as this, staff members who have an allegiance to theory get into the confrontational situation that Professor Dover described at Cardiff. And, in the light of this, the cautious approach of Stirling becomes more understandable. This puts a spotlight on an enormous teaching problem in the humanities. University students are the result of a rigorous process of selection. They value themselves inevitably by the criteria used to value them. They may have an urge to extend their range but their strongest urge is to continue doing what has brought them success and approval. They do want to see more things but the last thing they want to do is to change their ways of seeing. This applies to the staff as well, as we have seen from the story of their resistance to seeing differently. But they are not being required to learn and develop as the students are, so the conflict is less apparent. It seems highly unlikely that teachers, however prestigious and gifted, will get students to change genuinely and funda- mentally, to engage in what Bateson calls 'Learning II' and Marton calls 'deep learning', without some way of overcoming the fear, and without it being in their interest to change.

The future

PNL

There is one institution where these problems have been largely solved – PNL. The students at PNL make statements about theory which are not made anywhere else. Mary Thorpe, a mature student and single parent:

> I love it, I can't get enough. I am reading Saussure and Barthes, and Althusser, and I wonder what hit me, because at the beginning of the year I thought, 'I'll never be able to read this,' then it started to make a bit more sense, and because of the way the course was structured you gain interest. I've caught the bug, it's something to do with PNL. The number of ideas they put across to you. They say, 'Try it, see what happens.' (89)

Simon, a mature student from Macclesfield, who left his secondary modern school at 16:

> It suddenly dawned on me that this was the heart of what we were doing. The Shakespeares and Brontës won't go away, and this is my chance to learn the critical theories which are the tools to do the job. (81)

Jennifer, a first-year student from an independent school in Bedford:

> A real revelation. You take the world as a natural place and you don't ever think of the way it's constructed, you don't think of language as a construction. It really felt as if I was being stripped raw of all belief in a given society, and suddenly I stood on very shaky ground, I didn't know who, where, what, why – very scary, but exciting. You are aware that underneath the surface there are all these forces going on that before you didn't comprehend, and sometimes now you still can't comprehend but you know they are there. (89)

Why has PNL succeeded in gaining such general acceptance for theory when other institutions have achieved at most a conflictual presence? An external examiner at PNL expressed the view that PNL was 'better than anywhere else I've seen at introducing students to primary texts and theory simultaneously.' This seems to be the key, integration. Other institutions tend to split thinking and feeling, reading and reflecting on reading:

> In Sussex you either did the twentieth-century literature MA or the Critical Theory. We were the theorists and they were the ones who liked reading the books. You need integrations. PNL is wonderful for

that. Through the discourse option it allows them to take theoretical issues on board but relates them to traditional English lit. (42)

The suggestion is that it is not enough to offer competing viewpoints and allow students to pick and choose. The head of school at PNL:

> In higher education people want to say they are pluralist. The problem is whether you look at it from the staff level or the student experience. If that variety of views is not placed in some kind of structure which is coherent, it's bewildering. (40)

This structure is provided by an interdisciplinary first-year course called 'Discourse', which uses a specially developed dossier containing material and teaching strategies. It was developed between 1986 and 1988 by three research assistants. It is taught over 14 weeks through lectures and associated seminars. The topics are: discourse theory; semiology of the visual image (Barthes); semiology of language (Saussure); constructing 'the real'; linguistic analysis (newspaper headlines); communication (Jakobson); author and text (Barthes, Foucault); psychoanalysis and the subject (Freud, Lacan); ideology; history; contesting meaning; realism. Almost everyone in the department has taught on the course.

Another feature of PNL is that they have made several highly specific theory appointments. The age pyramid is reasonable, the male–female ratio fairly balanced, and the whole group shares a broad consensus. I have included this account of PNL in a section called 'The future' because there is a sense in which it can be seen as having gone beyond the situation in which the universities now are to one which they might conceivably reach in the coming years. But the move happened very quickly in PNL and in ways connected to its nature as an institution. It seems crude, but one has to conclude that the difference in the response to theory in PNL and Newcastle is explicable by the class interests of the students:

> There was conflict. We had two people on the staff. C was into feminism, M into structuralism. They said that we were teaching in an old-fashioned way, and what we should be doing is structuralism. There were bitter arguments. On occasions they would get up and walk out having had a blazing row with everyone else. We have always had working-class, politically motivated students. The students were saying, 'We demand structuralism.' It happened quite quickly after that. The students would start forcing us to talk about Jakobson, then they were using technical language. Books started to appear in the library, and everyone was seen around with Terence Hawkes's book. The bastion crumbled. (41)

Paradoxically, because the splitting has been reduced pluralism is more acceptable. It is not universally known that there is a popular PNL course on Old Norse sagas: 'That's the difference between now and five years ago. You can be eclectic, you don't have to take up a position as a Lacanian or whatever.' (47)

One form of theory which has developed at PNL more than elsewhere and which has contributed to the ending of the splitting is reader response theory: 'Critical Theory is a move up into the head, with the exception of reader response theory, where you can turn the tables on theory and bring it back to what individuals are actually feeling.' (44) The basic dilemma of teaching literature is being confronted here. English as a subject is based on an act – reading – which is private, interior and strictly unobservable by the ethnographer watching in the library. The gap will not be bridged by checking on accuracy of recall. A reader who could miraculously re-write *Bleak House* from memory would not be giving an account of the experience of reading it. The experience is one of transformation, and forgetting is an essential part ('Without forgetting one is a parrot' – Paul Valéry). The social reality of the subject has to be based on accounts of this reading act, or on accounts of the act of reading accounts. But between experience and account there is a gap which reader response theory attempts to bridge:

> What we start with is a sheet of paper with little black marks on it, and after a certain time we are sitting there crying. I said to them, 'Tell me how this comes about. You can do a lot towards unpicking the mystery but you have to unpick a lot about yourself on the way.' (44)

This ties in with the number of creative writing courses offered, courses which are not designed to produce Booker Prize winners, but to enable students to approach texts in a different way. Instead of splitting the creative and the analytic they approach a text from the point of view of the writer:

> We are not saying, 'Is this [*Death of a Salesman*] a good play, and what's Arthur Miller saying?' We are saying, 'He has got two big requirements. He needs to keep the audience's attention and he needs to give them information. How is he doing this?' (44)

As for the theoretical discourses, psychoanalysis is, not surprisingly in view of the above, a dominant interest at PNL. But again the split is avoided because some of the staff have experience as analysands. Their motivation for going into analysis seems to have been both scholarly (the need to understand Freud or Lacan) and personal, though it is an open question to what extent the scholarly reason was a rationalization: 'Well, that was the reason I gave myself for going into it, that was the conscious reason. I did have one breakthrough – with no help from Lacan but a lot from the analyst.' The influence of Marxist thought has declined with the move to pluralism:

> The theory I am interested in now is semiotics, post-structuralism, post-Marxist. The Marxist theory that I was taught was Marxism as a science, as a theory of history, the reason why certain kinds of ideas are dominant at a certain period. The influence of post-structuralism

and political events of the past five years means that a lot of people I know who once would have described themselves as Marxists, would do so now with a small M. They no longer believe in it as a science of history. It's increasingly regarded as just another discourse, which for historical reasons arose at a particular time to contest the ideology of Victorian Europe. It's the end of meta-narrative, you can no longer make the claim that this version stands above all others in theoretical purity. (43)

Overall, PNL represents the way that the various aspects of the subject can be integrated. The original experience of reading, the precognitive, is allowed to cross the institutional boundary rather than being seen as exclusively private, and the precognitive activity of writing is also allowed in, and both are theorized by a psychoanalytic awareness and made operational through pedagogical strategies which favour negotiation and exchange. A whole series of splits have been addressed: writing–reading, thinking–feeling, masculine–feminine, creative–receptive, private–public. This could well be the future for the universities. On the other hand it could well not.

Paradigms and generations

I have fallen again into the trap of seeing present and future neatly distinguished. In one sense the future already exists in the universities in the form of new lecturers who may be 30 years younger than those who introduced theory 20 years ago. This is consonant with what one knows of paradigm shifts. As Max Planck wrote, a new paradigm 'does not triumph by convincing its opponents and making them see the light, but rather because its opponents eventually die, and a new generation grows up that is familiar with it' (quoted in Kuhn 1970: 151). So while it is important to look at the experience of the older members of staff, new entrants to the subject are in some ways more significant. Dr Clay has just been appointed to his first post and compares himself with someone just ten years older:

He's a theorist, but he discovered it after he'd had his education, and realized it would be a good thing. For me it was part and parcel of my education. I had David Lodge as a tutor. The tutors I liked had taken feminism on board. I didn't have to go through the structuralist controversies, it was just part of the business of being aware of what we were doing. (54)

Dr Jameson is in his first year. His research in Oxford has been traditional scholarship. He sees theory as important 'not so much for my research, as for my teaching. I'm a fellow traveller as regards theory, and I want to teach myself by teaching students.' (59) The question is how the generations can coexist. A traditional scholar:

The last conference I went to, all the papers by anyone under 30 or 40 were critical theory. Bakhtin was the buzzword. I don't think they understand very much about what [that author] is going on about. The idea that we used to have that we could somehow link into these people and the worlds that they came from has gone. Subjects like that have become texts for theoretical discussion, whereas I have an inkling that you can tap into something that happened in the past and understand it. You're the agent somehow. I think that texts are repositories of truth, and although these ideas have been under fire, it still strikes me that's what we are doing and that's what the students are doing, when they are writing essays and so on. (16)

The older generation is established and may continue to propagate values like these. It may be possible to go on teaching without assimilating theory, or by gaining a nodding acquaintance. ('There are plenty of bluffer's guides around' (2).) But it is more and more difficult to publish: 'Critical Theory people have the market. That's where the publishing racket is.' (22) People's long-established specialities are being invaded by theory: 'The deconstructionists have moved in on Romantic studies in a big way.' (20) The new generation has to have something which the old generation doesn't know in order to compete, because the old generation by definition knows so many of those things which the younger generation doesn't know: 'It's a generational thing. You've got to have your place to stand.' (59)

I was fortunate to find a Canadian post-graduate who was actually looking for a job in America, and using the bi-annual MLA job information lists. He summarized:

1,500 jobs on offer, not more than 25 are for someone who is primarily interested in theory, and, of those, a dozen are looking for people who can teach theory to undergraduates, survey courses. What your own theoretical interests are, is irrelevant. You teach the tools. Most of the jobs say 'period plus theory'. Theory is a base for teaching and getting a job. If you're anti-theoretical it would be hard to get a job. (74)

There is no reason to think that the situation (apart from the number of jobs) is very different in Britain. So it seems as if to make a career now as an English Person you need two strings to your bow, and one of them must be theory. This is in contradiction to the fears of the older generation that theory is an alternative to 'knowledge': 'There's been a a brisk institutionalization of it, people who feel that they need to know nothing whatsoever about the eighteenth century or the twentieth century who still have to know about literary theory to be a Victorian specialist.' (53)

So the young are furthering their careers by theory. But they are also questioning theory, not at all from the Leavisite position of their elders, but in more radical ways. They seem to be questioning a use of theory which 'comes to the aid of conventional Eng. lit. – new ways to do old things'. (74) They are more purist about using translation, more European. They see theory as being over-cautious, particularly with regard to criticizing the educational institution itself and its forms. They are perhaps more systemic: 'There are a lot a drawbacks with theory and the way it's taught. It's important to see that the study of literature is all part of a system and it's not the only system. You must question the foundation and the boundaries.' (1)

This analysis does have long-term consequences for one institution in particular – Oxford. Oxford is important in Britain as a graduate centre. Dr Stone previously taught in a provincial university, and sees the number of graduate students she has at Oxford as the main advantage of her move. But Oxford's reticence about theory and its examination system means that it is not producing post-graduates as one might expect: 'My best students are being disenfranchised, the students that one would hand over the future to. Serious sustained work must be reduced to a one-hour answer in an examination paper. Who's going to come back to Oxford?' (25) There is an awareness of the problem – 'The colleges are not like market-led institutions responding to demand' – but there are pressures, 'because theory has been on the board everywhere else and post-graduates have theory interests, so they look for places where they can pursue them.' (74) This was one of the reasons for appointing Terry Eagleton to the Wharton Chair and overriding the hostility. A respondent closely involved in the selection process gave the reason: 'He would be a magnet for recruiting graduates, a figurehead. He would say that theory existed at Oxford. Otherwise, looking at the syllabus, they might get the impression it didn't.'

Following the advice of the young theorist cited above, we will now move to foundation and boundary matters: first the boundaries of English as a discipline and then, in the final chapter, the crucial foundation question of the link between English and England.

eight

Discipline

We with our quick dividing eyes
Measure, distinguish and are gone.
The forest burns, the tree frog dies,
Yet one is all and all are one.
              (Judith Wright, 1985, 'Phantom Dwelling', in *Rainforest*)

Global: group/discipline/subject

Since my whole project centres on the notion of discipline it behoves me
to address the difficult question of definition. What do people mean when
they say that they or others are 'English People'? The ambiguity of my title
is deliberate, since the problem is the same whether we are talking about
disciplines or nations, and indeed the analogy is commonly drawn (Becher
1989: 172, note 3).

Group

The essential notion is that of *group*. We see ourselves as members of various
groups, and we are seen by others as members of various groups. These
groups have two kinds of names: a generic name for the type of group they
are (discipline, profession, nation, tribe); and a specific, proper name for
each generic instance. So this is a tribe, the Apaches; this is a discipline,
English.

The group is used to deal with identity questions, to answer the questions
'Who am I?' or 'Who are you?' There are considerable advantages for an
individual in being able to answer both questions clearly, and disadvantages in not being able to. These advantages are: (a) practical, by being
recognized as a member of a group I gain group protection and multiply
myself; and (b) psychological, if I have a clear idea of who I am and who
others are this gives me a sense of permanence which makes the world
more secure and predictable. The paradigm case is a team game: if I know

(a) that I am a member of a team (generic) and this team is Welsh and plays rugby union, and (b) that you are a member of the French rugby union team, then we can get on with our business. There are advantages for groups as well as individuals: a group which is not sure what group it is, or even what generic group it is, is less effective than one which is sure.

Discipline

We will look at nationality in the next chapter. Here let us consider discipline.

When people use the generic term discipline, what are they doing? They are, I think, doing two things. They are referring to (a) an abstract map of knowledge, and (b) an institutional map of the way departments, schools, faculties, institutes, centres, etc. are organized. In *Language People* I called the first the *discipline* and the second the *subject*. An actual group is defined by reference to both.

The generic term discipline implies reference to some abstract structure, the world of knowledge seen as a whole. But while poets and Parmenides can affirm this, for practical purposes people need distinctions between trees and frogs. So this totality is comprised of various parts, which themselves are sub-divided. We may think of it as a computer tree: root, directory, sub-directory . . . ; language, linguistics, psycho-linguistics, bilingualism . . .

'Studying a field of knowledge means investigating its hierarchical structure', wrote Lowe in 1971 (p. 141). And at that time American epistemologists were developing this kind of cognitive model of knowledge: Bloom (of the taxonomy), Gagné, Bruner and Schwab shared the view that a discipline was a part of the whole world of knowledge, with a clear principle of coherence or core and a clear boundary separating it from other disciplines or sub-disciplines. The metaphor was a pyramid and it derived basically from the sciences. It coexisted with another metaphor, knowledge as a territory which could be mapped, with the map being coloured to reveal the explored and unexplored areas: even when one did not know where the unexplored areas actually were, one knew they were there, rather as fossil fuel resources are calculated to allow for still-to-be-discovered lakes and seams.

In my conclusion to *Language People* I went along with this notion to some extent, inventing my own pyramid, which had communication near the top and modern languages as a sub-directory of that. This metaphor of levels is deeply ingrained. Here is Becher (1990: 334) using it with a wide sweep:

> At a very general level, we can regard knowledge as an undifferentiated phenomenon . . . But we may also operate with broad sub-divisions, such as those between the sciences and the humanities or between

pure and applied investigations ... In more detailed discussion, we would in all probability need to focus on individual disciplinary fields ... However, there are also valid and useful distinctions to be made below this familiar level of analysis ... it is possible to explore the nature – both epistemological and social – of sub-units of varying scales within what is defined as a single discipline.

The key to knowing your discipline (your group) in this perspective is knowing your core, your essence, your principle of coherence. You also need to know your boundaries, but this is secondary because, if someone else's core is different, they are by definition beyond your boundaries. You should also know your place in the hierarchy (where you would be if you 'paged' up or down, what the other sub-directories are on your level).

The core can be generically various. It can be the *material*: rocks for the geologists, literature for English People. But it can also be a question of *technique*: crystallography, close reading or statistical analysis. And it could be *theory*: Marxist or Structuralist.

People need to place themselves on a mental map of knowledge, and the map is likely to be some combination of the territory and the pyramid, a set of coordinates involving material, technique and theory. People will have, as Becher says, a very large-scale, taken-for-granted map – science, humanities – to which they will not give much attention. But nearer their own area they will have, or attempt to have, a more detailed sense of where they are. In order to see themselves as part of a discipline, individuals refer to some abstract concept or label which they read off this map. The actual experience of belonging to the discipline (or joining it) is one whereby we continually check whether the label still suits, whether we still are where we think we are on the map and whether the map is still accurate. (In this context 'accurate' can only mean 'shared by others', since it is characteristic that these maps only exist in the mind; we may in fact spend time and energy trying to impose a particular map of the totality or of our part of the totality.)

Subject

This abstract map in the mind is in relationship with the actual organization of people and things. When I was writing *Language People* and thinking about these concepts, a committee in my university was engaged in redrawing the intellectual map of the university; for example, eliminating completely the Faculty of Social Science by merging it with the Faculty of Arts, putting psychology unequivocally in the Faculty of Sciences, grouping English literature, English language, journalism and philosophy into one school and cost centre. This particular exercise was effected for severely practical reasons by severely practical men (and one severely practical woman) but they still kept an eye on the abstract disciplinary map: a suggestion that the School of Architecture should be merged with the Centre for Population Studies and called the 'School of Town and Family Planning' was turned down. This institutional realization of the abstract map I call the 'subject'. In *Language People* I used the work of the British sociologists of education, Young, Bernstein and Lacey, in contrast to the American writers, to illustrate this aspect of the social organization of knowledge.

'Disciplinary culture' is really, it seems to me now, the interaction of discipline and subject and, as Becher and Huber point out in the special issue of the *European Journal of Education* on 'Disciplinary cultures' (1990), it is a new specialism in need of clear operational distinctions – something which is easier said than done. This publication and Becher's *Academic Tribes and Territories* (1989) have enabled me to see the issues with more clarity. I was helped by a useful difference of opinion between Huber and Becher. Huber sees disciplines ('subjects' in my terminology) anthropologically, predominantly as 'social constructions'. This is the relativist attitude. Huber is dubious about the realist attitude (represented by Becher and Clark), which 'sees the nature of knowledge as a clue to the key characteristics of disciplinary culture' (Becher and Huber 1990: 238) and 'the epistemological characteristics of the domain of knowledge . . . as causes of the disciplinary cultures which cultivate them' (242). In my own contribution to the journal issue I can now see that I was describing a mismatch between discipline and subject in modern languages and saying that the various cognitive maps in the mind which the inhabitants of modern languages departments hold are particularly heterogeneous. There was one paragraph where I used my experience of group relations work and my reading of Bateson to declare that

> a disciplinary culture is not to be understood in an essentialist way, as the variegated realization of some original essence; our job is not to work our way ethnographically through the leaves and branches of the oak to the original acorn. Like an individual, a disciplinary culture is a shifting and fragile homeostatic system – a particular and unique equilibrium of opposing forces, a method for avoiding or attempting to avoid *schismogenesis* (breakdown resulting from unchecked, dialectically heightened oppositions) while evolving and adapting to changing environments.
>
> (Evans 1990b: 275)

This statement seems to place me very much in the anthropological, social-construct camp with Huber. But in fact what I was attempting to say was that an essential part of the experience of the socially constructed group (subject) is one of perceived consonance or dissonance with the hypothesized (fantasized) platonic world of coherent, bounded entities in hierarchical relationship (this is not the same as the real or imagined belonging to *other* socially constructed groups – the 'invisible college' of researchers, the cosmopolites, living the conference life, as opposed to the localites and the administrative life).

In this sense the discipline/subject is a system of the type that Palmer and Reed (1992) call recursive or containing:

> Systems as patterns of relatedness which persist through time and so define an identity which can in principle be named . . . in the short term they exhibit homeostasis (like-standing) : they respond to changes and conditions so that their form does not vary outside narrow limits. In the longer term they change and unfold in accordance with their own internal logic . . . or they may undergo metamorphosis.

What this does, I think, is to change the dominant metaphor. A homeostatic system involving groups in the mind is not an oak tree or a computer tree or a map or a territory.

The homeostatic system is not the only alternative metaphor. Hoskin (1993) writes of a 'knowledge ecosystem' where 'there is no place for one overarching unitary truth'. Becher (1989), in his chapter on 'Overlaps, boundaries and specialisms', describes work which is based on other metaphors – the network (Polanyi), the chain (Polanyi), the honeycomb (Crane), the fish-scale (Campbell) – all of which have the characteristic of being horizontal, not vertical, and of excluding the notion of the superordinate. Small units (specialisms) exist and, like fish-scales, overlap with other small units. Operationally, what we have then are 'loose amalgamations of segments pursuing different objectives in different manners and more or less delicately held together under a common name at a particular period of history' (Bucher and Strauss, quoted in Becher 1989: 44). This is recognizably what happens and it is reconcilable with the homeostatic metaphor. It also has the virtue of incorporating a certain nominalism: the name or label which the group gives itself is an important factor in the recursive creation and maintenance of the group, specialism or amalgamation, and it can operate in a pre and post way: I join a group called English and become English; the name or label pre-exists my joining the group. But when I am in the group I may propose that the name should be changed because it no longer corresponds to my idea of what the group 'really' is; or else my own contributions may radically change the reality behind the label which is nevertheless unchanged.

The pure and the hybrid

Becher (1989) refers to one author whose reflections on these problems seem particularly useful, the cultural anthropologist Clifford Geertz. Geertz is relevant particularly for the insight he brings into the ways we conceptualize disciplines; and this as a specific case of the more general issue of how we divide up the world. But, as an anthropologist, he is also highly aware of the complex links between (a) the dominant pattern or metaphor, the way the world is punctuated, the choice of generic names for the divisions (what I call 'discipline'); and (b) social constructions linked to (not necessarily based on) that pattern or metaphor (what I call 'subject').

So the university has to divide up the work (indeed, in a way, universities are organizations for enacting maps of knowledge). And how it divides up the work – faculties, schools, departments, sections, centres – bears some relation to a particular model of knowledge. But what that relation is is obscure: one thing one can safely say is that it is out of synch – the institutional structure is likely to be at variance with the map in the mind.

I say this by way of preface to describing Geertz's views since one thing he underlines is the effect on institutions like universities of the intellectual development he describes. This development is that of the demise of the disciplinary paradigm based on 'hard–pure' science, according to which the soft–applied and the hard–applied (these terms are not his) were immature sciences and the social sciences were in the business of becoming more 'mature' sciences, maturity being defined by the criteria of physics (experiments, replicability, etc.). The soft–pure disciplines (the arts) were anomalous in the whole system: clearly hopelessly immature, but nevertheless wise in some other mysterious way which the model could not encompass (which did not stop individuals in the arts striving for maturity and scientific validity). Geertz's (1983) thesis is that the social sciences are moving away from being aspirant hard sciences. The nineteenth-century metaphors in which social phenomena were likened to interacting forces have not worked: 'Laws-and-causes social physics was not producing the triumphs of prediction, control and testability that had for so long been promised in its name' (Geertz 1983: 3). The move, then, is from a laws-and-instances ideal of explanation to a cases-and-interpretation one. The effect of this is the blurring of the genres which is the subject of Geertz's essay. The more significant blurring for our purposes is that between the humanistic and the social sciences. Geertz puts it like this:

> Grand rubrics like 'Natural Science', 'Biological Science', 'Social Science', and 'The Humanities' have their uses in organizing curricula, in sorting scholars into cliques and professional communities, and in distinguishing broad traditions of intellectual style. And, of course, the sorts of work conducted under any one of them do show some general resemblances to one another and some genuine differences from the sorts that are conducted under the others . . . But when these rubrics are taken to be the borders-and-territories map of modern intellectual life, or, worse, a Linnaean catalogue into which to classify scholarly species, they merely block from view what is really going on out there where men and women are thinking about things and writing down what it is they think.
>
> (Geertz 1983: 7)

In other words the tendency is to take the subject as an accurate mapping of the discipline, with the result that one fails to understand the subject; or rather that the discipline is being conceived in terms of a metaphor (map, territory, Linnaean catalogue) which hides the subject from view.

Geertz is able to refer to an impressive range of evidence for his blurred genre theory – that, over a whole range of phenomena, cultural producers and consumers are becoming less intolerant of the hybrid, less enamoured of the pure, more able to tolerate ambiguity. He invokes French writers Foucault and Barthes (whom he calls splendidly 'all purpose subversives'): 'Something is happening, not a change in the map but an alteration of the principle of mapping' (Geertz 1983: 4).

Another anthropologist, Mary Douglas (1966: 53) sees the demand for 'purity' or 'holiness' in Leviticus, for example, as the requirement that 'individuals shall conform strictly to the class to which they belong . . . and that different classes of things shall not be confused.' Clothes should not be made from 'two kinds of stuff', 'fields should not be sown with two kinds of seed'. The clear genre is a sign not of the modern but of the archaic.

Sartre, whom Douglas quotes, saw this attachment to purity and hatred of what he called the *visqueux* as constitutional of humanity. Human beings desire the solidity, the firm boundaries of the *en-soi*, of (classifiable) stones and crystals, and fear the fluidity of the *pour-soi* – existence, consciousness. Douglas, like Sartre, sees that life is a tension between these opposite needs:

> It is part of our condition that the purity for which we strive . . . turns out to be hard and dead as stone when we get it . . . Purity is the enemy of change, of ambiguity and compromise . . . the yearning for rigidity is in us all. It is part of our human condition to long for hard lines and clear concepts. When we have them we have either to face the fact that some realities elude them or else blind ourselves to the inadequacy of the concepts. The search for purity . . . is an attempt to force experience into logical categories of non-contradiction. But experience is not amenable, and those who make the attempt find themselves led into contradiction.
>
> (Douglas 1966: 161–2)

And she opposes order and disorder: 'Though we seek to create order, we do not simply condemn disorder. We recognize that it is destructive to existing patterns; also that it has potentiality' (Douglas 1966: 95). Primitive people recognize the power of the simpleton to wander in disorder and bring back order. The artist is a modern version of this and thus those who speak for the artist have a vested interest in resisting order, classification and purity.

It is not possible to resist them completely, however. The art for individuals is to hold on to the idea of *different forms of order*, different metaphors, while living and working in specific organizations as members of specific but multiple groups. We could put it differently: to be a member of a discipline means to be able to think metaphorically and to have a variety of metaphors at one's disposal rather than being locked in one. It also means, here as elsewhere, living a tension between the subject, the institutionalized face-to-face group, and the discipline, the mental construct, and the real or imaginary people who share it.

Local: cores and boundaries

It's a huge problem, isn't it? How do you define English? (42)

Reflections

Let us now make the leap from these abstract reflections back to real English People, an activity that Geertz (1983: 69) calls 'tacking between the most local of local detail and the most global of global structure ... hopping back and forth between the whole conceived through the parts that actualize it and the part conceived through the whole that motivates them.'

The English People who have reflected most about these issues are, not surprisingly, the theory people, though I would not say that it was a major intellectual focus for many. Professor Edgeworth expressed considerable scepticism about the whole question of disciplinary (subject) boundaries. He sees them as arbitrary or historically based: 'Most of them come from German universities in the nineteenth century, and they are used to keep people in or out.' His view of English at the moment is that 'we are teaching a whole range of things which are only peripherally related to the traditional idea of English,' and he would like his department to be renamed Critical and Cultural Studies: 'But you would need to open up to lots of other disciplines then, sociology, politics, history, philosophy and linguistics.' He rejects the idea of some master discipline (the pyramid), in favour of something that sounds like the fish-scale or network model. 'Cultural studies could be not a master discipline but a space where these other interests could come together.' But then suddenly he becomes aware of the institutional problems, of the advantages of professional identity: 'Literary critics talk about Husserl without the necessary technical background. Critical theorists get asked to give lectures in law departments or music departments but this may mean that those departments abandon their own forms of argument and therefore their standards.'

I might add that this is the difference between confident public utterance like that of Geertz and private communications like that of my respondents; uncertainty and ambivalence surface more in the latter than in the former. And this is a mirror of what happens when a personal interest enters the institution. The abstract notion of discipline (involving denial of contradiction and ambiguity) intervenes:

> Once you put it into a university and make it a discipline it has to be seen to be a discipline. The notion of what constitutes a discipline is scientific and mathematical. So you make it more scientific, Northrop Frye and so on. Not that those things aren't useful, but they are not the answer to the fundamental questions of the discipline. What you have to hang on to is that readers are individuals who have responses. (51)

Both subject and discipline are constraining with respect to the individual. Individuals negotiate with discipline and subject in order to find a container which will protect without excluding: 'I have a wide variety of interests, which I'm still trying to contain. The institutional framework in which to pursue these interests led by a process of elimination to English.' (74) Once they are in, they refer to disciplines while inhabiting the subject: 'I see myself as a cultural historian. Literature plus visual art, plus language, plus Italian. I teach English, but I don't see myself as an "English literature major". English is incredibly flexible.' (25)

There are great advantages in this flexibility and openness. One is that the subject is in touch with (or, if we redefine it, includes) people outside the institutional boundary. Barbara illustrates well the weak framing:

> When I used to tell people I was doing a psychology degree, before I stopped, I used to get a very strong reaction. I used to get things like, 'Are you going to analyse me?', or 'What's that?' My flatmate does environmental science, and they think she gets rats out of houses. But when you tell them you're doing English they feel quite cosy with it. They say, 'Oh, who's your favourite author then?'

And Dr James sees it as a virtue:

> I'm committed to the idea that criticism should be written in as plain a language as possible. Because I'm worried that the common reader will disappear. I am against the elitism of a critical theory which makes discussion of literature impossible for the man in the street. (29)

But there are weaknesses in this position. One respondent went with her husband (not an English Person) to a professor's inaugural lecture. At the end of it she said to her husband, 'I could have done that', and he replied, 'So could I.'

This is the strength of theory: 'At least you feel they're doing something that the ordinary man in the street couldn't do.' Without some disciplinary distinction, there are, as one lecturer put it 'very real problems in maintaining the strength of the group'. (29) For staff, ultimately, the *subject*, which could well be a group of people reading books, needs to meet the *discipline*. A theory person:

> There is resistance to professionalization, or to specialization. But why should a university have a faculty full of people who are simply as well-educated as any well-educated person? Why should you get paid to do what every articulate person does? (27)

The answer to this appears obvious and yet, while English People seem not to have a discipline like others, at the same time they are not seen as having no discipline at all.

People within the subject have a nervousness about it being a soft option but in actual experience of colleagues in other disciplines one detects in their attitudes towards people in the subject a certain kind of – reverence would be too strong a word – but a kind of respect as though there were something faintly magical about this ability to be so absorbed in literature. (6)

This is less likely to happen, it seems, with students. The weak framing makes them anxious about whether they have studied a subject at all, and this is most noticeable when they think of the attitude of employers, as mediated by fellow students who are doing subjects which are, in terms of materials and technique, more strongly framed:

What worries me is what is going to happen when I leave university with an English degree. I think people will get the impression that I did English at school, couldn't think of anything else to do, so I did English at university, whereas for me in fact it was the end of a long decision-making process. (66)

Students are aware of how curious the subject's techniques and working practices appear to others. Mark shares a flat with a business studies student, Pete:

In writing essays, I usually read the text and then sit down with my feet up for a couple of hours or a couple of weeks, and just think about it. I even worry myself that I'm not actually doing much here but when I actually sit down to write the essay it just comes out, and I suddenly realize that in my mind I have actually been weighing it up and putting it into some kind of order. This infuriates them. Pete is annoyed that I'm going to come out with a degree and he is as well. He just doesn't believe it when I say, 'Well okay, sometimes I stay in bed till 10 o'clock but I'm thinking when I'm doing it.' (65)

Nevertheless, Mark is confident: 'I think I have a much wider view of the world, a bigger concept of the way things are, than he has. I'm going to come out of university a lot better off than he does, I will come out of it understanding things more, which is the important thing for me.' (65)

Not all are as confident. Desperate for some specialized technical core (equivalent to the linguist's competence in a foreign language), students can be reduced to asserting that they can spell: 'I say to them [business studies people], "Your grammar's appalling, you don't know how to spell."' (94) 'Employers like to see a piece of paper saying "Degree in English literature", because they think, "At least they know how to speak the Queen's English reasonably well. Perhaps they won't make spelling mistakes." (70) And staff can go along with this. A Stirling student reports: 'For essay marking, absolutely everything is corrected, and in other subjects it wouldn't be.' (69) Anglo-Saxon is a more esoteric form of technical core serving the same purpose.

Everyone may recognize that 'the disciplinary boundary is really a boundary of convenience', that 'it's been fluid for a long time but people have refused to recognize its fluidity', that 'it's going to be more and more difficult to maintain a purity of disciplinary boundaries'. Nevertheless, the subject, that is the group of people in the institution, has to operate across boundaries with the environment, and for that it cannot rely on magic. It needs an identity and a label.

The environment means the university itself and also the market-place:

> We had this discussion at the staff level: should this degree be called an English degree, given that we do Australian literature and so on? We come up against this fact that the students come to do an English degree. It's not clear what you would call it that would continue to attract people and also describe what we do. (47)

In the market-place labels are important. They determine choice:

> You can't do English much in polytechnics, it's communication and media studies and things. I wanted to do something that wasn't journalism and radio and television, I wanted to do English literature. Polytechnics seem to be more vocationally orientated. (104)

But the need for definition is not only instrumental. There is a need in staff and especially in students for identity:

> What I want is not so much to reconstitute the subject of English as to give the students more identity as students of English. They find it quite hard to work out a pattern, or make sense of their degree as an English degree. If they are doing women's studies, film studies, Irish studies or whatever, I think they do have a strong sense of what it means to be in those subjects. They often say they feel English is very disparate. It also takes away from their understanding of the subject. If they just do an individual unit, where is the coherence, or the rationale for why they do one rather than another? They develop all sorts of rationales – the assessment pattern, stuff that they like, or how it fits in with their part-time job. There's not an internal rationale. (47)

In other words, the subject aspects (assessment etc.) cannot give identity, and the subject as practised (at PNL in this case) does not have the clarity of definition of the other subjects mentioned (film, women, Irish) because the *material* is not as precise: 'The poor things have nothing. They have very good, very interesting units, but no particular reason for putting them together.' (47)

One solution might be to base the core, the 'internal rationale', on theory rather than material, and PNL is indeed thinking of extending the interdisciplinary Discourse unit. But this is close to metamorphosis: 'Some people think that that might be the end of English as a subject.' Another suggestion: 'Instead of a content core – Shakespeare – have a methodological core – the spirit of enquiry, neural networks . . . '. But no sooner has this idea been expressed than it is seen to be impossible: 'This doesn't fit with any sort of institutional structure at all.' (53)

In the real world what counts, for a discipline, is the material: 'People have said to me, "But we really have to concentrate on what's central to the discipline." When we went over to a modular system the issue of the core – what was to be compulsory – became uppermost, and we had big fights about it.' (53)

What then is the core? If English must be a discipline what kind of discipline is it? 'English would like to think of itself as a summation.' (2) So would they all, but as I argued above, this computer tree, 'master-discipline' model is no longer available. What about a modest, clearly defined fish-scale? The proponents of cultural studies are open to this kind of thinking. But the reality of the experience of the discipline for most English people is that of competing, rather than overlapping, sub-groups. Individuals inhabit the subject English in a particular institution, while being conscious of particular disciplines which may or may not be subjects themselves. This will become clearer through some examples.

Language

Once a group starts to think in terms of a core, particularly a materials core, it is working at achieving group identity and escaping the weak framing but it is also risking break-up. 'English' has a deep split, with historical roots, between the notion that the core material is language and the notion that it is literature.[1] The split is enacted between institutions but also within institutions. As always, it is not so much on/off, either/or, as figure/ground. Either knowledge of language is used to illuminate texts or texts are used to illuminate language. In theory, it should be possible to switch easily between one and the other. In practice this division is a dramatic example of the problems of institutionalizing cognitive mind-maps when they are seen as territories.

Dr Daniels, linguistician in a department of literature, imagines a new pyramid which would have language as the superordinate term and literature as an 'instanciation' of language. He sees the importance of understanding language, and of having a meta-language in which to talk about it. Continental students and British modern languages students, he says, have this conceptual framework but students of English do not.

So, in a sense, Dr Daniels is one of the Language People, aware that, for the world, 'English' is language and not literature. (He has followed the transformation of the British Council from an organization devoted to literature to one devoted to language.) This is his experience in 'discipline' terms. In terms of the subject he is completely isolated: 'I do not have an academic life here because I've got no one to talk to'.

One would expect an alliance with theory people. One of these (from another place) stated clearly:

I do think language is at the heart of it. It's language we have to look at. Anyone who is working with language seems to be getting to where it really counts. (17)

But no, the disciplinary groups cannot meet as equals in the subject:

> There's no common cause with theory. They would say I ought to get my literary theory right, and I would say they ought to get their linguistics right. There's a conceptual boundary between me and my colleagues. I have to adopt their way of talking about texts. (4)

And he cannot use his linguistic knowledge with students either: 'I have to take my linguistic hat off when I'm teaching literature.'

In Newcastle, the split has progressed but is not complete, since the two departments remain within the same school. There are practical, institutional reasons for inter-group resentment:

> We have a lot of people applying for the literature degree, and a lot less for the language/literature degree. We've had equal quotas for those degrees. We're having to reject good candidates for the literature degree, take poorer candidates for the languages degree, who, after the first year, switch over. To put it at its rudest, we're bolstering up our language colleagues. And we're teaching like maniacs. When you've done a 16-hour week, in my case this week, and you meet a colleague who has just done three with classes of four, it's rather annoying. (53)

The students perceive the difference in status:

> When you are doing language in a department where there is English literature you do get marginalized. A lot of the English literature lecturers look at us as if we're inferior. There'll be a briefing for the whole department, but the head of department will come to us and say, 'Oh, I don't know about the English language courses, you'll have to ask someone else about them'. People don't recognize the English language as something of value. They see language very much as a kind of ancillary. (101)

Anglo-Saxon

It is impossible to discuss the notion of language as the core without considering the esoteric but burning question of compulsory Anglo-Saxon at Oxford. Teachers of Anglo-Saxon are language people, particularly with regard to the technique aspect; an Anglo-Saxon class is a translation class, identical in form with translation classes in the classics or in modern languages. Dr Sage specializes in Old Norse and teaches Anglo-Saxon. But is it English?

> No, it's not. It's a completely bogus connection. It's not a sensible place to have it. It ought really to be part of an Institute of

Scandinavian Studies, as it is in UCL. I'm conscious of the odd situation I'm in, which is researching something that really doesn't have much to do with English at all. (31)

This is one position. But there are others. Oxford is the quintessence of English, Anglo-Saxon is the quintessence of the quintessence. More than the tutorial system perhaps, compulsory Anglo-Saxon is perceived as the Ark of the Covenant. (Though there is also a move to make it less visibly different by speaking rather of 'Old English' and 'Middle English', which is a way of using language to incorporate that particular kind of text into the category which includes Shakespeare and James Joyce.)

The issue became controversial in 1991, when Valentine Cunningham, English tutor at Corpus Christi, published an article in *Oxford Magazine* calling for the abolition of compulsory Anglo-Saxon and in general attacking the curriculum for being a 'dinosauric museum-piece'. In the classical way, this was taken up by the quality press (an article by Nicolas de Jongh, *Guardian* 18 July 1991) and followed up by various letters and an editorial (19 July 1991, 22 July 1991), ending with a contrary view from a student, Freya Rowe, in the *Oxford Magazine* (no. 75, 1991). Rowe reports a survey she conducted which shows, she says, that 'students would like to maintain Oxford's traditionalism as a specialty'.

The relatively small number of students I interviewed seemed to confirm that there is, if anything, among students a majority in favour of retaining compulsory Anglo-Saxon – especially among those who have already done it. Julian, a final-year student:

> I'm in favour. It's an essential grounding. The danger is you learn the translation parrot-fashion, but even then it gives you a sense of continuity, a sense of feeding. In the sixties and seventies you did Anglo-Saxon all three years. I think that was wrong, but it's now placed very intelligently at the beginning. It's absolutely essential. (78)

For students it may be that the very fact that Anglo-Saxon (like the one-to-one tutorial) is eccentric is a positive feature. Its position at the beginning of the course also gives it a rite-of-passage aspect, which seems always to have been present: in Birmingham at one time, the prize for doing well in Anglo-Saxon was to be allowed to give it up. (5) For some students, this particular kind of study has a powerful impact: 'The thought of reading *Beowulf* actually used to make my heart leap. I was just thrilled at the idea of having to do with Anglo-Saxon.' (57)

Students are capable of responding to the singularity of Anglo-Saxon while still disapproving:

> We were looking forward to it. Our attitude was this is a joke. We are just going through it. Like at A level the things I enjoyed most are the things I wouldn't have chosen to study myself. But don't get me wrong. I think the idea of compulsory Anglo-Saxon is completely

barbaric, and it puts off hundreds and hundreds of people. The people who have done Latin and Greek got on much better. The people who haven't done Latin and Greek didn't have a clue what the tutor was talking about. (75a)

From the teacher's point of view there is of course a trade union aspect to this: there are a lot of medievalists in Oxford, and they need work: 'I've got a vested interest in keeping it compulsory, so that it keeps the hours for medievalists up and makes my chance of getting a permanant job better.' (31) The *Guardian* editorial I referred to makes a comparison with 'the shop-stewarded Cowley of 12 years ago'. But there are more lofty arguments, which come down to conservationism. 'If you don't have compulsory Anglo-Saxon, soon there will be no one reading that body of literature.' (50) What Oxford doesn't do today, London doesn't do tomorrow.

Anglo-Saxon can be seen as a metaphor for all sorts of valuable old things which are threatened by the modern world. Paul summed up what he thought Anglo-Saxon was saying in Oxford – 'We're not peripheral. We are central and we deal in this central canon' (75b) – and this may be the basic idea: the spatial idea of the core, the centre, has been made chronological and turned into a myth of origin. But ultimately, beyond abstract debate, the concrete reality of the pedagogic practice – or rather the unreality of it – affects everyone, especially the staff. Dr Sage, a specialist, says she passed the examination by using a crib 'and most people in the faculty did as well':

> That's what students are doing in reality. Everyone knows that they are, and I find it embarrassing to collude with the students in the pretence that this is actually an intellectual exercise, when it's memorizing the Everyman or the Penguin translation. I tell them, 'Don't put *chalice* there, find something else, cup or something.' To start off the whole Anglo-Saxon course with this, 'I know you're using translations to prepare your work, but I'll pretend I don't know,' and say, 'Oh well done' at the end of your stint of translation, is damaging because it means they don't take the rest of the subject at all seriously. I can't see myself, if I have a permanent post, teaching the same dreary course year after year. I'd get much more archaeology and art in as well, and translate less and give them a bigger variety of texts to look at. (31)

The problem is not ultimately the material itself or its arbitrary connection with other materials collected under the heading 'English': in that sense, Anglo-Saxon is no odder than *Singin' in the Rain*. It is the compulsory rite-of-passage aspect. It is not difficult to justify Anglo-Saxon as a specialist study (as in Cambridge, where it is an option in the Anglo-Saxon, Norse and Celtic tripos). It is difficult to justify *Beowulf* being compulsory while *Paradise Lost* is optional.

Literature

Where literature and language coexist to form the subject, literature is dominant, and, of the various contenders for the core position, literature is the most favoured. Language is a rival – the English language is a powerful organizing notion in a way that French or German are for language people. But the inhabitants of English departments do not see themselves as language people in that sense and where they do have an involvement with English as a foreign language, as in the Centre for Applied Language Studies in Cardiff, they may be institutionally connected but they are hardly seen as belonging to the same subject. In many places, this activity is split off into a (commercially orientated) language centre.

The question of whether the material is English literature or literature in English is one we will consider in the next chapter. For the moment we will look at the dominant idea that the core is literature. The answer to the question, 'What is the *material* which all English People work with?' (the equivalent of a geologist's rocks) is, according to this version, 'literary texts written in English'.

This is true even where theory is dominant. According to the head of school in Cardiff, post-graduates at the Centre for Cultural and Critical Theory are not encouraged to write theoretical work but to apply theory to literature. 'It will', he says, 'take a great revolution to displace literature from the centre.' This sounds specific enough and justifies the more precise label used in some institutions: 'literary studies'. But the term 'literature' manages to be both capacious and slippery (see Eagleton 1983: Introduction). English people are permanently oscillating between definitions that are too wide or too narrow.

For example, it is possible to respond as subjects do: to strengthen the frame, specify the technique, concentrate on one aspect of literature (typically poetry) as the 'core'. This produces a gain in clarity or 'purity' but engenders a sense of unacceptable limitation:

> Plenty of disciplines do narrow their frontiers and make a mystique of what they do, to publicize and raise the status of their group. What that has meant for literature is that you've tended to emphasize the purely linguistic or aesthetic. People feel that the pure heart of the subject is a poem. The pure heart is what distinguishes your discipline from others. I'm willing to say that that is the pure heart, students must be taught to read and talk about the language. But if that's what we were doing most of the time we would be doing our subject in a most uninteresting way. In most subjects the most interesting areas are the margins. If you didn't do that one would be sentencing most people to close reading for ever. (26)

This idea of a 'pure' discipline of English with a definite and uncontested material (poems in English) and a precise technique (close reading) has actually been proposed by Bergonzi (1990) as a specific solution to the problems of English. But, as we saw with reference to Mary Douglas, 'purity' is sterile.

The student, faced with an array of subject doors, goes through the one marked 'geology' and finds on the other side what he or she expects to find: rocks. The problem for the literature student is that the door is painted on a theatre flat: on the other side of the door marked 'literature' or even 'poetry' is once again life. For the geology student, subject selection operates like a powerful telescope. The territory/pyramid/tree metaphors are valid. For the literature student, selection does not produce a reduced and manageable subject matter. A mature student, Alison, sees this aspect very clearly. She recalls the Everyman books and their motto: 'All human life is here':

> You're introducing all sorts of ideas under the umbrella of English – absolutely everything is covered. All the things that are divided into separate subjects are actually under the umbrella. (69)

Literature is wider than social science subjects:

> You can look at the way that everything that really matters has been formulated and ask students, 'Where do you stand?' Literature does this better than sociology. Sociology takes language for granted, isn't aware of the unconscious, isn't aware of almost anything that makes life complicated. (17)

So the core material of English is 'life'. If one retreats from this unmanageable position to something involving technique (interpretation or reading) one still finds the remit very wide: 'Oxford English goes back to a time when literature didn't really exist, so you can read anything – Philosophy, Science . . . '. (75a)

To say the core is interpreting texts may be a useful framing move; but English People then switch again, redefining 'text' as co-terminous with life: 'I'm attracted to the everything-is-a-text idea.' (7) 'The interpretation of texts is part of everybody's everyday life, and the kinds of things one does in English can be a kind of psychology, a kind of philosophy, a kind of history.' (45)

So the subject English defines itself by reference to other disciplines which it seeks to use within its own subject boundaries.

Film and media studies

Film and media studies was one of the first major transgressions. It is linked with the rise of theory, since in Britain the new material of film was, as we have seen, dominated from the beginning by *Screen*.

Dr Ford provides a good case study. He was appointed to teach Renaissance literature but he had grown up in a culture where the sort of experiences I described in Chapter 3 were provided not by books but by films. When an opportunity came to bring those experiences across the boundary by professionalizing them he took it. And that meant mastering a completely new material:

> It was an extraordinary adventure. One discovered a subject and there was no question of specialization. If one was interested in the cinema, one was interested in Japanese cinema, as well as Ealing comedies. You look back and you think would you be capable again, over five or seven years, starting from nothing . . . ? At the end of it you were in relative mastery of a large field. (52)

He teamed up with a colleague and then tried to get film accepted as an option in the department. I was given a graphic account of the opposition such a move provoked in English (less in modern languages):

> It was a tremendous battle to get it through . . . the depth of conservatism throughout the university. People in English who were against it skipped the level of discussing it internally and discussed it at the higher level – a committee of non-entities who knew nothing about the subject. There the argument was that it was not a viable intellectual discipline.

The argument in favour was that film had 'extraordinary creative figures' – Lang, Buñuel, etc. But these arguments were not what won the day: 'It finally got through by internal pressure, people who felt they owed one something.' And when film started to be taught there were surprises for people who had supported it: 'It came as a shock to the professor that it was *Singin' in the Rain* as a text rather than *Richard III*.'

His publications on film have their root in literary study:

> Our work benefits from coming out of literary study, but then having undertaken sociological and anthropological research. If it had been the other way around those people don't have much to do with the cultural tradition out of which film comes.

But there are tensions, since the very people who have transgressed feel guilt about the transgression. Inevitably, to introduce a new subject area means detracting from the old. Students who study *The Searchers* are less likely to read *Paradise Lost*:

> I become shocked when students don't know major literary texts or film texts. I'd much rather have students who have read *Paradise Lost*, than students who hadn't. It's frightened me, the total breaking away from a historical canon. (52)

This particular respondent illustrates the moment when a disciplinary split is about to occur. There are various reasons for this. First, there are limits to the range of what can be offered to students within one subject and, although the notion of options extends this range, it is not extended infinitely. Then there is the need to expand and the need to escape from a subordinate position: 'You can't expand. I have to cut links some time, because otherwise one is tolerated, appreciated, but very minor in an English department.' (52)

In another of the institutions I visited the split had already occurred. A media studies unit which had started as part of the English department and as a way of teaching in that department in new (theoretically inspired) ways was now a separate department with its own professor, located in a different part of the building. It was striking that the professor was in fact a sociologist with no literary background. The process seems to be that a new *material* – film – is introduced (it has to be film *in English*) together with new theory (semiology). This cannot be contained within English and separates off to become a new subject, but the subject has different disciplinary references and the original instigators do not necessarily move from English. The film and media studies department interestingly takes on the role of upstart intruder that was, a century ago, that of English. A student reports: 'We had pats on the back for leaving FMS. There's a love/hate relationship between the media department and the rest of the arts departments.' (68)

Colin Cavendish was appointed to the department but has a background in fine art. He is not an English Person at all:

It's a film and media department, so its initial impetus came from English and from disaffected academics being able to import into that area all kinds of theory. We've got that. We've also got a professor of sociology, now a professor of film and media studies, who comes at things from an entirely different perspective, not very interested at all in textual analysis as such, much more interested in cultural production and cultural theory. (10)

Once the split has taken place the new subject then has to deal with tensions of its own, notably with the fact that it is closely connected with a particular industry, that it is vocational:

On the one hand we are saying to these people, 'You can interrogate the text more thoroughly, you can deconstruct it,' on the other hand we are saying, 'Yes, but when you go out there if you start talking to these people about deconstruction you are out of a job.' Think how much easier it is to be able to sit within your little ivory tower and say, 'This is my discipline. Here are its four walls.' And how attractive in a way because it just doesn't have these contradictions.

Here the disciplinary boundary meets the boundary of this book. Cavendish does not represent English People but Media People. What remains relevant, by contrast, is his conviction that the subject of film and media studies, by working at the academy–industry boundary, is in touch with modern reality. This is the soft–applied position and the suggestion is that the soft–pure position of English may be becoming unsustainable: 'The walls of the tower are getting thinner and thinner. It's part of a push towards vocationality within higher education.' Also relevant is his tentative espousal of the fish-scale model. The department has individuals with a wide variety of disciplinary connections and no ideological line or principle of coherence.

The media studies example seems to demonstrate a standard move in disciplinary change. The core definition by material expands either (a) by extending the definition of the material or (b) by incorporating another different but similar material. A specific technique and a specific theory are applied to the new material. There follows a process whereby the extended definition or the incorporated material provokes a division. The reasons for this process are, as we have seen, connected with the prestige of the teachers and questions about the relative size of fish and ponds, but also connected with the teaching reality. In theory, students should study everything (expansion); in practice there has to be a choice (splitting). This can cause dilemmas to those committed to the new while being attached to the old.

Cultural studies

From a simple market perspective there is no reason why differentiation of product should not occur: if there is a large number of consumers, they don't all have to consume the same product any more than we all have to drive red Ford Sierras. Some can consume 'English', others 'film and media studies', others 'women's studies' or 'cultural studies'. This solves the question of a student's incapacity to study everything, and reduces tension around questions about the relative value of different products, by letting a consumer decide.

So, to take a particularly contemporary question, that of cultural studies, there is, on the market-place model, no requirement for English to dissolve into cultural studies as Easthope suggests. English (literature) can define itself in a particular way – eliminate any unattractive aspects of the product, such as association with nationalism, and continue to operate side by side with cultural studies. There may be arguments about which product should have prime eye-level position by the check-out, but basically they are both on the shelves. Dr Draper thinks he might like to move into a cultural studies department but sees no reason why English should turn itself into cultural studies. 'This misrecognizes the fact that there are plenty of places where cultural studies already exist.' (28) He sees this move as an example of the imperialism of English. 'Cultural studies may be a new discipline but that doesn't mean it has to be born at the expense of the death of another.'

The same would apply to women's studies, Caribbean studies, or Bergonzi's idealistic project for a department of poetry. There are advantages for all concerned: students choose precisely what they want and teachers get to teach precisely what they want to teach.

The difficulty with such a simple model is that it ignores the discipline aspect. Any particular grouping has within it a haunting sense of its own incompleteness in the light of the imagined whole. English, as we will see in the next chapter, can no longer be defined as the study of English people and their heritage. But even in situations where the focused sense of a group is much more viable – women's studies, Caribbean studies, Asian studies – there is the sense of the incomplete. Dr May, a feminist, told me of her dislike of women's studies because it excluded men. It was she who, as admissions tutor, picked up that an Asian student was being pressured into taking an Asian studies course because she was Asian, whereas what she wanted was English: not a place where you 'belonged' automatically because you were an Asian (or a woman) but 'an institutionalized place where fragments can be integrated'. (48) The commercial model of the subject and its specialisms ignores the reality of the discipline, the larger world of knowledge and the desire to integrate, to draw energy from the margins, from difference.

The burning issue between 'English' and 'cultural studies' can only be understood by seeing that the opposition itself is construed in two different ways. Either cultural studies is an alternative to English (as are film and media studies), with different material, techniques and theories; and in this case the commercial model applies, as we have just seen. Or it is a new formulation encompassing and abolishing English. This is the position of Anthony Easthope and, as we saw earlier, of Professor Dover. It is the logical consequence of theory's critique of the subject. This is Professor Edgeworth giving his approval to Easthope's position:

English has come up with so many arguments for abolishing itself, people can't continue believing in it . . . The only solution to these internecine wars of English is transforming it into something else with another title and another name. (12)

'Cultural studies' is a different entity according to whether it is an extra product on the shelf or an attempt to eliminate English:

It's one thing to have an option in cultural studies, it's another thing to make the whole thing cultural studies. The resistance to that is less critical than political. You have got to have some touchstones, they say, of the values that we live by, and we have got to have some place where they are conveniently embodied and crystallized, and that's what literature does. If these arguments were about literature in a narrow sense, I don't think there would be so much dust and heat. (23)

There is, it seems, a great deal of tolerance and play, but there are limits, and people are concerned if the gap seems too great between what they do and what the label says:

English – I wonder if that is what I am doing. This time next year I'll have a piece of paper which says 'English literature degree'. This semester I haven't got any novels to study at all. But I am doing semiotics, I wrote about an advertisement. There's creative writing. (81)

Philosophy

I shall conclude this chapter by suggesting one more core distinction, one which seems to be at a profounder level than the language in which materials are produced or the media through which those materials are transmitted, or indeed than the materials themselves. This concerns ways of thinking, specifically the difference between logical and analogical thinking or between argument and metaphor:

> An argument either flies or doesn't fly. Whether a poem flies or doesn't fly is different. It's a different kind of question and it's certainly not as easy to answer. (12)

> I couldn't conceive of a life that didn't have metaphor at its centre. Philosophers on the whole are very distrustful of metaphor and they want to leach metaphor out, and for me metaphor is a condition of knowing anything at all. A connection with religion and language. The key for me is the communication of an experience. (19)

I am not suggesting that metaphorical thinking is the 'real' core of the subject but here as elsewhere I am saying that this tension determines experience. The material (literature or film) involves metaphorical or analogical thinking and the problem for the subject then becomes whether digital thinking is appropriate for understanding or responding to it. But, however that problem is resolved, the actual opposition remains basic. Human beings need to function in both ways. It is a question of what aspect predominates in an individual or a group and how the minority aspect is dealt with. There are in English many people whose basic cast of mind is predominantly logical, and these are the people who have developed 'theory'. They would have perhaps been less contentiously professionalized in a philosophy department. Alas, nothing is simple, and the kind of philosophy they became interested in was more literary or analogical than is prevalent in Anglo-Saxon philosophy departments. So these people may be too philosophical for English departments but they are also too metaphorical for philosophy departments: 'Had I grown up in a French culture, I'd have ended up in philosophy, but there wasn't that space.' (74)

Even those English People who were most philosophical are still hybrids, or people transgressing, which is another way of saying attempting integration, specifically between the two ways of knowing. However, they may see themselves as actually being philosophers and find their hybrid status untenable:

> I spend most of my time reading, thinking, writing about philosophy, I feel my life's got out of kilter. I'm paid to teach novels and poems and literary theory whereas I'd much rather be teaching philosophy. To get things back in line. I'd feel more honest about it. (12)

The simple and preferred solution for this respondent would be to change departments (or 'subjects'). The fact that this is extraordinarily difficult says a lot about the nature of subjects.

Another respondent, on the other hand, feels he is in the same situation but would not seek the same solution: 'I'd say I'm over the boundary into philosophy. I teach literature but I don't actually write about it much. I wouldn't like to be in a philosophy department though.' (28)

We are now looking at the relations between two subjects and two disciplines. In particular we are seeing how a subject, philosophy, which in Britain made itself pure, sees that purity threatened by another subject and reacts, according to one respondent, in a dog-in-the-manger way: 'A lot of the resistance to theory comes from philosophers who bitterly resent people like me encroaching on their territory, which I see them having actually vacated.' While staying in the subject 'English', he refers to a sub-discipline which does not yet have a name:

> It's become almost a sub-discipline: it's not literary theory, it's not philosophy, it isn't any of these things. It's a place you can do things that you can't do elsewhere, such as read continental philosophy, and it's a place where you can do psychoanalysis. There are very few places that can read Freud apart from literature departments. A lot of my work is on the boundaries of anthropology. I like that. (28)

This brings us neatly back to Geertz and blurred genres. Once again we see that two forces exist in tension, on the one hand the urge to merge and mate, to blur the genres, the categories, to put fish-scale upon fish-scale; on the other, the urge to be pure, fish or fowl, to divide and distinguish – discipline from discipline, but also tribe from tribe, nation from nation. And this is the topic of our final chapter. But first, by way of conclusion to this chapter, I offer the reader an opportunity to respond to a practical example of blurring the genres. Should the poem printed on the next page be in this book?

On the cusp

The year itself is on the cusp
Mid-on mid-off the wing three-quarter
Languish on the same turf
The girls who cling to Summer clinging dresses
Shiver in the evening breeze
And hug their arms
Fading tan and goose-flesh
The wise virgins itch at noon
Beneath their prudent wool

To be clearly Ram or Crab or Bull in the ascendant
To tread unequivocal snow
To feel the scorch of sand
To go completely metric
To know the genre the category with certainty
To make a massacre of hyphens and obliques
To be smooth-chinned or white-haired draw a pension
To have it all before you veiled enticing
Or recollect in sharp and cherished pictures
To slide off this cusp the slippery ivory slope
Down the throat of darkness
To serenity simplicity
Is the blandishment
Which I resist

O Lord give me serenity one day
But now crampons for my hands and feet.[2]

nine

English, Englishes and the English

Quand le destin . . . a fait de chacun un poids précieux et différent pour peser le plaisir, la conscience et jusqu' à la nature . . . L'univers sait bien qu'il n'entend pas préparer aux hommes deux chemins de couleur et d'épanouissement, mais se ménager son festival, le déchaînement de cette brutalité et de cette folie humaines qui seules rassurent les dieux.

(Jean Giraudoux, 1935, *La Guerre de Troie n'aura pas lieu*, II: 13)

Sets and sub-sets

The basic question raised in Chapter 8 was: how do we make sense? How do we recognize and define a totality in space and time and how do we structure and sub-divide that totality so that it is available for academic scrutiny and purposive activity by individuals with limited capacities and life-spans, seeking to locate themselves and to achieve knowledge? Individuals may wish to know about the history of the world or the geography of the planet: in practice, they are likely to eschew such grandiosity by choosing to study Outer Mongolia, the late Middle Ages in Europe, or a village in the Vaucluse. This assumes, on one model, that others will study other parts of the totality (Inner Mongolia, early Middle Ages . . .), and, on another, that the part is somehow analogous with the whole, that, for example, by studying one disciplinary culture one learns something about them all. The problem (especially acute for the first model) is that there is a lack of consensus about the principles by which the totality may be defined and divided and the work shared out: the terms themselves – Middle Ages, Mongolia, Europe, village, Vaucluse – are generically ambiguous, their boundaries uncertain.

We also saw in Chapter 8 that the various mind-maps that individuals have for making manageable the totality and for knowing their own place and task within it have somehow to be wedded to actual institutions for knowledge-making and knowledge-transmitting.

As we have seen, a common way of illustrating these epistemological problems is to use the metaphors of territory and tribe. But it is not a question, as with some metaphors, of explaining the unknown (discipline) by reference to the known (tribe). The intellectual problem is in fact the same when we are concerned not with knowledge but with real people and real territory. What is the totality? How is it divided in the mind? How is it divided institutionally and politically? For most disciplines the two sets of questions are distinct: physicists may need to 'police their boundary' in order to defend against pollution or 'illegal immigrants' (Becher, 1989: 50, 24); but they do not have actually to consider real frontiers and real tribes as part of their work.

English People do.

The title of the subject (and of this book) proclaims the fact that this particular area is fundamentally about ethnicity – about the real and imaginary divisions of people and places into sub-sets. This is the conclusion of an eminent theorist: 'The more I think about it, the more I think that the whole thing is about nationality, ethnicity; it sure isn't about literary theory.' (23)

The point about 'English' as the name of a subject is that it is an adjective being made to serve as a noun. So 'English' is always pointing towards an absence – the noun. Is the subject English literature, language, society, culture, people? As Christophe Campos, to whom I owe this point, puts it (not of 'English' but of 'French'): 'Adjectives can serve as nouns, but they are not very good denotative nouns because they have an arbitrary field of reference . . . and an unpredictable denotation when they are substantivized' (Campos 1992: 33).

Another tree – global

Let us imagine, as we did with knowledge, a computer tree metaphor for the problems we have just considered.

Level 1: the world

The root is the world, the society of mankind, the totality of all human beings and of the planet. I am down among the twigs, part of that whole, sharing a common humanity with the other 5,500,000,000 odd members of the human group. In terms of place, I also feel solidarity with the planet, so that the Amazonian rain forest is my place, just as Blaen-y-Glyn is my place. This global belonging is not new; the poets have declared that 'no man is an island' and 'all is one and one is all', and environmentalism has increased our holistic sense. This way of thinking foregrounds similarity and communality, and backgrounds difference.

Level 2: empires and federations

If we page down a level we come to the directory 'empires and federations'. The sub-directories here include: the British Empire; the USSR; the Russian Federation; Yugoslavia; Czechoslovakia; Switzerland; the European Community; the USA; the United Kingdom. This rather odd collection (some files are, in fact, deleted) does have one principle of coherence: all these groupings are smaller than the world and larger than the entities whose agglomeration composes them. They are also all in varying stages of composition or decomposition.

Mainly decomposition. If individuals' sense of belonging to the world (level 1) has increased somewhat, even perhaps in institutional terms through the increased activity of the United Nations, it would seem that their sense of belonging to any kind of level 2 federation has declined dramatically. The collapse, first of colonial empires and then of the Soviet empire, has blown away that tier. Even a stable confederation like Switzerland is affected as the economic gap between the Germanic majority and the French-speaking minority gets wider (see Hennebelle 1992: 173.) The efforts of the European nations to move in the opposite direction demonstrate that history is not a river. But as I write, the Danes have rejected the Maastricht Treaty and the movement towards European federation seems less assured than it was. In any case the EC is one of the major fissiparous forces acting on other agglomerations like Switzerland and the United Kingdom.

For the sub-directory that interests us particularly – the United Kingdom – also seems fragile. The break-up started with the creation of the Republic of Ireland in 1920, and Northern Ireland bears appalling witness to the agonizing difficulties of real-world redefinition. As Raphael Samuel says, the Northern Ireland question has 'exposed the fragility of the United Kingdom and the uncertainty of its territorial boundaries' (Samuel 1989: Vol. II, xxiv).

The last British general election (1992) was characterized by serious discussion about the end of the Union. Gavin Stamp in *The Times* asked 'Should auld acquaintance be forgot?' and considered whether Scotland's destiny was not now in Europe, that is, whether the level of the United Kingdom was now needed. He lives in Scotland and speculates whether he, a Londoner, will be sent away 'like the Sudeten Germans, the Hungarians in Transylvania, or for that matter, the English in Ireland. For that is what can happen when empires collapse' (*Times Saturday Review* 23 January 1991: 4–6). Norman Stone, Professor of History at Oxford, made the same point about Europe being potentially a substitute for other level 2 groupings: 'The Italians are frightfully good Europeans because they basically don't believe in Italy, and actually neither do I' (*The Guardian* 9 February 1991: 6).

Welsh separatism is still a force to be reckoned with. Plaid Cymru won the Ceredigion and Pembroke North constituency with a swing of 13 per cent. A poll in the *Western Mail* indicated that four out of five people in Wales want a devolved assembly.

Not to be outdone, Christopher Monckton in the *Evening Standard* (27 January 1992: 9) asked, 'Should the South-East break away from Britain?', and attempted to demonstrate that South-East England is subsidizing a mass of 'querulous Celts' who would be 'banana republics without bananas' were it not for (South-East, *Standard*-reading) English largesse.

Level 3: ethnicity

If we page down again, we come to a very large set of sub-directories: Scotland, Wales, Ireland, England, but also Ulster, Croatia, the Basque Country, Serbia, Estonia, Kurdistan, Lithuania, Catalonia, Slovakia, as well as all the ethnic groupings in Africa and the Islamic world which artificial colonial boundaries ignored. It is at this ethnic level that individuals have the most powerful emotional sense of belonging to a political and cultural entity. It is at this level that discontinuities between the mental map and the institutional one generate the 'brutality' and the 'madness' that Giraudoux, writing in 1935, refers to. What is novel in the contemporary situation is that, unlike what happened during the rise of the European states, when non-state entities were agglomerated to produce the European countries we know, we are seeing level 3 entities engaging in what the *Economist* (13 June 1992: 13) called 'a Gadarene rush to statehood'. The Serbian leaders, for example, seem to be demanding a particular kind of purity: Serbs should not be a minority in a state nor should there be minorities in a Serbian state. The Serbs represent the extreme form of the search for purity and clarity in group definition (the Poles are already in a similar position, though not from choice). The quest for purity in group-definition means purity in self-definition. It is the opposite of what Salman Rushdie declared to be his positive ideal – the acknowledgement and encouragement of hybridization (*Fin de Siècle*, Channel 4, 10 June 1992).

Level 4: regions

The next level is the region, small entities like Cornwall, Yorkshire, Oxford, London or the South Wales Valleys, entities which share a language with level 3 entities, but which have a characteristic dialect or accent and a particular history and geography. People's sense of place seems located powerfully at this level. I myself do not have a particularly strong sense of being in 'my' place in North Wales; I am just as much at home in the Lake District, the Salzkammergut or the Pyrenees. I feel at home when I go beyond Merthyr Tydfil to the Brecon Beacons (which incidentally does not stop me preferring the Lake District). It is as if ease of travel has actually homogenized everything beyond the area that can be reached in a day from one's home, so that the distinction is between that and everything else, everywhere else. And this area called 'home' is also likely to be the area where the child made primary identifications (if this sounds Proustian, it is because it is).

There are alternative ways of mapping the regions: the North–South divide can be seen as existing at the regional level (Samuel 1989: Vol. III, xii), as can other important divisions: city–country, metropolis–periphery. Religious affiliation may be a powerful principle and may or may not be mapped on to ethnicity and national groupings (e.g. Jews). It is, as Samuel says, 'a far more ancient form of belonging in this country than any notion of national allegiance'. The Irish poor in Manchester in 1871 told the census enumerators that their nationality was 'Catholic' (Samuel 1989: Vol. II, xxix). John Lucas (1991: 40) points to the 'determination of many Welsh, Irish and Scottish people to resist absorption into England/ Britannia'; they resorted to religious non-conformity for this purpose, since it conveys 'a sense of belonging, of social identity, different from the Englishness which was being developed at the time'.

Social class is yet another powerful principle of association, both in the mind and in institutional reality, in trades, professions and their guilds, as well as specificities of place.

A crude taxonomy like this does have some capacity to clarify: it is possible to see how one can be a member of groups at all levels and have more or less powerful feelings about each group.

This complex reality, which the various schemas attempt vainly to corral, is the stuff of art and literature. Individuals with their own mind-maps and institutional allegiances produce imaginative works which represent some aspect of the totality as seen from their position in time and space. These representations are then used by others and may be taken up as the shared way a group sees the world and itself. This process, whereby artistic works come to represent the accepted fantasy-self of the group, is – to put it mildly – not an unmediated one. The process of image creation is of crucial political importance: a group which sees itself as a powerful defender of the weak against the strong, slow to anger but fearsome when roused, capable of taking on and overcoming more powerful adversaries, will behave differently in certain situations from a group which sees itself as neutral, detached, sceptical, unheroic, concerned above all to survive and to pick up the pieces. Samuel (1989: Vol. II, xi–xxxvi) gives due importance to these imaginative components of national identity, to which, he says, sociologists and historians give a wide berth.[1]

English People, in the sense of people involved in teaching and writing about these imaginary productions, are deeply involved in this process of mediation. They may be involved at the level of actually mediating – broadcasting the work, affirming, confirming (possibly disconfirming) its particular view – or they may be concerned at a meta-level with the process of mediation itself; but they are always concerned with images of groups, one or more of the various levels of the tree. And, like the authors of the works they mediate, like everyone else, they too are individuals seeking to make sense, seeking to develop individual and group identity.

How do they experience the relatedness of their subject and their group affiliation?

Another tree – local

In an attempt to answer this question let us now work down the tree again, this time concretely with real English People.

Citizens of the world

An Australian in Oxford declared, early in the interview: 'I would never call myself an Anglophile, and I hope I am not a citizen of the world either.' (111) Yet half an hour later, after describing her sense of dislocation – not at home in Oxford and yet, having, for the first time in twenty years forgotten the Marylebone Cup, thinking she could never go back – she wondered: 'Maybe I am a citizen of the world, after all. I don't know.' Another Oxford student, Irish this time, had studied within the Atlantic College organization in Canada, where he had felt most integrated. Yet he said he had always felt an outsider everywhere – indeed he had *L'Etranger* on his desk as we talked.

So the universalist stance may be one which precludes belonging altogether. To belong to such a common denominator group is not to belong at all. This is connected with a debate about rootedness and a general ambivalence about the *déraciné*. John Lucas (1991: 6) suggests that 'rootedness is always something wished on others ... those who are rooted are not free', and implies that the wanderer is emancipated in some way. Yet there is also a great deal of scepticism on the left about universalist, humanistic, 'unrooted' values:

> If you want to be racist and sexist and still be in civilized society, you talk about human values. That is understood to be the code for those deep essential values which transcend the relatively trivial distinctions between nation, race and gender. That's a very powerful ideology, but it sees itself as talking about the human. (23)

In the narrower terms of literature, a global view is very acceptable:

> I'll happily read any translation from anywhere, Caribbean, American. I'm doing South American literature. I don't see it as exclusively English. (97)

> We studied Chekhov. I've seen the play. I sat there and I listened to it and it was in English. I understood it. It wasn't a Russian play, specifically. (88)

In one institution I visited, three students wanted to do a dissertation on Dostoyevsky, and, after some resistance, this was allowed. So 'English' is doubly inadequate as a label: not only does a noun have to be supplied – literature – but the adjective here means 'written in English, or translated into English, from anywhere in the world'.

Europe

I suggested in *Language People* that the discipline of modern languages had, as its 'specialized work task' on behalf of society, dealing with difference; and I concluded with the assertion that, for that discipline, the time was extremely propitious because Britain's identity crisis seemed to be resolving itself in the direction of the Channel rather than the Atlantic. I believe this movement towards Europe has continued (Margaret Thatcher quit the scene after the publication of *Language People*, though there was no causal connection as far as I and the Open University Press know). Language People, then, have a very necessary and visible task. What about English People?

Professor Peter Hennessy devoted two Radio 4 *Analysis* programmes in 1990 to the 'special relationship' with America: one of the views expressed was that Britain's agreement, as part of the special relationship, to quadruple the defence estimates in 1950, making them 12 per cent of national wealth, in order to help the USA in Korea, was the ultimate source of Britain's current economic weakness. And it was pointed out that at the same time Britain was refusing to join the Coal and Steel Community. Sir Nicholas Henderson told Hennessy:

> I feel bitter about it, that my generation should have allowed this British insularity, narrow-mindedness and lack of vision, to dominate British policy towards the continent of Europe . . . The inability of the British to see where their interests lie, that is to say in close integration with Europe, is a thing that, well, I feel almost a sense of despair about.
> (*Analysis*, 'Money bags and brains: 1: A dependency culture', BBC Radio 4, 25 August 1990)

Hennessy summed up: 'When trouble struck, whether economic or military, the British instinct was to pick up the phone to our American cousins rather than to our European neighbours. English-speaking blood will out.'

The position now is that the USA is anxious for Britain to be part of Europe and is itself diminishing the special relationship. Michael Heseltine made it clear that, in his view, if Britain were not at the 'centre' of Europe, then America would pursue its relationship with those who were. The idea of Britain as the honest broker between Europe and America is untenable. Hennessy concluded: 'Forty years of reluctant Europeanism in the face of continual American encouragement to integrate fully may finally result in our ceasing to be the dependable ally. Where would that leave us? All dressed up in our finest sovereignty with no place to go.'

Where do English People stand on this? An American respondent sees striking similarities between Britain and the USA, both 'island cultures, each terribly wrapped up in its own concerns, insular, provincial, incompatible with cosmopolitanism.' (13) He compares them with cosmopolitan, magpie Sweden where he once lived: the Swedes have no qualms about borrowing from other cultures (the supermarket system from America, for example) whereas Britain and America think they have nothing to learn from others. The question then is: what is the role of the subject English in Britain in terms of this? Is it like modern languages (which would encourage the cosmopolitan) or does it reinforce the insularity?

As I have already said, English People in my sense could well have become Language People. They are in no way inward-looking or insular: 'The first book I found really interesting turned out to be by Thomas Mann. Then it was French literature.' (20) Those who are monoglot are unhappy about it:

> I do feel ashamed that, amongst my equipment, I do not have languages. I won't be able to live out my life with it. I shall have to do something. It's partly a sense of fraud really and it also has to do with this sense that things English do not have the kind of natural superiority that I was taught they had, and that my ignorance is simply cutting me off. (7)

> I can only speak English. I can barely speak French fluently, it's disgusting to be so ignorant. (49)

Dr Stone was very anxious that I, a linguist,[2] should see her as a European:

> I miss Europe when I'm in the States. I don't miss England. I say that hastily, in case you mark me down as someone who is at heart a kind of closet English-literature-for-the-English person. I'm a European. I had read Flaubert and Balzac before Jane Austen. (25)

Indeed I was surprised at the extent to which my respondents insisted that they felt European in America:

> I've always thought of myself as a European. When I was in East Berlin I felt much more at home than in Chicago. (21)

> I came home sensing that I could never really live in America, and America seemed an awfully shallow country after being here. The language didn't really matter. My society and my culture had more to do with the Germans, or the French, or even the Italians. I suddenly started considering myself as a European for the first time. (65)

> I'm interested in English as one blossom on the tree of European literature. (3)

There is an awareness that the wider context of Europe (level 2) can actually encompass and facilitate small entities (level 4), missing out level 3.

> This is happening in Scottish studies. Previously, if you were lucky you got a conference in Dundee but I've been to Germany and France, talking about Scottish subjects. I've published quite a lot in German periodicals. (8)

This new relation between a level 3 or 4 identity and the level 2 one is still being worked out. One respondent's 12-year-old daughter triggered the hyphen idea. She was with a group of American students who were saying 'I'm Italian-American' and she said afterwards to her mother, rather anxiously, 'We are just English aren't we?' (42) In fact, she is English-British and English-European.

Institutionally, however, none of the places I visited had dismantled or even pierced the wall between English and modern languages. Institutionally 'Europe' excludes Britain: (European studies, in Cardiff, includes some British politics, but excludes all literature and film in English; and the English department in Cardiff studies nothing in a foreign language). Joint degrees in English and modern languages are possible, but it is in fact an option rarely taken up. The subject English tends to perpetuate the classification based on the English language and therefore to avoid the European dimension.

Britain

> My mother was not English so much as British; an intrinsically efficient mixture of English, Scottish and Irish . . . She would refer to herself as Scottish or Irish according to what mood she was in, but not, as far as I can remember, as English.
> (Doris Lessing, 1960, *In Pursuit of the English*: 5)

> It is indeed an open question whether such a thing as the British nation exists . . . it will take more than a 'core curriculum' to restore even the fiction of a people at one with itself.
> (Samuel, 1989, *Patriotism*, Vol. II: xxxiv)

There is a lot of confusion about 'Britain', a term which seems to have come into existence as a legal designation in 1707 with the Act of Union. Nairn (1990) sees the United Kingdom or Britain as highly artificial and, in the absence of a written constitution, very dependent on the dubious symbol of a monarchy.

A mature student in her sixties has a sense of being British which is connected with the Second World War and is specific to a generation:

> I don't feel I'm Anglo-Saxon. I do feel British, I was a child of the Second World War, and I still have a strong British identity. I do love

the British Isles. I still wear my poppy. They don't, the younger generation. I'm here because of all that. (79)

An English student uses 'British' as a way of not being English: 'I like the idea of being British more than the idea of being English. I don't like the jingoism, I think if you're British you're more of a European.' (104) It can also be used to describe a mixed origin: 'I actually see myself as British, because my Dad is Scottish.' (93) Dr Holmes, a Scot, links this with the post-modern idea of fictions:

> The sense of Great Britain. I see it as an imperial fiction, a construction, to do with imperial intentions on the world which I was uneasy about when I was a student and it hasn't changed much to this day. And I think we can now look at that as literature. It's all literature, it's all fiction, it's all construction. I think that that is helpful. (8)

One conclusion might be that 'Britain' is an outworn level 2 fiction. Agglomerations like this are breaking up everywhere. The new federation of Europe is being seen as an alternative to the old nation states, so that the future could be much smaller entities (than Britain, France or Italy) in a European federation. (There is even a possible solution to the Northern Ireland problem here: if the difficulty is Northern Ireland's relation with the United Kingdom, do away with the United Kingdom.) I suspect, however, that this European federation is also a fiction, or more specifically a dream, based on the fantasy that one can have all the cultural advantages of the level 3 entity (including not having to deal with difference internally) *and* the economic and political advantages of the level 2 entity; briefly, that one can belong to a federation without giving up sovereignty.

The Celtic fringe

Wales

We saw in Chapter 1 that one way of understanding the story of Britain is through the concept of 'internal colonialism'. Tim Williams (1989: 199) calls this notion 'theoretically threadbare', and says it is 'a strange colony which is more prosperous in the period of coal industrialization than most parts of the colonizing power'.

I think it is possible to agree with Williams's account of the Welsh and their pragmatic readiness to speak English as the language of power, while still recognizing that Hechter's notion does have considerable explanatory power. There are, as shown by the authors of *The Empire Writes Back* (Ashcroft *et al.* 1989), levels of dominance; a country can be dominated and dominant (Australians between Britain and the Aborigines); a country can be colonized but also complicit with the colonizer power (Scotland especially, but also Ireland and Wales), since different classes profit differently. As for the language, it depends, it seems, on the period: at the end of the nineteenth century, says Williams (1989: 199), the British imperial government was encouraging the Welsh language, and the Welsh were reluctant; this is hardly the behaviour of a colonizer. But in the same volume Samuel (1989: Vol. 2, xxiv) reports that in 1856 the British government was making strenuous attempts to put down the Welsh language. I can offer the evidence that my father and his brothers were still forbidden to speak Welsh at their South Wales elementary school in the 1920s.

Britishness can be, as Williams (1989: 179) says, 'a positive set of practices and possibilities', but it can certainly also impose dominant/ dominated relations. This is precisely the paradox of colonialism, seen most vividly in India, where the English language is a powerful unifying and emancipatory force *as well as* a threat to authentic indigenous ways. Colonization is hybridization, with the consequential loss of purity and simultaneous potential for change.

One striking fact is the absence of Welshness in the English department at Cardiff. This contrasts strongly with Stirling. Both departments have English, Cambridge-educated heads and a majority of English staff. Of 19 full-time members of staff in Stirling, 11 have a degree from Oxbridge, nine a Scottish degree. In Cardiff the English literature section also has 19 staff members: 11 have degrees from Oxbridge (mainly Cambridge) and four have degrees from the University of Wales. In Stirling, Scottish culture and literature is a presence in a way that it is not in Cardiff. Modern Scottish literature is, with creative writing, the most popular of all the options in Stirling, well ahead of the next most popular, American drama. There is no equivalent option in Cardiff. Indeed, to get the point of view of a Welsh-speaking lecturer I had to go north, outside the sample, to another college of the University of Wales.

Dr Mercer went to a Welsh-language school. At university, she had to choose between studying Welsh and English, and chose English, because, she says, of the seductiveness of the literature. English literature, for her, was actually literature written in English, and when it came to choosing between that and a narrower, male-dominated Welsh literature, the allure of 'English' proved too strong. Yet after years studying and teaching, in Oxford and in another English university, she began to feel that the whole journey had been inauthentic:

> It was not actually as if I was living in this experience, but using it for rebellious purposes without actually having to rebel. I think particularly, when I was teaching in X, I had more and more the sensation of emptiness, a feeling of 'What am I doing here?' It took me a little while to realize it was about slipping further and further away from the Welsh side, and I guess then all the pluralism bit felt much more obviously empty. It was not actually my experience, it was only an alternative experience, which meant release from the negative side of my experience. So that more and more I decided I had to go back to Wales. (11)

She returned to Wales and is now concerned to teach not Welsh literature ('I am not professionally qualified for that'), but women's studies in Welsh. Her experience puts flesh on the abstract ideas outlined above: English is a colonizing process, but it is also, via its literature (or parts of its literature), seductive and liberating, allowing a rebellion against the 'given' identity which leads to a new identity, often, as here, via a spiral-like return to the old. This is very much the process of 'Language People' (*Language People*: 96–102).

Julian has a very similar background and is also Welsh-speaking. He is in his final year at Oxford. He seems now to be a case of complete bi-culturalism, though whether he may later have the same reaction as Dr Mercer remains to be seen. He spent his childhood in Oxford, and there his Welsh-speaking parents pragmatically spoke English to him, but then the family moved to Wales and he learned Welsh. He studies Medieval Welsh as part of his English degree in Oxford:

> People ask, 'Where does your allegiance lie?' I say it's always going to be Wales and the Welsh but it's nice to feel that you've got some grasp of another culture. I feel at home in Wales and at home in the heart of England. (78)

Scotland

'People have said to me, "It's rather strange that you're a Welshman in Scotland doing English."' (62) An individual's origin is of great relevance to the way he or she experiences the subject; some Scots will stay in Scotland, some Northern English will stay in Northern England, but for many the formative experience is of discovering identity by crossing boundaries and possibly, like Dr Mercer, re-crossing them. The boundaries themselves may be in the mind: for example, I would have thought Dr Soper, who was born in Motherwell, studied in Glasgow and taught in Stirling, was Scottish, but this is not his view:

> There's no sense in which I'm not English. I don't belong to these wild Celts. They're going to steal all my cattle. I'm Lowlands, the Angles, Northern England, I'm working-class Northern Britain, a natural Labour supporter, not SNP. (3)

He used English as an escape from 'a poor, mean culture' and 'the power of this wailing voice that had lost its way'. 'All that emotion which you could not cope with . . . you had to protect yourself. I found protection in a higher culture, the culture of the landed people.' (3)

The issue comes down to the paradox of rootedness which I mentioned earlier. The local identity can be either a means of shutting out the world or a powerful springboard for reaching it. Dr Holmes teaches options in Scottish literature:

> I have a small prejudice sometimes against the students I get in Scottish literature courses. There are sometimes people who want to be told

what they already know and where they already are is enough. They want Scotland to be the world and not really to tackle the world and Scotland's place in it. (8)

The alternative is 'A way of dealing with Scottishness which takes it out of the ghetto and brings it into a wider and less neurotic engagement with the world at large, whereas historically Scots have been sitting in a small dark corner and calling it home.' For Dr Holmes, the starting point is 'the proliferation of small cultural identities'. 'Human value in general is in multiplicity, difference, variety, and finding ways in which these varieties should flourish together.' He quotes MacDiarmid: 'No internationalism without nations', but he seems almost to be saying also 'No nations without internationalism'.

The Stirling undergraduate prospectus states clearly: 'Because of its wide-ranging nature, the Part 1 course is described as literature rather than English literature' (1991: 65). The prospectus goes on to refer to 'English literature' for Part 2, but in fact the initial statement applies to both parts. There is some uneasiness about the whole question of the label in Stirling. 'It's a tricky question, the one question one doesn't want to ask oneself up here, but think of all the hassle if you called it something else.' (62)

English in Stirling means international literature, including Scottish literature. English students in Scotland have their Anglo-centric attitudes ('saying English when you mean British') challenged, not only by Scotland but by writers like Achebe, Ngugi Wa Thiong'o, Pirandello and Dostoyevsky. 'I'm certainly not studying England's literature.' (69) 'The last thing you could accuse the course of is being Anglo-centric.' (64)

It is tempting to suggest that 'Celtic' English departments are undermining Englishness – Stirling by the emphasis on Commonwealth literature, Cardiff by the emphasis on universalist (and continental) theory. The sense of a subordinated, non-metropolitan culture enables the Scots to empathize particularly with other such cultures and with pluralist, non-centrist attitudes in general. They move down the tree to 'small cultural identities' whereas the theory people in Cardiff, disaffected in different ways, move up it – towards universalism. Both move away from the level where English and England are coterminous.

Ireland

It is one of the many limitations of this study that it does not include an Irish or a Northern Irish institution. However, I did interview a significant number of staff and students of Irish or Irish-immigrant origins. One of these (from PNL) gave a graphic illustration of how significant a part Irish writers have played in 'English' literature:

> We now have an Irish studies course. The Irish studies lecturers argued that books by Irish writers ought properly to go into the Irish studies section of the library, so they were all moved out. Of course it takes a huge chunk out of English literature to do that. One of my colleagues

on the English course said seriously, 'I rather resent this kind of imperialism.' I said 'Well the Irish resented it for quite a long time too.' (43)

This same respondent illustrates the uncertainty people have about the salience of these distinctions. He can say, 'I see myself as Irish by ancestry but English by where I have always lived. British doesn't mean very much, or perhaps when I say English I mean British. I tend to think most people in these islands are sort of hybrids.' But the 'ancestry' is powerful: 'If you're Irish, even if you are brought up in England, you are given a different sort of history, so the idea of the Reformation is different. I remember a priest in school putting up a picture of Henry VIII and saying, "This man is a bastard." Good objective history!' Dr Kelly's background is similar, though he has always taught in Oxford: 'England is a pretty comfortable place. I have a detached affection but I have no sense of belonging.' (24)

Patrick is different in that he is Irish-speaking. He illustrates the complexities within the Celtic communities, the striving for the kind of bi-culturalism illustrated by the Welsh student, Julian, above. But, for a variety of historical reasons, it is much more difficult for the Irish than for the Welsh to achieve that. He was brought up in an Irish-speaking part of Ireland; Irish is his first language:

There's a fight going on in my life to show that you can be an Irish speaker but not an introverted Irish speaker, not be afraid of English. I spent so much time with cultural nationalists, who are, it seems to me, afraid of English, not proud of Irish. It's actually common – the experience is identical to that of the Africans. (72)

Indeed, in post-colonial situations educated people are required to live the contradictions: English is 'snobby', the key to upward mobility; the school he went to played rugby, not hurling; Irish is (literally) beyond the Pale. But it is still the core of the identity.

One can see how these tensions get resolved, both in individuals like Patrick and in authors like Beckett and Joyce – it is a version of the process I described in *Language People*, but less extreme, more ironic and para-doxical. It is the choice of the jester:

I worried whether it wasn't like the court jester. Someone who is allowed to say the outrageous things about British society, like Oscar Wilde. They need to be said so that the British can continue with the same thing. The king needed to be insulted, but as long as the jester was doing it, no one of any importance had to do it. It would be said, but it would be said by the authorized figure of transgression. Joyce, Beckett, those people did such strange things to the English language, partly because it wasn't theirs. It wasn't as serious as it is for some-one who is English. The English language has a much more powerful resonance than it does for someone who is Irish. (72)

Dr O'Hare is from Dublin and teaches English in Scotland. She is from what she calls 'the sub-culture of West Brits', Protestants from the Republic of Ireland 'concerned to emulate British culture'. (1) She grew up with a sense of displacement: 'You were always aware that you were on the edge of things. My cultural home was not Dublin, but neither was it Britain.' She uses the same word as Patrick to describe English: 'snobby'. English, the subject, was perceived socially as a prestige thing. 'I had a sense of superiority, "Gosh, I'm studying English" . . . I feel embarrassed about that now.' She went to university in Dublin ('Trinity, not UCD'). The way she describes herself is not dissimilar to the bi-culturalism of Julian, but, unlike Julian (and more like Dr Mercer before she returned to Wales), she still feels 'displaced' in spite of having been accepted, through the subject, as 'one of us'. 'I have no sense of a fixed national identity. I am not a proper Irishwoman.' And 'English studies is a garment I wear, it isn't me.' Like Patrick, who saw Canada as the place where difference was accepted, she sees North America (the USA in her case) as a potential resolution: 'America wouldn't be a problem. It's a place for displaced persons'. (1)

The question for the Celts is: how important is the ancestral belonging? For some, like Dr Mercer, it is clearly crucial; for others the status of outsider is comfortable and English the subject can fit that status very well.

England

> My friend and I laid delighted hands on him. At last, we said, we are
> meeting the English. He drew himself up. His mild blue eyes flashed
> at last. 'I am not,' he said, with a blunt but basically forgiving hauteur,
> 'English. I have a Welsh grandmother.'
>
> (Doris Lessing, 1960, *In Pursuit of the English*: 7)

The unmarked case

And so we come to the unmarked case. In *Language People* I claimed there was a paradox: 'Language people are not language people' because of their lack of concern for what the world sees as their role – teaching language. Were it not for a fear of becoming predictable, I could say that English People are not English people. Among the hundred or so teachers and students of English I interviewed were Welsh, Scottish and Irish people, Australians and New Zealanders, Americans and Canadians, people born in Britain of Indian or African or Greek parents. When I thought I had found the *rara avis*, it turned out to be '5/16ths Jewish', or to deny the ascription English in favour of a level 4 term – Cornwall, Yorkshire, 'the North' – or to have 'Jersey tendencies'. (94) (Outside my sample, I note Frank Kermode referring to himself as a Manxman.)

Stuart Hall pointed to the key to this when he said on the Channel 4 programme *Fin de Siècle*: 'The dominant culture never recognizes itself as an ethnic group.' To see one's group as a group among groups is to assume a base of equality: to be dominant means not dominant on the same level – *primus inter pares* – but from a higher level. Nairn puts it like this:

> The . . . English attitude towards nationalism . . . consists in indicating . . . that the English are above that sort of thing . . . The vein of truth here is of course that the English are not above but below 'that sort of thing'. They have not yet got there. Empire, crown, establishment and Labour Party have prevented them forging a modern democratic national identity.
>
> (In Samuel 1989: Vol. III, 84)

Professor Thomas in Oxford sees this in his students:

> Where are the natives? The English didn't have to develop an identity, and suddenly when they need it they've got problems. I find with my students, if they could invent for themselves a non-English lineage – a Jewish grandfather or a Serbo-Croatian uncle – they would. There's a lot of post-imperial guilt. I think the younger generation are worried about being English, basically, and somewhat envious of those who have an alternative identity. (23)

There is plenty of evidence from my sample to support this idea of English people not having a national identity (because in the past their claim was to be on a different level) but feeling the lack of one now. The reference is usually to a 'blind spot', to an incapacity to see Englishness. Professor Leigh:

> This might be my blind spot because I am English and middle class. I am not on the edges of it, I am in the centre of it, and if I were from Newcastle or Scotland, maybe the visibility of England and the oppressive nature of it would get to me. But it doesn't. (17)

What the English lack, and the Scots, Welsh and Irish have, is the sense of the other that comes from acknowledging being constructed by the other. A Southern English student in Stirling:

> The Scottish have a very strong feeling about the English but the English don't have any strong feelings about the Scottish. We don't have this historical legacy of being put down by the Scottish and so we simply don't think about Scotland. (66)

Even the road signs seem to indicate this. Professor Pool pointed out that when you drive to Scotland there are signs saying 'Welcome to Scotland' but no signs in the other direction saying 'Welcome to England'; 'Unless you're out of England you're assumed to be in it.' The Welsh position is semiologically complex; when you leave Wales by the Severn Bridge you do get a sign saying 'Welcome to England', but it is written in Welsh – *Croeso i Loegr* – and so was presumably put there for the departing Welsh (as a reproach or a warning?).

English people deal with their concerns about Englishness in a variety of ways. Here is a student from England (but, typically, 'partly Irish') expressing 'post-imperial guilt' and retreating to level 1 universalism (a human being), level 2 federationism (Britain) and level 4 localism (Wessex), as well as illustrating what I described earlier as the Proustian element in this last kind of identification:

> I don't think the English have an identity. All they've done is to suppress the Irish, the Scots and the Welsh, and that is their identity. English people with a brain in their heads are rather embarrassed about it. I don't feel English – I suppose I feel like a human being, a bod on Earth. If I was pressed I would have to say 'I'm British'. I'd never say English though. I was born in Bedford and I hate the place. The home I identify with is my grandparent's home, and that's in Somerset, that's Hardy's Wessex. I spent the whole of my summers there until I was seven. It was very idyllic and me-centred, and it snowed at Christmas. (88)

The obstacle to the English national identity is shame about power relations with the other groups: 'Asserting pride in being English means asserting pride in things that have had a certain cultural domination.' (47) So when you *are* dominant you don't think to assert it and when you are no longer dominant you are embarrassed to.[3]

England and Britain
There is also the deep confusion already referred to between England – the level 3 cultural identity, one of several – and Britain – the level 2 (federated) nation state. Dr Forrest made the comparison with the United States:

> I went to a baseball game and they played 'God Bless America', and, regardless of political persuasion, people stand up. All Americans can sing 'God Bless America', but all Britons can't sing 'God Save the Queen'. It's not the same tradition here. The notion of Britain is supposed to do that, but it doesn't have the same sort of democratic traditions, it can't. Britishness and Englishness have always been equated, and that's the problem. When it's English nationalism it gets called British. (47)

This is connected with Nairn's argument about the monarchy: the Queen is Queen of *England*. She is not normally described as Queen of Britain or of the United Kingdom. There are similar confusions in the world of sport, where sometimes it is a British, sometimes an English, team competing. At the Barcelona Olympics medals were announced as won by 'Great Britain and Northern Ireland'.

English studies? Yes
The problem for the English is that as a group they are not free to develop self-understanding and identity as other groups are. Women's studies, Irish

studies, Asian studies, Scottish or Caribbean studies, all these assume a legitimate field whose principle of coherence (based on the material) is the group itself, whereas 'English' is either world literature or literature of the British Isles, or English literature presenting itself as British literature. In no case is there a sense of one group legitimately investigating its own bounded identity via its traditions and its cultural productions over time. 'We are not doing English studies like they are doing Caribbean studies. We are doing English literature.' (81) Yes, but what does this mean?

Professor Thomas in Oxford claimed that 'English literature' meant what it said: 'They may not say so, but if you look at the structure and the syllabus of most English departments around the country we [in Oxford] are not out of line.' (23) Whatever the terminology, he claims, university departments are actually doing what Oxford does, teaching the literature of England. Dr Paisley agrees: 'There is a terrible insularity about a lot of English literature courses. There is an awful lot of little England stuff around. "American literature? Oh, is there any?"' (53) And she sees evidence for this in the market-place: 'There's a lot of profit in that stuff; if you work on Thomas Hardy it's very easy to publish lots of books, TV adaptations. It can be sold in all sorts of ways; people go off and pontificate and show slides of Dorset.' I did indeed hear clear, unabashed declarations of a specifically English rather than British identification, together with cultural pride and a wish to study a heritage, all this free of guilt. Dr Singer, for example:

> I feel I am in touch with the roots of Englishness. I feel quite strongly about the English language. I feel it's part of the heritage, as is the literature. Some of it is pure sentimentality – hearing Elgar in the Malvern Hills and Vaughan Williams. (57)

A student, Patricia, says she is

> a hundred per cent English. I wouldn't want to be anything else. That sounds awfully pompous, doesn't it? I have a very strong sense of English about me. I get this funny feeling in the pit of my stomach when I fly over English land. It's all green, just little things like that. I would like to live in other countries and I've travelled quite a lot, but I've always wanted to come home. Cambridge is home. (102)

This is not an uncommon sentiment, especially in Newcastle: students have pride in their 'heritage': 'Shakespeare, Chaucer, and things like that. It's a good heritage to have.' (104) 'I can't think of any nation that's produced as many outstanding writers as we have. I don't know what it is, but it obviously is something about the English race.' (102) The students who express these views are English and may well be from conservative backgrounds: 'I only feel that way because of all the books that have been shoved under my nose in the past by my mother. I'm a reluctant Tory, and I'm to the left of my parents. They are definitely the product of a Tory government.' (94)

There is a rationale: 'You can only be at home in other literatures once you're at home in your own.' (49) There is also a recognition that the fact that the tradition is not all positive is not a reason for ignoring it. On the contrary:

> If you mean does doing an English course makes you a better Englishman? No, I find myself teaching against that, but at the same time in *The Faerie Queene* for example you are looking at the origin of the current Irish situation, the history of Englishness, the way in which English attitudes, particularly attitudes to foreigners, were formed. (54)

When Professor Weston says 'You can't know what it is to be English or British [the usual slippage] if you haven't studied canonical English texts,' (50) he is not asserting that the texts give you a glorified view of Englishness. They may be used for that, but that remains to be seen; for a group to ignore them in favour of the texts and traditions of other groups is what needs justification. The authors of *The Empire Writes Back* affirm that 'A study of national traditions is the first and most vital stage of the process of rejecting the claims of the centre to exclusivity' (Ashcroft *et al.* 1989: 17). They might not, but others would apply this to the centre itself:

> The history of the subject as a construction of a certain kind of Englishness means that it's very fruitful ground for a critique of what it means to be English. (47)

Even if the 'heritage' is seen differently ('mine would involve illiteracy, illegitimacy and people starving to death in the slums' (53)) it can still be studied. 'What you are doing is studying the history of your culture, and part of that history is profoundly racist.' (43)

English Studies? No
Most of my respondents claimed that the idea of English as formative of national identity was dead:

> That nationalist idea is a straw dog. People don't actually believe it. I'm much more conscious of French as a national literary identity than I am of English. (25)

> I have heard it said that literature contributes to the national identity, but I haven't heard it held with spluttering vigour. (28)

> I think it's still rare, but I can't imagine there are many departments in English where it survives in its original form, as a straightforward set of claims about the essence of Englishness, or the greatness of English culture, or the best that has been thought and said. There is a residual sense of that, simply because we continue to teach canonical texts. You are still giving reasons to find them worth reading. You

can't get away from that, nor would you want to. But that unquestioning allegiance to a notion of Englishness is disappearing now. (12)

The result is that Shakespeare can be treated as level 1 material – part of the grand narrative of universal human culture, one of those, like Dante, Cervantes or Tolstoy, who transcend nationality:

> Shakespeare is international. It seems to me so long ago. It's almost as if a modern Italian, making spaghetti, were to say, 'My ancestors ran the Roman Empire.' And I would say, 'Yes, but it was a long time ago,' so to evoke Shakespeare as evidence that the English are great seems to me to be a bit thin. (17)

Belonging

This is true. Shakespeare wrote a long time ago, has meaning for all sorts of groups and cannot be logically used as an alternative to better British trade figures (or better plays) today. But this does not prevent him, 400 years on, having a meaning for the English which he has for no one else. To deny this is to deny that groups exist over time and that even humble spaghetti-makers have a sense of their past as well as their pasta. The same respondent recognized the difference between the productions of her group over the centuries and those of other groups:

> When I read black American writers, I think they are great but I don't feel qualified to talk about them. Because they are talking about things I don't know about. I can understand what George Eliot is saying about class. My mother talked in the same way about trade and land. (17)

This link between past authors ('our' authors) and present readers, both seen as members of the same group over time, may not be rational but it is powerful. As we have seen, many students believe it strongly: 'One of the guys in the house doesn't like Shakespeare and I find that insulting to the heritage.' (94) It seems unrealistic to claim that the view a British Racine specialist has of Racine is not different in kind from the view a French Racine specialist has.[4] I interviewed an English expert in American literature who is considering a move to the States, but not to teach American literature:

> I think I'm less marketable in America. They'd rather me teach Hardy. Especially when you come to reading bits of it aloud. It's accent again. When John Wayne says, 'Truly he is the Son of God', everyone winces. (53)

This may be discussed in terms of 'authenticity' (Hamlet with an American accent, Racine with a North African one) but it is essentially about insiders and outsiders, about belonging. The experience of outsiders with insider professional qualifications is ambiguous. Professional knowledge may not be enough to bestow belonging (which links with our previous discussion about institutionalization and competing forms of legitimacy). Lavita, of Indian origin:

> A study of literature in this country is often based around an unac-knowledged notion of national identity but it's a mysterious national identity. One of the fictions about literary education is the idea of harking back to the national identity, a true identity. What happens in the teaching of English literature is that you fictionalize that rela-tion to nationality through cultural education. It's not there already. Although I've felt at anxious moments that some people really *know*, I don't really think that's the case. Teaching English is actively fictionalizing a national identity through a school system. (71)

Lavita believes that her professional qualification is not enough:

> I teach a course with 50 per cent Americans and I have this embar-rassment because I think, 'You come to Britain to do English litera-ture and to have an embodiment of the English identity, and I'm just not it.' Shakespeare is one of the things that had been taught accord-ing to a notion of belonging. I haven't taught Shakespeare and I don't think I ever could. I still think that someone of Indian birth teaching English literature is not tenable. (71)

Other Englishes
I think this puts into perspective the widely held view that 'it just happens to be written in English', that 'English isn't the language of the English anymore' and that English is what is written in English: 'I've become more and more interested in other Englishes. The development of interest in Australian literature, of West African literature, Indian literature.' (56) There is the positive aspect – escaping insularity, avoiding the 'Little Englander' narrowness – but this approach may be ignoring the problem of *English* literature which Lavita is confronting, and therefore the problem of England which this section is about. The dynamic here is, I think, very similar to the one I detected among *Language People*: an urge to migrate to the exotic other rather than explore the local self with all its skeletons. It is less obvious because the language is the same. The consequence may be that Englishness is not explored adequately but simply evaded. In Nairn's terms 'the drama of unresolved national identity' (in Samuel 1989: Vol. III, 76) does not progress. Leavis can now be seen as someone who was actually engaged in doing this work: 'We may look at Leavis afresh now and say here is a great tradition which he was postulating for reasons which weren't clear to himself at all.' (8)

Sub-sets of the English

> 4 words only of *mi 'art aches* and . . . 'Mine's broken,
> you barbarian, T.W.!' *He* was nicely spoken.
> 'Can't have our glorious heritage done to death!'
>
> I played the Drunken Porter in *Macbeth*.
> (Tony Harrison, 1987, 'Them & [uz]', in *Selected Poems*: 122)

The question is: in what way has the work continued to be done after
Leavis? The problem with English People, as the case of Leavis himself
illustrates, is that the 'local self' is riven by class and caste. To explore
Englishness is to explore not only the relation of that group with other
groups – Welsh, Scots, Irish – but its own inner divisions, to consider
intra- as well as inter-group reality. In a word, class. In two words, class
and accent. Here is a working-class grammar school boy, now a lecturer,
recalling a traumatic moment in his life:

> I remember the head of English in school saying 'We won't bother
> with Oxbridge for you,' and I thought, 'What does he mean?' And in
> a way I've never ever forgiven him – why did he do it? It was about
> saving the school's reputation, saving Oxbridge. The very fact that I
> remember it, I remember it was said in the library. It was enormously
> significant for me, and I went on to interpret a great many events on
> the basis of that. It was a serious matter getting into Oxbridge. The
> whole school was devoted to this, and yet I was top in A level, and
> other people with lesser grades were put in. (20)

Here is another incident also based on accent:

> I am English. My mother was English. My father was English. I was
> born in the middle of England. I couldn't be more English. And yet
> I was told that there was something wrong with my use of the lan-
> guage. I had a Birmingham accent. It's surprising how wounding it is
> when someone says you speak in a funny way. I suppose I've got
> some sense of what it is to be an immigrant. My feeling has always
> been that of being an immigrant in my own country, of being shown
> by people who are better than I the treasures of my own country. I
> was born within 24 miles of where Shakespeare was born. I remem-
> ber saying to a schoolmaster, 'but Shakespeare probably had a Bir-
> mingham accent as well'. His response to this was detention.

He was offered elocution lessons ('You are, after all, going to teach English') so that he would learn (like T. S. Eliot) to speak 'this peculiar, non-
locatable patois which is a class symbol'. 'It was an obvious way out. It
was like having your teeth straightened at the dentist, or changing your
name if you were Jewish.' But he refused. 'You could say that my whole
career in English has been to find out what one could do about all that in
terms of the subject that bears the name English.' (15)

This is the link with theory: for this respondent, theory does not mean a preference for the exotic or the universal; it means using foreign weapons to attack another sub-group of the English:

> I don't represent the incursion of foreign ideas, I represent the rise of a genuine Englishness which was overlaid by a false Englishness. But we got our weapons from abroad. We took up the disintegrative ideas that were becoming available in France, Germany and North America. It's a rationalization of outrage that I felt from a very early age.

The grammar school boys, through theory, are actually working on Englishness. By proposing to change what 'English' is they are proposing to change what Englishness is or rather to modify the power relations between sub-sets of the English.

The requirement to change your accent – one of the most deep-rooted parts of an identity – as a condition for changing social class may be peculiarly English. The Celts are not pressured in the same way. Could this be because what is being signified by the RP accent – membership or eligibility for membership of a dominant class – is in any case not open to those who do not meet the initial requirement of being English? It is certainly widespread: 'When I was at school we had to have elocution lessons so that we wouldn't speak Norfolk. They wanted us to talk with what was called an Oxford accent, which has peculiar vowel sounds that I've never been able to master. I've resisted it. It's a class barrier you see.' (79)

'Small cultural identities'

As we saw earlier, many English People (possibly for the reasons described above) quite strongly reject the national level in favour of a lower one, which they call region or province.

> I like to consider places like provinces. I'd like to go to Cornwall, I'd like to go to Devon, I'd like to go to London, I'd like to go to Newcastle, but I wouldn't like to go to England. Even in Wales normally I say I come from North Wales, not Wales. I think there was a time when I thought of Scotland as Scotland, but now I tend to think of it as the Highlands and the Islands, the East coast and the West coast . . . (61)

> I identify myself with Kent more than with England. (100)

> Localism. I don't like nationalism; I'm more of a Shropshire lad. (4)

Oxford

One of these regions is special: 'Some small cultural identities punch heavier than others, that's for sure; the Oxbridge/metropolitan nexus is one.' (8) Oxford, which can stand for the nexus, is a locality with great symbolic power. 'A place like this is the centre of Englishness, village churches and Shakespeare and all that.' (24)

I interviewed two students, Paul and Virginia, who live within five minutes' walk of the *Oxford English Dictionary* offices. Their analysis of Oxford was revealing. Virginia:

> I think that Oxford has become more of a centre for the idea of Englishness while I've been there. I spoke to some Americans the other day, and for them, to live within five minutes of where the English language is created . . .

Englishness may be a myth but in Oxford it's a saleable myth. Paul:

> It's partly why Oxford survives. When we had the Oxford appeal two years ago 97 per cent of sponsorship money to higher education went to Oxford in that year. The reason we can go on going to the Bodleian and having tutorials is because of Englishness centred on Oxford, because most of that money was foreign money. It's a foreign idea of Englishness which centres very much on Oxford, not on Cambridge because the Oxford English course is what it is. The English course is part of what the Japanese tourists come to take photographs of. Most of the work I've done this year has been Shakespeare and nationality. It's a figurehead of Englishness. (75a)

This also explains why compulsory Anglo-Saxon survives: 'It shows we have a pedigree. We have roots that go far back.' (23) Attitudes to this vary. There are students who are prepared to be quite cynical: 'I've always had a fairly negative attitude towards the English actually, but that didn't affect me going to Oxford. I wanted the best of what their educational system could give me. It's quite a mercenary attitude, using the weapons of the oppressors against them.' (76) There are staff who see the myth of origins as particularly disturbing. A respondent went to the inaugural lecture of the new Professor of Anglo-Saxon, who said, in defence of Anglo-Saxon, that we enlarge our minds by going back to our origins: 'All the overtones were fascist. He had no idea of how racist his talk of origins was.' There are English people who for one reason or another – religion or class – feel excluded from this version of Englishness: 'As a Roman Catholic here I feel far more that it's an Anglican establishment. Very much Church of England. That's not a national thing. It's a religious thing.' (76) 'I was an internal émigré in England as long as I lived in the working-class North. I've been long enough in the middle-class South to feel less of an émigré, but I can still encounter a kind of upper middle-class Englishness which will remind me what a peculiar bunch of people they actually are.' (23)

So Oxford continues to represent Englishness and in the eyes of some to exercise power that is far from that of the theme park. Out on the periphery there is still great hostility:

> When it comes to research selectivity, who is it run by? The Professor of Anglo-Saxon at Oxford. That has to be the most bizarre cultural event of the late twentieth century. A man who has loathing for

English literature after 1200. The Professor of Anglo-Saxon at Oxford University is the man calling the shots over English literature. I'm back where I started, I'm on the outside being judged by people who won't talk to me, and where I can't go. That feeling is shared by a huge number of people. (20)

I always think it's a very great pity that the Germans did not bomb Oxford and Cambridge to the ground. It would have been an excellent thing. What we have got now is a situation where two institutions have a stranglehold on the rest. They represent Englishness, and they still do, in its most rampant and constricting form. (15)

Multi-cultural Britain

The question of the relatedness of a level 2 notion of Britishness and a level 3 notion of Englishness is already complex enough when it is restricted to indigenous sub-groups and their relative power to influence the higher-order definition. But internal colonialism or immigration (such as that from Devon to South Wales at the beginning of the century) is only one aspect. There is also the phenomenon of individuals from the Empire immigrating to the centre, and of settlers returning. Living in Britain today and considering it their home are: people who were born, say, in India or the West Indies; the British-born and educated children and parents of those people; people who were born, say, in Australia; and their British-born or Australian-born children or parents. One can add to this European immigration: the British-born children of Italians, Greeks, Jews and so on. Britain is a multi-cultural, multi-ethnic society, both because of the original, internal ethnic variety and because of the number of people who have memories of, and allegiance to, other places and other customs, either directly or through older generations.

The state, faced with this multiplicity of sub-groups, has to create a unity. In theory the unity could be purely contractual and legal: the various cultural groups would all agree to pay taxes, obey laws, fight wars, in exchange for the security of belonging to a larger group. They would not modify their cultural and religious practices in any way. In reality, such rationally based, contractual group behaviour seems possible only where there are shared cultural group beliefs and practices. These, in theory, can coexist with lower-level sub-group beliefs and practices but again, in reality, are likely to conflict with them. The whole thing is a matter of negotiation and the communities themselves balance out painfully the costs and benefits of becoming British. But the state sees great benefits in unity, first because it needs power *vis-à-vis* other states – and there is a correlation between unity and power – and second because the sub-groups themselves can turn on each other in the absence of this combination of a unifying culture and an external rival. The break-up of the Soviet Union and of Yugoslavia illustrates this dramatically: take away the grand narrative and you have some extremely brutal short stories.

So the level 2 groupings have great potential for avoiding inter-group fighting. Dr Holmes describes the nature of this level of national cultural identity:

> You look for a larger fictional identity or a larger group identity, the kind of myth that the group will accede to – a notion of Englishness or Scottishness which many English or many Scots will agree to, will accept, and yet they themselves don't live like that. Scotland does have a national identity, and it's by mutual consent. (8)

This shows how fragile a creation it is and how it may not be possible to develop it above a certain level (can Europe ever have that kind of identity?). The onus for producing this mutual consent, this over-arching shared culture which the state requires for external and internal purposes, has been allocated largely to the education system (though the media are also powerfully involved, as is sport), and within that system, to the subject which usually bears the name of the dominant language – 'English' in Britain, 'French' in France. The society may be multi-cultural and multi-lingual but there has to be one culture and one language which is common (countries like Switzerland are special cases). Ideally, the Welsh and the Bengalis will keep their language and customs while mastering the *lingua franca*, English; in practice it may be necessary to make Welsh and Bengali the language of the home and allow the common language and culture monopoly in the school. This process is one of integration or assimilation. It may be, as one of my respondents believed, a painful but necessary business:

> People have to make up their minds. There is the pain of immigration which you can't avoid. Are you going to live in a ghetto of your own culture, or do you say you learn the language, the literature, the culture? (21)

This assimilationist process (which, opponents say, sees blacks as 'trainee whites') may be softened by universalism: the culture learned in school is opposed to the home culture, by being not only that of the federation (level 2) but also that of humanity (level 1). Shakespeare is not English but human, therefore Welsh and Bengali. Basically though, it is about the acquisition of the culture of the federation.

France is a classic example of a school system being used to create a common culture and language out of sub-groups who, at the time of the Revolution, as Balibar (1974) demonstrated, could not understand one another (the school was not all, and compulsory military service has always played an important role, one significantly missing in Britain). There is still some belief in this capacity to assimilate; Georges Hourin (*La Vie* no. 2388, 6 June 1991), writing after the riots at Mantes-la-Jolie, says (my translation) 'I do not believe any more in the co-habitation of cultures. My experience convinces me that the assimilative power of France, her culture, her universal values, her way of life, are still very powerful.' The fact that the immigrants are Muslim can be mitigated, he says, by the secular nature of the French school system: 'The insertion of a religious community into our country can lead, given the force of our secular education system, to the individual integration of its members.' French philosopher Alain Finkielkraut, on the other hand (*Fin de Siècle*, Channel 4), believes that this process of cultural integration is crumbling. The school system cannot produce integration. The 'assimilationist discourse' is seen as racist.

For Britain, Samuel (1989: Vol. II, xxxiv) agrees: 'British society has lost its assimilative power'. One of my respondents said the same of the United States, another classic example of education producing assimilation. He spelled out the consequences in terms of the development of the national language:

> The subject and Englishness has language as the middle term. There has to be a community of language, a sustaining level of language activity. Arthur Miller has said that the New York theatre is falling apart because there no longer is a consensus and theatre needs a consensus. (13)

The *Economist* sees more dramatic consequences for the USA in the collapse of a linguistic consensus at level 2: 'the evolution of a Spanish-speaking majority in much of the west, leading in time to claims for the secession of Arizona, California or Texas' (*Economist* 13 March 1992: 13).

As far as Britain is concerned, this uncertainty about Britain's assimilative power must be connected with the problem of Britishness discussed above. The uncertainties about the British identity brought about by the greater consciousness of the constituent indigenous cultures means that there is a weakening of the assimilative power *vis-à-vis* the immigrants. Place is not enough it seems: the Bracchis and Carpaninis of the South Wales valleys had to be British before they could be Welsh. Perhaps, indeed, they can never be Welsh: the superordinate category is the only one with assimilationist power.

More generally, the cultures of origin are no longer prepared to efface themselves as the price for federal belonging. It is not the idea of being a citizen of a federated state that is rejected, but rather the notion of imposed cultural unity as a precondition of asymmetric bi-culturalism. In particular there is an awareness of, and a resistance to, the dominant myths; an example is the myth of the English countryside. 'To be English was not to be English' says Lucas (1991: 97), pointing to the fact that 'the heart of England is to be found in rural circumstance', while most people lived in cities. Immigrants have a different sense of place and cannot relate to that myth.

This puts the subject English at the very centre of political debate; it explains a great deal about the passions it arouses. The problem is acute in primary and secondary schools, especially because Britain does not have France's secular defence. The problem of Muslim children in a Catholic primary school is one which a French state headteacher does not confront.

In universities it is not a practical difficulty, simply because immigrants and the children of immigrants do not usually get that far, or if they do it is in safer subjects, not the one which forces them to confront their deepest dilemmas. I have already discussed the experience of an exception, Lavita, a British-born Oxford student of Bengali parents. She feels that going to Oxford was, for her, a mistake: 'I was socially freaked. It was an extremely white environment and there were not just white kids, but white kids from private schools. They hadn't had to do with black Britain before.' (71)

The universities I visited were not very different from Oxford with regard to whiteness. But the public sector is different. An evening class at PNL:

> There's an evening class in Romantic poetry. I've got two Iraqis, a Nigerian, a guy whose father is from Sri Lanka, eight Irish, a woman who is Canadian, a woman who is Finnish. The English are a minority in that group, and that's fairly typical of the evening degree. (44)

It would scarcely be an exaggeration to say that the British problem of multi-culturalism is, at the higher education level, being dealt with entirely by the public sector. Even in Stirling and Newcastle, where students are certainly being made aware of literature in English, as opposed to English literature, they are not actually meeting the complexities of black Britain in the classroom. Jennifer, a PNL first-year student from Cambridgeshire, *is* meeting them:

> To come here and see a lot of black faces, in London too, it's a funny feeling. Not a a nasty feeling, a different feeling. I read *Heart of Darkness*. The African woman stood on the bank in the book, she's strong. I've got a lot of respect for her. Then this black student in the seminar said, 'That's racist'. She said 'She's screaming, she's naked, she has no dignity,' and I thought 'Help, what have I said?' You now look at things very differently, and I re-read Conrad. (88)

So, in a different way, is Dave, who was born in Lincoln, whose father was from Sierra Leone and whose mother was half Banjara Asian:

> To a certain extent I am looking at my past when I study Shakespeare because I was born here. But then when I think of my colour I think 'No. Am I English?' . . . Lincoln Cathedral – ah, yes, that thing. It's a lovely piece of work but it can never be mine. I can never say, 'This is my country,' I don't feel it is. I don't know, maybe I don't want it to be mine. I can't explain it, it's difficult, last night I was driving through Chelsea looking at these large white houses, and they looked nice, and I was thinking how did they come about, and I thought of the slave trade, when all the money came back and they built their big houses. You are aware of these things, and you can see that it's not yours, the suffering that's gone on for these things to be . . . Is

anything English mine? Not the football team – that's Brazil or the Cameroons. London now I suppose, because it's multi-cultural. It's very, very difficult. All this is coming up in our course on 'Shakespeare and ideology'. (80)

Dr Perrin was born and educated in an ex-colony – India. He was the child of a senior officer in the Indian Air Force. At the age of nine he went to an English boarding school near Delhi. 'Everything – church, war memorial – was English. The headmaster was very Anglicized himself; he had been to Cambridge.' (46) When he came to England to study, his languages reversed and Hindi is now his second language; but he teaches English at PNL and, unlike Lavita, he would be prepared to teach Shakespeare. For me this is less an indication that the boundary is not so strong as we think, and more an indication of something special about PNL. Indeed, before joining PNL, when he was teaching English as a foreign language, he remembers being turned down for jobs: 'I was told students preferred being taught English by an English person. It was illegal, but still . . .' (46)

Settlers
There is a basic distinction between the settler colonies (Australia, New Zealand) and those that were invaded (India, Kenya). An Indian like Dr Perrin has a difficult position between the British and non-Anglicized Indians, but this is in some ways less uncomfortable than the position of the New Zealander between the British and the native Maoris. English for Dr Perrin was a totally imposed alien culture, and England a foreign country. For settlers, England is home, where the journey started, maybe generations ago. However long they have been away, or whatever the political changes that have occurred, they can feel that they are dispersed members of the same group – English, Welsh, Scottish, Irish, according to their ancestors. The teaching of English in the colonies maintained that fantasy:

I'm really conscious about being placed by the texts that I read then. No joke, *The Daffodils*, a real founding text, and *Alice in Wonderland*. It was a colonial society, and the material we read was English. (48)

What shocks them is to find, on arrival in Britain, that they are not part of that group, that they are exiles: 'I was shocked to be excluded. I hadn't expected that. I can remember thinking I don't like the way these people are treating me, but I'm going to put up with this because I want to get to a certain position in this society.' (48)

Another respondent describes the bitter feelings of 'cultural cringe' in Oxford, and contrasts her own openness with what she perceives as a culture of reserve and bitter class distinction:

I find it terrifying. One day they are going to know it was a mistake and that this little fish has slipped through the net. It's a cultural thing too, English people are not so open about their experiences whereas I think more and more, 'why lie?' Why bother? You can lie or tell the truth, it seems best to me to tell the truth. I can't believe the class thing here . . . An American friend of mine said to me the other day, 'I've never been in such a bitter society. If I'm walking along the street,' she said, 'and I'm singing [because she was happy about some career thing], people look at me with absolute venom.' And that's true. English people hate anyone who is too successful. Too happy. It's a fascinating society, it really interests me, but the class thing is awful and terrible, and the gowns and the dinner jackets, and the people begging in the streets. It's a real dilemma living in England. (111)

When I interviewed him, Dr Ford had another two hours in which to decide whether or not to return to New Zealand after 20 years. He went to New Zealand with his English parents, aged six, came back to England aged 20, thinking that he would be returning to his roots, but now still thinks of himself as a New Zealander: 'I had not thought that those years in New Zealand would be so defining. One really feels an outsider in England.'

I would prefer to live in New Zealand, except, it sounds trivial, for the newspapers and the television. Lots of people from overseas must think that there is something decaying and rather awful about urban England, urban culture, but because it's a large place and the culture is so deep and long at a certain level, there is a place on the top there and you would miss that. (52)

Europeans
Another group are the children of European immigrants, often political refugees. Martina's father was one of the dissidents who left Prague in 1967:

I was in this weird situation that I knew the history of Eastern European countries better than I knew the history of England, because Dad'll talk about it at home a lot. I've got dual nationality now, but only since the government was overthrown and it was all changed. I see myself as British. (101)

Christina was born in London of Greek parents. She made a clear distinction between citizenship and cultural belonging. 'I've got a British passport and British citizenship, but I would say that I was Greek; part of me is Greek, why should I forget it?' (86) In general, she is practical about her studies; she did Greek A level and found the literature difficult, but she also did Chaucer and found that difficult. 'The rest of the class, who were English, found it just as hard to understand. It doesn't make any difference what your origins are when you come to someone like Chaucer.' Rather like Martina, she represents an uncomplicated, matter-of-fact approach to multi-culturalism, in contrast to the Indian Lavita (which is surely not just a matter of personality):

> I don't feel any more English or less Greek for doing this subject. English is important to me because I live here. Okay, I'm Greek, but I was born here, and that's probably where my life is going to be. My mother couldn't understand English, but I speak to her in Greek. She'll say, 'Speak Greek, I don't understand what you're saying.' For marriage I think my parents would prefer a Greek but that doesn't mean it's going to happen. A lot of English people want their daughters to marry English people. (86)

Finally, Werner is an example of a student who is unusual at the moment, although we may well see more like him in the future. He is German. He decided in Germany that he wanted to study English (which makes him one of the Language People), but decided that it made no sense to study English in Germany, and so came and did a degree in English at PNL. The experience was very positive for him, but not in terms of incorporation.

> I still see myself as an outsider, even with the degree. At the moment I still don't feel that I will ever be fully accepted in this society, I'm sure that everyone who goes into another society feels the same way. I used to go and visit friends in Bavaria, and I used to joke, 'You are not German, you're Bavarian,' even though we were speaking a similar language. (84)

The degree has been a passport to the language, but not a magical entry into the society. He is currently looking for a job in London in the Civil Service, and is wondering whether his lack of success has to do with his being German: 'I do get the impression that although I have a degree in English, from an English institution, I am not considered as good as someone who was born and brought up here. It makes me wonder.' This links up with the question of different levels of belonging which we considered earlier.

On the rind

Britain is a complex system of groups and sub-groups. The idea that they can all be unified by one super-ordinate culture – 'British' or, worse, 'English' – is viewed with scepticism. Some believe that an elite might be inducted into an elite unifying culture; but a higher education system which allows itself to be so cut off from the non-elite social realities is in serious trouble; and a discipline which is concerned with cultural production but which ignores the multi-cultural realities is at risk of irrelevance.

English the subject is the place where a fundamental question about inter-cultural relations is being addressed. It could be that a particular strategy for dealing with difference has ceased to be available: the imposition of some powerful notion at the level of the federation. When one idea dominates, the sub-groups may not appreciate each other but they will not tear each other apart. Lucas (1991: 160) describes this move: the habitual strategy, he says, 'is to try to accept the divisions by imposing solutions – that is, identities – which can then be produced as evidence of agreed social arrangements in which separations are themselves somehow "natural".' What is being worked at in English is the optimistic idea that, as the single unified tradition falls apart, so smaller cultural identities learn to coexist. Internationalism does not mean eradicating difference through broader and broader generalizations, as in the tree metaphor; it means the interconnected variety of fish-scales, honeycombs and nets. And here the parallel with the world of disciplines is clear.

Many believe that the break-down of English may be necessary before the subject can reflect this move towards molecular pluralism:

> I would be happy to see English breaking down. When people start talking about English studies with the emphasis on the English it's with this siege mentality – 'All these modern people are taking over, all these damn continentals' – and you're left thinking what exactly is English literature? It's an empire mentality. I would like to see it as an anachronism but it's been preserved. (1)

So the alternative to the grand narrative could be strong level 3 or level 4 identities coexisting. But the students among my respondents give some indication of a different response again, a variant of the 'citizen of the world' theme. Some seem to be at home in a world where personal identity does not depend to any great extent on group identity. Werner again:

> That's already started to take hold in continental Europe, but not yet in Britain. People are still holding on to what I consider nineteenth-century notions of nationalism. There are more people like me in continental Europe, there are even people like me in certain areas of the States, New York for example. People are much more global, so it doesn't worry me that I'll never be accepted here. A little bit of vanity in me would like to be accepted, but I know that it doesn't really make that much difference. (84)

An English example:

> The reason why I feel close to Europe and to Ireland, Scotland and Wales is that I've done English. So many texts come from all these cultures, we are a mixture of all these cultures, and I don't really believe in nationalities. I don't believe you can say I am definitely this nationality, or this text believes in this nationality. All cultures are mixed together, they have been for a very long time. (107)

Another way of saying this is to use the metaphor of margin and centre. Marginality can be valued over centredness; the authors of *The Empire Writes Back* (p. 13) put it well: 'The alienating process which initially served to relegate the post-colonial world to the "margin" turned upon itself and acted to push that world through a kind of mental barrier into a position from which all experience could be viewed as uncentred, pluralistic and multifarious.'

Some of my respondents agree with this revaluation of marginality: 'I think what is exciting is that the power relationships are shifting and I think that now's the time for margins to stand up and be counted.' (8) 'I feel pretty marginal, but the margins feel like the place to be. The margins have become the centre.' (12) One of my respondents quoted Robert Graves's poem 'The Cuirassiers of the Frontier' (*We, not the City, are the Empire's soul:/A rotten tree lives only in its rind*) and commented: 'The Empire lives on the margins, on the frontiers, on the growing points, the places where you are guarding the wall, where you are actually invading enemy territory. And if you go back to Rome or go back to the heart of things, it's rotten, or there's nothing there.' (13) He has a hopeful view of Britain and of what Britain is working at on behalf of everyone:

> Britain is on the frontier in that sense. People here do want to find out how their lives are to be lived. We are central in that, more even than in the States. The States is the leader, but nevertheless in Britain it's more complicated and more advanced because the States has been locked into the cold war. They've got a lot of catching up to do.

What we are doing in Britain, he says, is living with post-industrial failure, living with the failure of Empire, the failure of that dream, and building something spiritual on top of the failure but also on top of prosperity. 'English is where that learning is taking place, that's why English is important. English is where one studies the breaking down of the juggernaut. This in a sense is the mission of English.' (13)

Some may see this as over-generous to Britain, but it is certain that English the subject is deeply involved at a practical and theoretical level with the most basic questions about how societies and cultures will function at the end of the millenium.

Postface

A portrait is neither an argument nor a blueprint. Individual English People or groups may perhaps use this book as part of the exploration stage
which precedes or accompanies strategy, policy or decision. This book
may perhaps contribute to answering the question, 'Where are we?' But
my role is not to make suggestions about where English People should be
going nor how they should get there. Nor do I feel able to produce at the
end a handy thumb-nail sketch for skilled readers who may have turned
to this page first. I think this would be to negate what I see as the reality
of English People (in both senses). The essentialist urge towards summation meets resistance from the present-day reality of the subject and the
society. Like the British Isles, 'English' is an archipelago, not a land mass.[1]
There is a great variety of practice, belief and institutional structure. The
island of PNL has a different terrain and different fauna from the island
of Oxford. Theory Isle has a much more severe climate than the balmy Isle
of Practical Criticism; the air, though rarefied, can be hot and there are
occasional severe storms. The Rock of Anglo-Saxon guards the dark blue
Sea of Dreams and is pre-Cambrian. We call the whole archipelago 'English' as we speak of 'The Bahamas', or 'Greece'. But as we sail from one
island to another we cannot use Linnaean species-and-genus charts to
organize the exploration. We have to use the map – analogical form *par
excellence* – which simply represents the islands' spatial relationships and
gives each a name.

The temptation to which I have yielded is to see English as the archipelago and other disciplines as land masses. I wonder rather whether *all*
disciplines are not archipelagos which *others* see as land masses. This would
be to transpose the Sartrean notion of identity to groups: I know myself
to be fluid but construct the other as solid and coherent, as I myself am
constructed as solid and coherent by the other. But, whether surrounded
by land masses or other archipelagos, English itself is scattered.

The archipelago image takes one so far. But it is a static image. And in
this it is like another image I have used in this book – that of a tension

between opposing forces, or, more ambitiously, a force-field. I have described English People's experience as a collection of tensions: public/private, masculine/feminine, Cavalier/Roundhead, subversive/establishment, purposive/ 'undesigning', cognitive/precognitive, merging/separating (e-merging?), dream/reality, pure/hybrid, teaching/researching, professional/dilettante, critical/creative . . . However, the static nature of a tension is an illusion. Let go of one end of the spring and the change is catastrophic. Pull one end harder and the situation changes in response. These metaphors are attempts to deal with the core problem: how to articulate the experience of difference – of opposing forces within the self and between groups – over time.

The recognition of difference is based on *either/or* thinking, which divides. But there is also *both/and* thinking, which joins. To say that we have to choose between one and the other is in fact to have already chosen either/or thinking. To choose both/and means choosing both/and *as well as* either/or. In other words the binary oppositions have to be posited before they can be reconciled.

This ties in with the practical work of Hampden-Turner (1990), from whom I have already quoted. He investigates a corporate culture (Apple, Thorn, Shell, etc.) and, in collaboration with the leaders of the company, attempts to articulate what he calls the key *dilemmas*. The aim is to specify the two horns – which are likely to be *values* – while not being impaled on either. His basic belief is that 'any one value or criterion of excellence pursued in isolation is almost bound to steer you into trouble' (Hampden-Turner 1990: chapter entitled 'The Hunt for the Unicorn', p. 223). Once the dilemmas have been articulated and clarified, the process of *reconciling*, the search for synergy, can begin. Reconciling may be a misleading term since it implies a once-and-for-all event, whereas the process is unending.

This is just one articulation of the problem. Another is the psychoanalytical one of *splitting*, which I have used at times in this book. Parts of the self or the group are denied and rejected. They then get projected on to other individuals or groups who are seen to represent these parts exclusively (the others can be seen as good or bad but usually they are seen as wholly bad so that the original individual or group can be seen as wholly good). Here again the process consists in seeing what part has been projected (what the split is) before taking back the projection; that is, acknowledging the denial, reintegrating the split part. To take the most obvious example, English People can deny 'thinking' and project this on to another group, the 'theory' people. The latter can deny 'feeling' (or 'intuition') and project this on to the 'sensitive' Leavisites. Yet the exercise of the subject, to say nothing of the exercise of being a human being, clearly requires both thinking and feeling.[2]

There is ample evidence in this book of either/or thinking, or splitting. But there is also evidence of reconciling, either consciously or unconsciously (what I have called 'accommodating'). Take a comment like this from the oldest of my respondents, one-time associate of Leavis:

METHOD

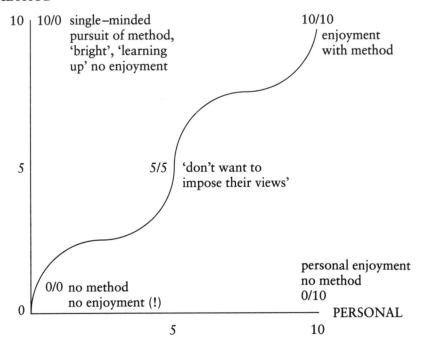

Figure 10.1

My hope for the future of English is that it would be taught by people who enjoy it, and who are highly intelligent, and who don't want to impose their views. It's a personal thing, you can't have a method. That's the trouble in America at the moment. There's a method, anyone can learn it up if they are bright enough. It's not a thing you can learn up. (49)

This respondent sees the 'dilemma': *given the personal nature of the material can there be method?* Using Hampden-Turner's method for charting dilemmas we have something like Figure 10.1. This respondent is saying that single-minded pursuit of 'method' (10/0) as exemplified (he says) by America is unsatisfactory. But he is not saying that the answer is 0/10 – personal pleasure – since his requirement is for people who enjoy it *and* are 'highly intelligent'. The 'don't want to impose their views' also represents the urge for reconciliation.

The problem with this kind of conclusion is that, compared to strong affirmations of either horn, it sounds boringly bland. But this preference for sharp dichotomies may (as Hampden-Turner suggests in an interesting chapter on Japanese business practices) be culturally specific to the West.

In any case 'reconciliation' is bland ('the truth lies in between', 'let us avoid extremes') only to the extent that the initial thinking was bland or experientially empty. Genuine reconciling is dynamic and challenging.

English represents quite fundamental dilemmas, for the humanities, for the university and for post-industrial society. Thinking/feeling, logic/imagination: these dilemmas, and the others I have mentioned, many of which are linked to them, must be addressed and reconciled. The university is impaled on the horn of cognitive power and English promises escape from that uncomfortable position (this is what the various references to 'magic' may mean). But *within* English, theory represents one horn of a dilemma and offers escape from an entrapment on the horn of intuition. The point is that the university's *thinking* and the subject's *intuition* are both *less* effective for being *unicorn*. The subject would have more impact on the larger system of the university for being less hypertrophied and more reconciled or integrated, as the university would have more impact on society.

English has the capacity to achieve these reconciliations. I have referred to two concepts in this concluding section – 'dilemmas' and 'splitting'. But there are other powerful explanatory theories to which English People have access, to say nothing of those complex verbal reconciliations of dilemmas, the symbolic artefacts – poems, novels, plays – which constitute a large part of their material and which are available as models or challenges for their own writing and teaching. Writing does not have to be wholly abstract or wholly metaphorical, but can reconcile both; teaching does not have to be wholly planned or wholly inspirational, but can be both.

Ultimately, what is required is that the capacities – theoretical and imaginative – that English People have should be used *reflexively*, not to denigrate other sub-groups but to further the understanding of their own experience. This book is intended as a contribution to that process.

Appendix

Details of respondents: Staff

Reference	Professor or equivalent	Senior lecturer or equivalent	Lecturer or equivalent	Male	Female
1			X		X
2		X		X	
3			X	X	
4			X	X	
5			X		X
6		X		X	
7		X		X	
8		X		X	
9	X			X	
10			X	X	
11			X		X
12	X			X	
13			X	X	
14			X	X	
15	X			X	
16			X	X	
17	X				X
18	X			X	
19		X		X	
20			X	X	
21	X			X	
22			X	X	
23	X			X	
24			X	X	
25			X		X
26	X				X

Reference	Professor or equivalent	Senior lecturer or equivalent	Lecturer or equivalent	Male	Female
27			X		X
28			X	X	
29			X	X	
31			X		X
40	X			X	
41			X		X
42			X		X
43			X	X	
44			X	X	
45			X	X	
46			X	X	
47			X		X
48			X		X
49	X			X	
50	X			X	
51		X		X	
52		X		X	
53		X			X
54			X	X	
55	X			X	
56		X			X
57			X		X
58			X		X
59			X	X	

Details of respondents: Students

Reference	Male	Female	First year	Second year	Final year	Post-graduate	Mature student
60		X			X		
61		X			X		
62	X					X	
63	X				X		X
64		X			X		
65	X				X		
66		X		X			
67		X		X			
68	X				X		X
69		X			X		X
70		X		X			X
71		X				X	X
72	X					X	
73	X					X	

Reference	Male	Female	First year	Second year	Final year	Post-graduate	Mature student
74	X					X	
75a	X				X		
75b		X			X		
76	X			X			
77		X		X			
78		X			X		
79		X	X				X
80	X			X			X
81	X				X		X
82		X	X				
83	X				X		X
84	X				X		
85		X		X			X
86		X		X			
87	X			X			X
88		X	X				
89		X		X			X
90	X			X			X
91	X		X				
92	X				X		
93		X		X			
94		X		X			
95	X			X			
96	X						X
97	X		X				
98	X			X			
99	X			X			
100	X			X			
101		X	X				
102		X		X			
103	X			X			
104		X		X			
105		X			X		
106		X		X			
107		X			X		
108		X			X		
109		X		X			
110	X				X		
111		X				X	

Notes

Preface

1 I derive this notion of the metalogue from Gregory Bateson who, in the American edition of *Steps to an Ecology of Mind* (1972), uses it to refer to an activity whose process mirrors the issue being dealt with (these are my terms, not his). See my article 'Teaching the humanities: seminars as metalogues' (Evans, 1990a).

2 I choose not to merge all the voices into my voice, distinguished from it (but not from each other) only by the faint accent of the quotation mark, but rather to give each a number and occasionally (purely for variety) an invented name. This protects the respondents' anonymity (which was the condition of their talking to me) while enabling the reader to recognize each of their contributions and get some sense of their variety. Occasionally I have omitted the reference where I thought the respondent's anonymity might be affected. A table at the end gives basic details, though I have not distinguished the different grades in the different institutions. The reader may care to note that a number below 60 will be that of a staff respondent and that I also distinguish staff and student names: staff have title and surname; students have first name. On one occasion I interviewed two students together and these are distinguished by a and b. In all other cases the number refers to a unique interview and to a unique tape-recording. As with quotations from books and articles, quotations from interviews are all verifiable.

3 Source: USR Tables U26711 (1990) and P26712 (1990).

4 Source: Department for Education (1990), England only.

5 Collecting even simple head-count statistics like these is not easy. The Universities Statistical Record collects statistics for universities in the United Kingdom, whereas the Department for Education's Analytical Services Branch collects them for England only. For my purposes in this preface this is, I feel, sufficient, but the totals for polytechnics and colleges need to be increased by the numbers of students in Scotland, Wales and Northern Ireland. The figures include part-time students (not a high proportion) and those combining English with another subject. The polytechnic figures include various designations. The largest entry by far is for Q300, 'English language and literature', followed by Q306, 'English

literature'. I have excluded Q1, 'Linguistics', and Q375, 'English as a foreign language'.

6 Source: USR Table S26739 (1990).

7 The figure 500 is a guess, based on student numbers and an assumption that the staff–student ratio is the same as that of universities (though it probably is worse). Staff figures for the public sector are not broken down by the Department for Education into units as small as English. SCEPCHE has a database, but this is incomplete (returns from 21 out of 40 member institutions). Source: USR Table U26711 (1990).

8 Source: Department for Education. These figures include leavers from further education institutions. Another way of describing the phenomenon is to say that in 1991, 4.2 per cent of the boys and 9.6 per cent of the girls of the population aged 18 passed English at A or AS level. The pass figures represent 88 per cent of those sitting the examination. Protherough (1989: 11) includes GCSE candidates and concludes that 'something like a million young people every year in England and Wales seek external qualifications in English literature'. He adds 'the 300 million or so world-wide who speak it as their first language' and a similar number who learn it as a foreign language.

9 See *Language People*, p. 197, note 3. I discovered that, of the modern languages cohort entering university service in 1972, 80 per cent were still in the university to which they were recruited. There is no reason to suppose English is very different.

Chapter 1

1 There is a sense in which the Book itself, the university's most revered object, is emblematically complicit in this respect, denying as it does its own production in time, eliminating, in a final edit, internal contradiction from chapter to chapter. Frank Smith expresses this very well at the beginning of his *Writing and the Writer* (1982: 2): 'One of the paradoxes of writing is that a text will erase its own history but can look into its own future'. This book is no exception. The reader will find no trace of the changes which occurred as a result of the events that happened during the writing – the result of the 1992 British General Election, the violent break-up of Yugoslavia, etc.

2 To get the sense of it as a living power it is probably necessary to go to a different culture altogether – to France, say, where the classics have clung on much more effectively – and to speak to academics who have experience of the way in which the classical subjects were used to create a wall between the classes that had studied them and those who had not. Even today, French government proposals for reform of higher education, involving a reduction in the degree to which Latin and Greek are available or compulsory, are met by impassioned pleas for the preservation and restoration to their former glory of Latin and Greek. Delpeche, writing in *Le Monde* on 4 March 1992, says (my translation) 'By compromising the study of ancient languages and of French as they have been bequeathed to us in the greatest works of humanity, the reformers are taking away from children the chance for better jobs, but also the chance to live more intensely.' *Le Figaro* organized a dinner debate to protect Latin and Greek. And even today 'French' in secondary schools is likely to mean 'French and Latin'. A teacher of French is likely to be a teacher of *lettres classiques* and to have been trained in that way.

3 Hoskin (forthcoming) argues convincingly that the examination system is the prime agent for change in these areas.

4 Behind this metaphor is a disturbing notion of the sadistic aspects of the teaching process.

5 The production of readers and anthologies is a crucial factor in the history of disciplines: I am thinking particularly of a book like Lagarde and Michaud's French anthology, which has played a major role in determining what French literature means in the French educational system.

6 The history of the discipline of philology has been dealt with in detail by the contributors to *Philologiques I* (Espagne and Werner 1990), especially Chapter 1, 'A propos de la notion de philologie moderne; problèmes de définition dans l'espace franco-allemand', and Chapter 2, 'Philologie classique et légitimée: quelques questions sur le "modèle"'.

7 For an account of the early Chairs in the University of London, see A. Bacon, 'English at King's College', *Victorian Studies*, Summer 1986.

8 My rather sympathetic view of Richards is not shared by Baldick (1983: 152–3).

Chapter 2

1 More work has been done on *career* choice than on subject choice. Researchers like Ginzberg, Super and Blau (usefully summarized by Sofer in Williams 1974) say little about subject choice, making the assumption that this is driven by occupational choice. But for pupils choosing English, the subject represents a means of *not* making an occupational choice or of postponing it. Having said this, this early research (and the articles in the Williams book) exemplifies the general theories of Heap *et al.* (1992) – choice of occupation is rational and purposive but not necessarily objective and conscious. With regard to subject choice itself, the more recent work of Woods (in Hammersley and Woods 1984) deals with secondary modern pupils. Garratt (1985) does deal with A-level choices and concludes that the 'interest value' of subjects is the main factor in choice. Protherough (1989: 26) usefully summarizes the work on subject choice and reports on a survey of his own.

2 There is a suggestion of *plus ça change*, however. A former don made the following revelation: 'There is an extraordinary number of hopeless Japanese students reading English at Oxford. Why? Because rich grandfathers have written endowments. It's a deeply corrupt place. We had a proposal in X College from some Japanese industrialist, that he was going to give a million quid or something. A necessary element of this package was to take his grandson. The debate was not over the morality of this but whether a million quid was enough. We decided in the end that it wasn't, so we turned him down. It's a question of the size of the bribe, and always has been. I'm sure the medieval university was like that.'

3 See Protherough (1989: 48). BBC or better was the norm in 1986.

Chapter 3

1 The authors of *Rewriting English* devote a chapter to 'Some women reading' and give further examples of what they call an 'ethnography of readers', including

accounts of their own use of reading. They focus particularly on the work–indulgence opposition and the hostility to analysis ('tearing books apart') (Batsleer *et al.* 1985: 142).

Chapter 4

1 Work began on a £3.2 million extension to the humanities building in Cardiff in July 1992.
2 Various recent publications address this question of teaching large groups. See Gibbs and Jenkins (1992) and Cryer and Elton (1992). See also Ramsden's (1992) review of Gibbs and Jenkins.
3 DUET – the Development of University English Teaching project – puts on annual participative workshops in Britain and abroad. See note 1 to Chapter 7, below.
4 For a spirited attack on the opponents of coursework see Greenwell (1992).

Chapter 5

1 See Hoskin (1993).
2 I made use of the life-cycle theorists in *Language People* (Chapter 3, Table 3.1).
3 See Lewis (1984: Chapter 2) for vivid accounts of the difficulties first-year students can have.
4 Belbin has since modified some of his terms. In particular, the 'chairman' role has become the 'co-ordinator' and the 'company worker' the 'implementer'. He has also added the 'specialist'. See Belbin (1988).
5 For the distinction between authority and power see my chapter in Evans (1993). Basically authority is the right to engage in a task on behalf of others within a social system, by taking on a role. Power refers to personal attributes (mental, physical, social). These may be used to replace authority (banging on the desk with your shoe) but they are also needed by the person in authority as resources to perform the task: authority without power is as unsatisfactory as power without authority.
6 The reference is to an exhibition, *Traum und Wirklichkeit* (Dream and reality), held in Vienna in 1985 and devoted to psychoanalysis and politics.
7 I suspect even Cambridge is seen as not part of the dream, and certainly the reflections on Cambridge I collected make me think of it as much more 'real', in institutional terms: concerned with the business of practical criticism, fanatical about the subject's relevance to life; in a way, 'Roundhead'. 'Cambridge still has the Leavisite fervour washing about,' (26) though the institutional reality seems to have been unpleasant for many: 'I had the misfortune to be there in the 1960s. It was the most quarrelsome faculty I've ever been in in my life. I hated it. Kermode woke up one morning and said "Why should I put up with this any more?" and resigned. Ricks resigned. Cambridge stinks. It's so acerbic, which is the opposite of that Oxford suavity.' (49)

Chapter 6

1 Source: USR Table U26711 (1990).
2 Source: Department for Education (1990), England only.

3 Source: Standing Conference on English in Polytechnics and Colleges of Higher Education (SCEPCHE).
4 Source: USR Table U26711 (1990).
5 My evidence for this statement depends on some unpublished considerations of mine based on television coverage of the Falklands War (the return of the QE2) and of sport (Wimbledon), as well as on French cinema – particularly Truffaut, who repeatedly asks the question 'Are women magical?' The Hollywood Western also offers numerous examples of men doing what they have to do and women trying to stop them.

Chapter 7

1 More scepticism about the Anderson thesis has recently been expressed by Ellen Meiksins Wood (1991).
2 My impression is that the conferences had a preponderance of polytechnic teachers but that the publication was mainly university. Of the New Accents authors, 35 are university-based (including overseas universities) and 11 polytechnic-based (this includes editors of multiple-authored books). Virtually none are from Oxbridge, though Terry Eagleton's Influential *Literary Theory: an Introduction*, published by Blackwell, was originally scheduled for the New Accents series. DUET was a university initiative (with a grant from Nuffield). It was the idea of Professor John Broadbent, who moved from Cambridge to the University of East Anglia, but has always been staffed by a mixture of university and polytechnic people, together with individuals from outside the university altogether, from the world of group relations. It has always attracted more participants from polytechnics and colleges than from universities and has also worked with 'English People' from overseas. I have been involved with the DUET project since its inception and am currently editing a book about it, to be published by Free Association Books.

Chapter 8

1 See Protherough (1989: 21–6) 'One subject or two?'
2 Colin Evans, 'Four poems', *Interactions*, June 1991.

Chapter 9

1 He is not quite right to say there is no scholarly research: Hofstede (1980) gives the result of a massive piece of survey research in 66 countries. The employees of a large multinational company, 'HERMES' (actually IBM), completed 116,000 questionnaires. The conclusion is that 'modern nations do have dominant national characteristics'.
2 This may be one instance where the 'observer' modifies the thing observed. My identity as a linguist and as a Welshman may well have produced certain kinds of response from the people I interviewed.
3 I am aware of how this analysis can be applied to the question of masculine identity.
4 With my own French state doctorate from the University of Paris came a note reminding me that it did not entitle me to teach in the French university!

Chapter 10

1 These final thoughts owe a great deal to a discussion with Barry Palmer. In particular, the image of the archipelago is his – though the subsequent whimsy is all my own.

2 According to Jung it requires *four* functions: sensation; feeling; thinking; intuition. See Evans (1986) and the account of the DUET 'Difference' event, using Jung's functions (Evans and Palmer 1989).

Bibliography

Aers, L. and Wherle, N. (eds) (1991) *Shakespeare in the Changing Curriculum.* London and New York, Routledge.

Anderson, T. (1968) 'Components of the national culture', *New Left Review*, 50: 3–57.

Ashcroft, B. *et al.* (1989) *The Empire Writes Back: Theory and Practice in Post-colonial Literatures.* London and New York, Routledge.

Bailey, F. G. (1977) *Morality and Expediency: the Folklore of Academic Politics.* Oxford, Blackwell.

Baldick, C. (1983) *The Social Mission of English Criticism 1848–1932.* Oxford, Clarendon Press.

Balibar, R. (1974) *Les français fictifs: le rapport des styles littéraires au français national.* Paris, Hachette Littérature.

Barker, F. *et al.* (1986) *Literature, Politics and Theory. Papers from the Essex Conferences, 1976–1984.* London, Methuen.

Bateson, G. (1973) *Steps to an Ecology of Mind.* St Albans, Paladin.

Batsleer, J. *et al.* (1985) *Rewriting English: Cultural Politics of Gender and Class.* London and New York, Methuen.

Becher, T. (1989) *Academic Tribes and Territories.* Milton Keynes, Open University Press.

Becher, T. (1990) 'The counter-culture of specialization'. In T. Becher and L. Huber (eds), 'Disciplinary cultures', special issue of *European Journal of Education*, 25 (3): 333–46.

Becher, T. and Huber, L. (eds) (1990) 'Disciplinary cultures', special issue of *European Journal of Education*, 25 (3).

Belbin, R. M. (1981) *Management Teams: Why They Succeed or Fail. London,* Heinemann.

Belbin, R. M. (1988) *Interplace: Matching People to Jobs: User's Manual.* Oxford, Belbin Associates.

Belsey, C. (1980) *Critical Practice.* London, Methuen.

Bergonzi, B. (1990) *Exploding English: Criticism, Theory, Culture.* Oxford, Clarendon Press.

Bernstein, B. (1972) 'On the classification and framing of educational knowledge'.

In M. F. D. Young, *Knowledge and Control: New Directions for the Sociology of Education*. London, Collier Macmillan, pp. 47–69.

Birkett, J. and Kelly, M. (eds) (1992) *French in the 90s*. Birmingham, University of Birmingham.

Bleich, D. (1978) *Subjective Criticism*. Baltimore, Johns Hopkins University Press.

Bleich, D. (1988) *The Double Perspective*. New York and Oxford, Oxford University Press.

Bligh, D. (1971) *What's the Use of Lectures?* Harmondsworth, Penguin.

Bourdieu, P. (1984) *Homo academicus*. Paris, Editions de Minuit.

Broadbent, J. (1981) 'Untwining all the chains: an account of the DUET workshop by its director', *Quinquereme: New Studies in Modern Languages*, 4 (2): 225–30.

Brooker, P. and Humm, P. (1989) *Dialogue and Difference: English into the Nineties*. London and New York, Routledge.

Campbell, D. (1969) 'Ethnocentrism and the fish-scale model of omniscience'. In M. Sherif and C. Sherif (eds), *Interdisciplinary Relationships in the Social Sciences*. Chicago, Aldine, pp. 328–48.

Campos, C. (1992) 'The scope and methodology of French'. In J. Birkett and M. Kelly (eds), *French in the 90s*. Birmingham, University of Birmingham.

Carter, R. (1991) *The National Curriculum for English*. London, British Council.

Cornford, F. M. (1908) *Microcosmographica: Being a Guide for the Young Academic Politician*. London, Bowes and Bowes.

Cox, B. (1988) *National Curriculum English Working Party* (the Cox Report). London, HMSO.

Coyle, M. *et al.* (eds) (1991) *The Encyclopaedia of Literature and Criticism*. London, Routledge.

Cryer, P. and Elton, L. (1992) *Active Learning in Large Classes and with Increasing Student Numbers*. Sheffield, CVCP USDTU.

Davies, T. (1982) 'Common sense and critical practice: teaching literature'. In P. Widdowson (ed.), *Re-reading English*. London, Methuen.

Dixon, J. (1991) *A Schooling in 'English'*. Milton Keynes, Open University Press.

Doyle, B. (1989) *English and Englishness*. London, Routledge.

Douglas, M. (1966) *Purity and Danger: an Analysis of the Concepts of Pollution and Taboo*. London, Routledge and Kegan Paul.

Duckworth, D. and Entwhistle, N. J. (1974) 'Attitudes to school subjects: a repertory grid technique', *British Journal of Educational Technology*, 44: 76–88.

Eagleton, T. (1983) *Literary Theory: an Introduction*. Oxford, Blackwell.

Easthope, A. (1988) *British Post-structuralism since 1968*. London and New York, Routledge.

Easthope, A. (1991) *Literary into Cultural Studies*. London and New York, Routledge.

Espagne, M. and Werner, M. (eds) (1990) *Philologiques I: Contribution à l'histoire des disciplines littéraires en France et en Allemagne au XIXe siècle*. Paris, Maison des Sciences de l'Homme.

Evans, C. (1986) 'Humanistic psychology, higher education and HEART: reflections with a little help from Jung', *Self and Society*, 4 (6): 245–54.

Evans, C. (1988) *Language People: the Experience of Teaching and Learning Modern Languages in British Universities*. Milton Keynes, Open University Press.

Evans, C. (1990a) 'Teaching the humanities: seminars as metalogues', *Studies in Higher Education*, 15 (3): 287–97.

Evans, C. (1990b) 'A cultural view of the discipline of modern languages'. In
T. Becher and L. Huber (eds), 'Disciplinary cultures', special issue of *European
Journal of Education*, 25 (3): 273–82.
Evans, C. (ed.) (1993) *Developing English Teaching: the DUET Project*. London,
Free Association Books, forthcoming.
Evans, C. and Palmer, B. (1989) 'Intergroup encounters of a different kind', *Studies
in Higher Education*, 14 (3), 304–5.
Farrar, F. W. (ed.) (1868) *Essays on a Liberal Education*. London, Macmillan.
Firth, C. (1929) *Modern Languages at Oxford 1724–1929*. Oxford, Oxford
University Press.
Garratt, L. (1985) 'Factors affecting subject choice at A level', *Journal of Edu-
cational Studies*, 11: 127–32.
Geertz, C. (1973) 'Thick description: towards an interpretative theory of culture'.
In *The Interpretation of Cultures: Selected Essays*. New York, Basic Books,
pp. 3–30.
Geertz, C. (1983) *Local Knowledge*. New York, Basic Books.
Gibbs, G. (1982) *Twenty Terrible Reasons for Lecturing*. Oxford, SCED, Occa-
sional Papers No. 8.
Gibbs, G. and Jenkins, A. (1992) *Teaching Large Classes*. London, Kogan
Page.
Glock, M. E. (ed.) (1971) *Guiding Learning: Readings in Educational Psychology*.
Chichester, Wiley.
Goffman, E. (1981) *Forms of Talk*. Oxford, Blackwell.
Graff, G. (1980) 'Who killed criticism?', *American Scholar*, 49: 337–55.
Graff, G. (1987) *Professing Literature*. Chicago, University of Chicago Press.
Graff, G. and Warner, M. (eds) (1989) *The Origin of Literary Studies in America:
a Documentary Anthology*. London and New York, Routledge.
Greenwell, B. (1992) 'Gradgrind's return', *New Statesman and New Society*, 24
January: 26.
Hammersley, M. and Woods, P. (eds) (1984) *Life in School: the Sociology of Pupil
Culture*. Milton Keynes, Open University Press.
Hampden-Turner, C. (1990) *Charting the Corporate Mind: from Dilemma to
Strategy*. Oxford, Blackwell.
Heap, S. et al. (1992) *The Theory of Choice: a Critical Guide*. Oxford: Blackwell.
Hennebelle, G. (ed.) (1992) *Le tribalisme planétaire*. Paris, Arléa Corlet.
Hofstede, G. (1980, 1984) *Culture's Consequences: International Differences in
Work-related Values*, abridged edition. London, Sage.
Holloway, W. (1989) *Subjectivity and Method in Psychology: Gender, Meaning
and Science*. London, Sage.
Hoskin, K. (1993) 'Education and the genesis of disciplinarity: the unexpected
reversal'. In E. Messmer-Davidow, et al. (eds), *Knowledges: Historical and
Critical Studies in Disciplinarity*. Charlottesville, University of Virginia Press.
Hudson, L. (1966) *Contrary Imaginations*. London, Methuen.
Hunt, F. J. (1987) *The Incorporation of Education: an International Study in the
Transformation of Educational Priorities*. London, Routledge and Kegan Paul.
Jaques, D. (1984) *Learning in Groups*. London, Croom Helm.
Kerr, C. (1963) *The Use of the University*. Cambridge, MA, Harvard University
Press.
Keys, W. and Ormerod, M. B. (1976) 'Some factors affecting pupils' subject
preferences', *Durham Research Review*, 3 (36): 1109–15.

Kingman, J. (1988) *Report of the Committee of Enquiry into the Teaching of English Language*. London: HMSO.

Kuhn, T. (1970) *The Structure of Scientific Revolutions*. Chicago, University of Chicago Press.

Lakoff, G. and Johnson, M. (1980) *Metaphors We Live By*. Chicago, Chicago University Press.

Lapeyronnie, D. and Marie, J.-L. (1992) *Campus Blues: les étudiants face à leurs études*. Paris, Seuil.

Leavis, F. R. (1965) *Education and the University: a Sketch for an 'English School'*. London, Chatto and Windus.

Leftwich, A. (1991) 'Pedagogy for the depressed: the political economy of teaching development in British universities', *Studies in Higher Education*, 16: 277–90.

Lewis, I. (1984) *The Student Experience of Higher Education*. London, Croom Helm.

Lowe, W. (1971) 'Structure and related ideas'. In M. E. Glock (ed.), *Guiding Learning: Readings in Educational Psychology*. Chichester, Wiley.

Lucas, J. (1991) *England and Englishness*. London, Hogarth.

Marris, P. (1964) *The Experience of Higher Education*. London, Routledge and Kegan Paul.

Marris, P. (1974) *Loss and Change*. London, Routledge and Kegan Paul.

Marton, P. and Entwhistle, N. (1984) *The Experience of Learning*. Edinburgh, Scottish Academic Press.

Mathieson, M. (1975) *The Preachers of Culture: a Study of English and its Teachers*. London, Allen and Unwin.

McCabe, C. (1988) *Futures for English*. Manchester, Manchester University Press.

Meek, M. and Miller, J. (eds) (1984) *Changing English: Essays for Harold Rosen*. London, Heinemann.

Miall, D. S. (1989) 'Welcome the crisis! Rethinking learning methods in English studies', *Studies in Higher Education*, 14: 69–82.

Michael, A. (1987) *The Teaching of English from the Sixteenth Century to 1870*. Cambridge, Cambridge University Press.

Miller, C. and Parlett, M. (1974) *Up to the Mark: a Study of the Examination Game*. Guildford, Society for Research into Higher Education.

Mulhern, F. (1979) *The Moment of Scrutiny*. London, NLB.

Nairn, T. (1990) *The Enchanted Glass: Britain and Its Monarchy*. London, Picador.

Newbolt, H. (1921) *The Newbolt Report: the Teaching of English in England*. London, HMSO.

Norris, C. (1985) *The Contest of Faculties: Philosophy and Theory after Deconstruction*. London and New York, Methuen.

Norris, C. (1991) 'Criticism'. In M. Coyle *et al.* (eds), *The Encyclopaedia of Literature and Criticism*. London, Routledge, pp. 27–65.

Palmer, B. and Reed, B. (1992) *An Introduction to Organizational Behaviour*, revised edition. London, Grubb Institute.

Palmer, D. J. (1965) *The Rise of English Studies*. Oxford, Oxford University Press.

Plumb, J. H. (ed.) (1964) *Crisis in the Humanities*. Harmondsworth, Penguin.

Potter, S. (1937) *The Muse in Chains: a Study in Education*. London, Cape.

Protherough, R. (1989) *Students of English*. London and New York, Routledge.

Punter, D. (1986) 'University English teaching'. In W. Godzich, *et al.* (eds), *Demarcating the Disciplines: Philosophy, Literature, Art*. Glyph Textual Studies No. 1. Minneapolis, University of Minnesota Press.

Ramsden, P. (1992) 'Lost in the crowd?', *Times Higher Educational Supplement*, 17 July: 15.

Richards, I. A. (1929) *Practical Criticism*. London, Routledge and Kegan Paul.

Robinson, I. (1983) 'UCCA to what?', *Use of English*, 34: 23–33.

Rudduck, J. (1990) *Innovation and Change: Developing Involvement and Understanding*. Milton Keynes, Open University Press.

Russo, J. P. (1989) *I. A. Richards: His Life and Work*. London, Routledge.

Ryle, G. (1949) *The Concept of Mind*. Harmondsworth, Penguin.

Samuel, R. (ed.) (1989) *Patriotism: the Making and Unmaking of British National Identity. Vol. II: Minorities and Outsiders. Vol. III: National Fictions*. London and New York, Routledge.

Sartre, J.-P. (1947) 'Qu'est-ce que la littérature?', in *Situations II*. Paris, Gallimard.

Scholes, R. (1985) *Textual Power: Literary Theory and the Teaching of English*. New Haven, CT, Yale University Press.

Scott, P. (1984) *The Crisis of the University*. London, Croom Helm.

Selden, R. (1980) *Practising Theory and Reading Literature: an Introduction*. London, Harvester Wheatsheaf.

Sherif, M. and Sherif, C. (eds) (1969) *Interdisciplinary Relationships in the Social Sciences*. Chicago, Aldine.

Shotter, J. and Gergen, K. J. (eds) (1989) *Texts of Identity*. London, Sage.

Smith, F. (1982) *Writing and the Writer*. London, Heinemann.

Tapper, T. and Salter, B. (1992) *Oxford, Cambridge and the Changing Idea of the University. The Challenge to Donnish Domination*. Buckingham, Open University Press.

Tillyard, E. M. W. (1958) *The Muse Unchained: an Intimate Account of the Revolution in English Studies at Cambridge*. London, Bowes and Bowes.

Walsh, W. (1980) *F. R. Leavis*. London, Chatto and Windus.

Watson, G. (1978) *The Discipline of English: a Guide to Critical Theory and Practice*. London, Macmillan.

Whiston, T. G. and Geiger, R. L. (eds) (1992) *Research and Higher Education: the United Kingdom and the United States*. Buckingham, Open University Press.

Widdowson, P. (ed.) (1982) *Re-reading English*. London, Methuen.

Wiegand, P. and Rayner, M. (1989) *Curriculum Progress 5–16: School Subjects and the National Curriculum Debate*. Lewis, Falmer Press.

Williams, R. (1961) *The Long Revolution*. Harmondsworth, Penguin.

Williams, T. (1989) 'The Anglicisation of South Wales'. In R. Samuel (ed.), *Patriotism: the Making and Unmaking of British National Identity, Vol. II: Minorities and Outsiders*, London and New York, Routledge.

Williams, W. M. (ed.) (1974) *Occupational Choice*. London, Allen and Unwin.

Wood, E. M. (1991) *The Pristine Culture of Capitalism: A Historical Essay of Old Regimes and Modern States*. London, Verso.

Young, M. F. D. (1972) *Knowledge and Control: New Directions for the Sociology of Education*. London, Collier Macmillan.

Index